LOOKING AT PHILOSOPHY

The Unbearable Heaviness of Philosophy Made Lighter

Text and Illustrations
by

DONALD PALMER

LOOKING AT PHILOSOPHY

The Unbearable Heaviness of Philosophy Made Lighter

DONALD PALMER

College of Marin

Mayfield Publishing Company

Mountain View, California

Library of Congress Cataloging-in-Publication Data

Palmer, Donald.
Looking at philosophy.

Includes index.
1. Philosophy — History. I. Title.
B74.P26 1988 190 88-1406
ISBN 0-87484-839-3

Manufactured in the United States of America
10 9 8 7 6 5 4 3 2 1

Mayfield Publishing Company
1240 Villa Street
Mountain View, California 94041

Sponsoring editor, James Bull; production editor, Linda Toy. Illustrations by Donald Palmer; hand lettering by Robin Mouat; cover design by Cynthia Bassett.

LOOKING AT PHILOSOPHY

Foreword ix
Introduction 1
I. The Pre-Socratic Philosophers 6
Thales 6
Anaximander 11
Anaximenes 13
Pythagoras 16
Heraclitus 19
Parmenides 25
Zeno 28
Empedocles 32
Anaxagoras 35
Leucippus 36
Democritus 36

II. The Athenian Period 42
The Sophists 42
Protagoras 43
Gorgias 45
Thrasymachus 46
Callicles 47
Critias 47
Socrates 50
Plato 57
Aristotle 74

III. The Hellenistic Period 88
Epicureanism 89
Stoicism 95
Neo-Platonism 100

IV. Medieval Philosophy 103

St. Augustine 103
The Encyclopediasts 110
John Scotus Erigena 111
St. Anselm 116
The Problem of Faith and Reason 120
The Problem of Universals 121
St. Thomas Aquinas 124

V. The 17th and 18th Centuries 135

Descartes 135
Hobbes 158
Spinoza 163
Leibniz 169
Locke 177
Berkeley 188
Hume 195
Kant 206

VI. The 19th Century 222

Hegel 223
Schopenhauer 234
Kierkegaard 248
Marx 263
Nietzsche 280
Utilitarianism 291

VII. The 20th Century 303

Pragmatism 303
G.E. Moore 312
Russell 319
Logical Positivism 330
Husserl 338
Wittgenstein 344
Sartre 360

Afterword 376

Glossary 381

Index 391

Foreword

Wittgenstein once said that a whole philosophy book could be written consisting of nothing but jokes. THIS IS NOT THAT BOOK, nor does this book treat the history of philosophy as a joke. This book takes philosophy seriously, but not gravely. As the subtitle indicates, the goal of the book is to lighten the load a bit. How to do this without simply throwing the cargo overboard? First, by presenting an overview of Western philosophy from the sixth century B.C. to the middle of the twentieth century in a way that introduces the central philosophical ideas of the West and their evolution in a concise, readable format without trivializing them, but at the same time, without pretending to have exhausted them nor to have plumbed their depths. Secondly, following a time-honored Medieval tradition, by illuminating the margins of the text. Some of these illuminations, namely, those which attempt to schematize difficult ideas, I hope will be literally illuminating. Most of them, however, are simply attempts in a lighter vein to interrupt the natural propensity of the philosophers to succumb to the pull of gravity. (Nietzsche said that only the grave lay in that direction.) But even these philosophical jokes, I hope, have a pedagogical function. They should serve to help the reader to retain the ideas which are thereby gently mocked. Twenty years of teaching the subject which I love — and which has provoked more than a few laughs on the part of my students — convinces me that this technique should work. I do not claim to have achieved Nietzsche's "joyful wisdom," but I agree with him that there is such a thing and that we should strive for it.

Before turning you over to Thales and his metaphysical water (the first truly heavy water), I want to say a word about the women and their absence. Why are there no women in a book of this nature? There are a number of possible explanations, including these:

1. Women really are deficient in the capacity for sublimation, hence are incapable of participating in higher culture (as Schopenhauer and Freud suggested).
2. Women have in fact contributed greatly to the history of philosophy, but their contributions have been denied or suppressed by the chauvinistic male writers of the histories of philosophy.
3. Women have been (intentionally or unintentionally) systematically eliminated from the history of philosophy by political, social, religious, and psychological manipulations of power by a deeply entrenched, jealous, and fearful patriarchy.

I am certain that the first thesis does not merit our serious attention. I think there is some truth to the second thesis, and I may be partially guilty of suppressing that truth. For example, the names of at least seventy women philosophers in the late Classical period alone have been recorded, foremost of which are Aspasia, Diotima, Arete, and Hypatia. (Hypatia has been belatedly honored by having a journal of feminist philosophy recently named after her.) Jumping over centuries to our own age, we find a number of well-known women contributing to the history of philosophy in the first half of the current century, including Simone de Beauvoir, Susanne Langer, and L. Susan Stebbing.

However, no matter how original, deep, and thought-provoking were the ideas of these philosophers, I believe that, for a number of reasons (those reasons given in the second and third theses are probably most pertinent here), none of them has been as historically significant as those philosophers which have been dealt with in this book. Fortunately, things have begun to change in the last few years. An adequate account of contemporary philosophy could not in good faith ignore the major contributions to the analytic tradition of philosophers like Iris Murdoch, Philippa Foot, G.E.M. Anscombe, and Judith Jarvis Thompson, nor those contributions to the Continental tradition made by Gayatri Chakravorty Spivak, Monique Wittig, Luce Irigaray, and Julia Kristeva. Furthermore, a new wave of feminist philosophers is already beginning to have considerable impact on the <u>content</u> of contemporary philosophy and not merely on its style.

So, in spite of the risks, I defend the third thesis. I truly believe that if women had not been systematically excluded from major participation in the history of philosophy, that history would be even richer, deeper, more compassionate, and more interesting (not to mention more joyful) than it already is.

Finally, I want to say that I've had some help with this book. Kerry Walk and reviewers Job Clement, Daytona Beach Community College; Hans Hansen, Wayne State University; Yukio Shirahama, San Antonio College; and William Tinsley, Foothill College, read parts of the manuscript and provided helpful suggestions. Donald Porter, College of San Mateo, read the whole thing. He clearly understood exactly what I was trying to achieve and gave me many good ideas for doing it better. Jim Bull, my editor at Mayfield Publishing Company, had faith in this project from its inception. He has provided unqualified support from start to finish. My thanks to Mary Forkner and Linda Toy of Mayfield's Production Department for their help and expertise. Also, thanks to Robin Mouat, whose hand lettering helped give this book the look I wanted. Leila May has been my most acute critic and my greatest source of inspiration. She kept me laughing during the dreariest stages of the production of the manuscript, often finding on its pages jokes which weren't meant to be there. I hope she managed to catch most of them. There probably are still a few pages which are funnier than I intended them to be.

«»

For Katarina & Christian

The story of Western philosophy begins in

GREECE

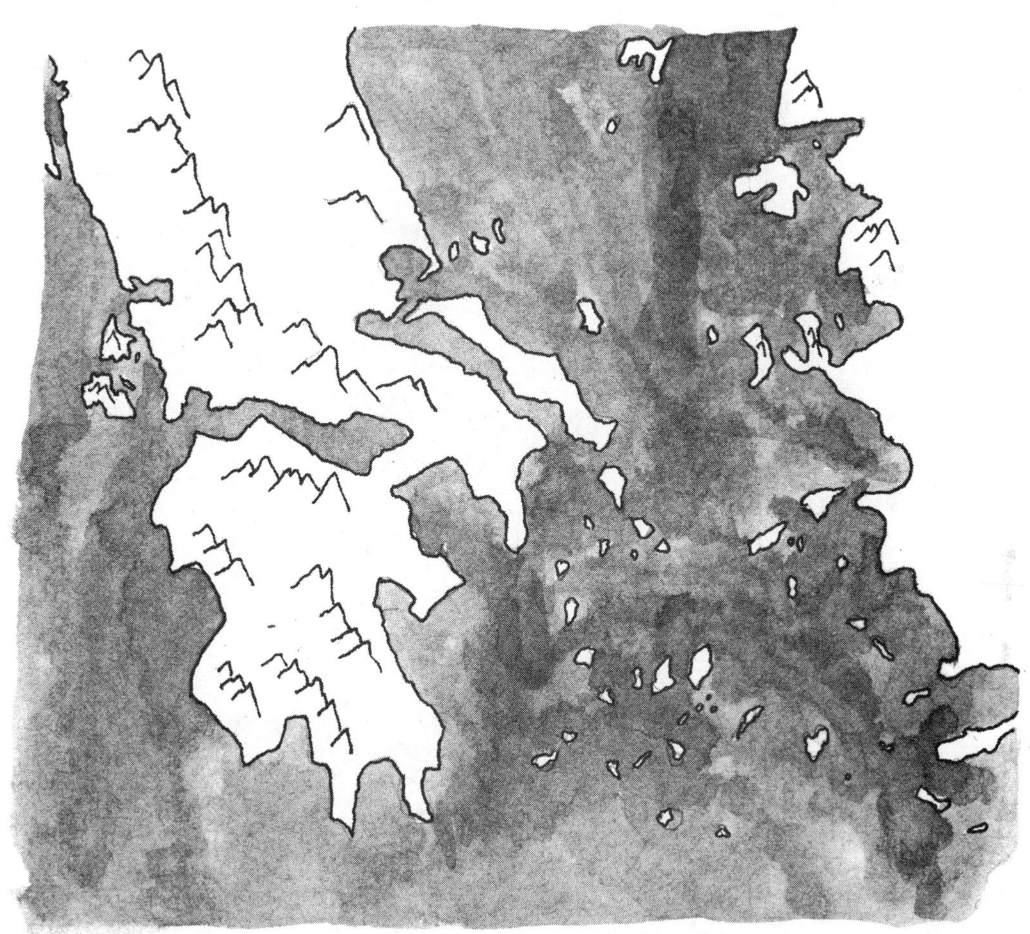

Why Greece, and not, for example, Egypt or Judea?

Well, for one reason, there was no PRIESTLY CLASS of CENSORS in Greece.

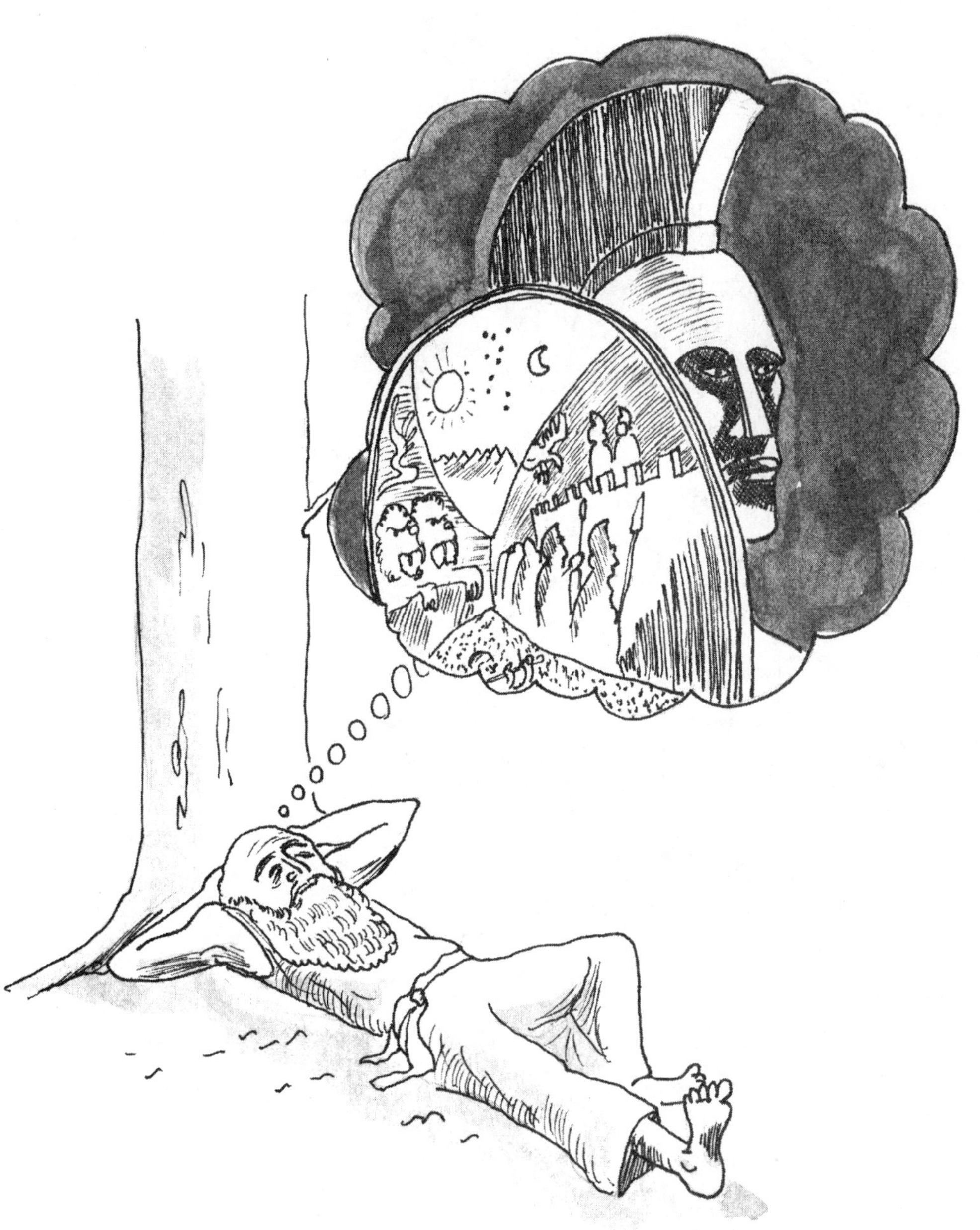

For another, the Greek imagination had always been fertile, and concerned with intimate detail. For example, Homer's description of Achilles' shield takes up four pages of the Iliad.

Furthermore, the Greeks were particularly aware of CHANGE, of the war of the opposites, summer to winter, hot to cold, light to dark, and that most dramatic change of all, life to death.

Indeed, this sensitivity to the transitory nature of all things sometimes led the Greeks to PESSIMISM. (The poet Simonides wrote, "Generations of men fall like the leaves of the forest.")

But it also led them to demand an EXPLANATION.

1. The Pre-Socratic Philosophers

The first dispassionate attempt at such an explanation was carried out by THALES OF MILETUS (c. 580 B.C.), who is recognized by all as the first true philosopher.

If there is change, there must be some THING which changes, yet does not change.

Thales was familiar with the four elements: AIR, FIRE, WATER and EARTH. He assumed that all things

must ultimately be reducible to one of these four— BUT WHICH ONE?

Of all the elements, WATER is the most obvious in its transformations: rivers turn into deltas, water turns into ice, then back into water, which in turn can be changed into steam, which becomes air, and air, in the form of wind, fans fire.

Then water it is!

ALL THINGS ARE COMPOSED OF WATER.

This obviously false conclusion is valued today not for its CONTENT, but for its FORM (... it is not a great leap between the claim, "All things are composed of water," and the claim, "All things are composed of atoms"), and for the presupposition behind it (... that there is an ultimate stuff behind appearances which explains change while remaining itself unchanged).

Still, not all of Thales' contemporaries accepted his formulation. ANAXIMANDER (c. 610 - c. 546), for one, said, "If all things were water, then long ago everything would have returned to water." He asked how water could become its deadly enemy, fire — how a quality could give rise to its opposite.

No, for Anaximander, the ultimate stuff behind the four elements could not itself be one of the elements. It would have to be an unobservable, unspecific, indeterminate something-or-other, which he called "the Unlimited."

But his followers asked, "How much better is an 'unspecific, indeterminate something-or-other' than nothing at all?" They decided that it was NO better, in fact, it was the SAME as nothing at all, and, knowing that EX NIHILO NIHIL (from nothing comes nothing), they went on searching for the mysterious ultimate stuff.

ANAXIMENES (c. 545) thought it was AIR.

The air which we experience ("common sense" air) is a half-way house between all the other forms into which "primordial air" can be transformed through CONDENSATION and RAREFACTION.

rarefaction

condensation

With the idea of condensation and rarefaction Anaximenes introduced the important claim that all differences in quality are really differences in quantity. (just more or less STUFF packed into a specific space), an idea with which many scientists would agree today.

These first three philosophers, Thales, Anaximander and Anaximenes, are known as the MILESIANS because they all came from the Greek colony of Miletus on the Persian coast, and because they constitute the first school of philosophy. In spite of the differences among them, they shared a number of characteristics, some of which would eventually become part of the Western scientific tradition — a desire for simple explanations, a reliance on observation to support their theories, a commitment to naturalism (the view that natural phenomena should be explained in terms of other natural phenomena), and monism (the view that ultimately there is only one kind of "stuff").

The School of Miletus ended when the tenuous peace between the Greek outpost and Persia collapsed, and the Persians overran the city.

The Milesians' successor, PYTHAGORAS (c. 572 - c. 500), did not seek ultimacy in some material element, as his predecessors had done. Rather, he held the curious view that all things are numbers. Literally understood, this seems absurd, but among other things, Pythagoras meant that a correct description of reality must be expressed in terms of mathematical formulas.

Furthermore, he anticipated the bulk of Euclid's writings on geometry, and discovered the ratios of concord between musical sound and number. From this, he deduced a mathematical harmony throughout the universe, a view which led to the doctrine of "the Music of the Spheres."

The influence of Pythagoras was so great that the School of Pythagoreans lasted almost 400 years. The spell he cast on Plato alone would be enough to guarantee Pythagoras a permanent place in the history of philosophy.

There was another, less scientific aspect of Pythagoras' teachings which should be noted. He was the leader of a religious cult whose members had to obey a strict number of esoteric rules based on asceticism, numerology and vegetarianism.

In spite of their vegetarianism, Pythagoreans had to forswear eating beans. This is because eating beans is a form of cannibalism. A close look at the inside of a bean reveals that each one contains a small, embryonic human being (or human bean, as the case may be).

The next philosopher, HERACLITUS (c. 470 B.C.), had a new insight: The basic stuff is FIRE!

though he seems to have understood this idea more in a metaphorical than in a literal sense.

There is something about the nature of fire which explains both the appearance of STABILITY (the flame's FORM is stable) . . .

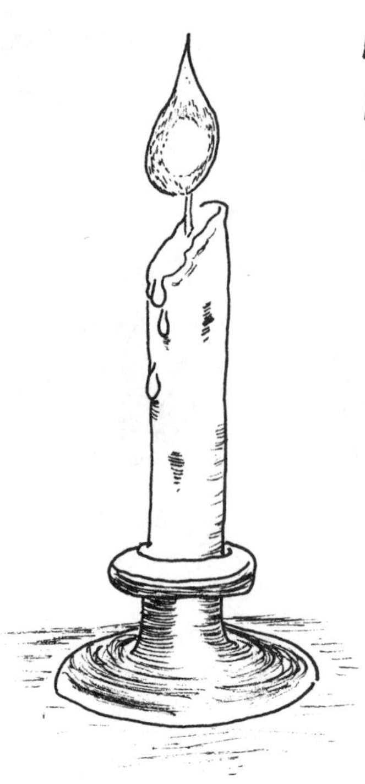

. . . and the FACT of CHANGE (in the flame, everything changes).

Heraclitus drew some striking conclusions from this insight.

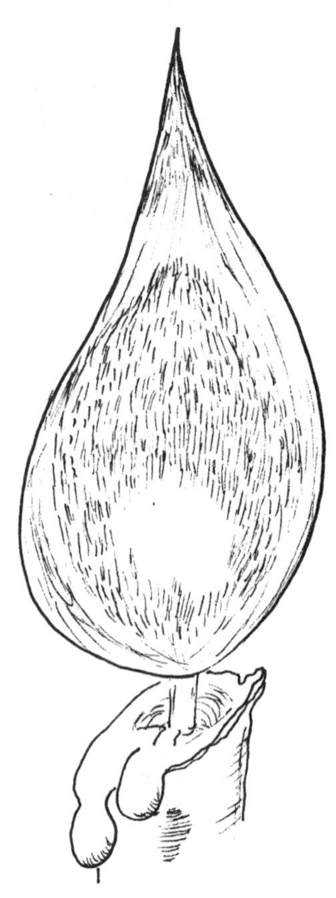

Reality is composed not of a number of THINGS, but of a PROCESS of continual creation and destruction.
"War is King."

"You can't step in the same river twice."

"Everything changes but change itself."

Heraclitus was called "the Dark One." His ideas were interpreted pessimistically. They create more than merely a philosophy – they constitute a MOOD, almost a "world-view" of nostalgia and loss.

You can't go home again. Your childhood is lost.
The friends of your youth are gone.
Your present is slipping away from you.
Nothing is ever the same.

Nevertheless, there was something positive in the Heraclitian philosophy. There existed an unobservable "LOGOS" — a logic — governing change which made change a rational phenomenon rather than the chaotic, arbitrary one it appeared to be. This Logos doctrine deeply impressed Plato, and eventually became the basis of the notion of natural law.

Heraclitus' successor, PARMENIDES (c. 515-c. 440), went a step further than his predecessor.

In effect, he said that you can't step in the same river ONCE.

Parmenides saw reality as an absolute plenum, chock-full of Being. His central thesis was simple: Being Is; Not Being is Not. Being is uncreated, indestructible, eternal, indivisible, and equally real in all directions. Being has no holes (no vacuum), because if Being IS, there can't be any place where Being is NOT.

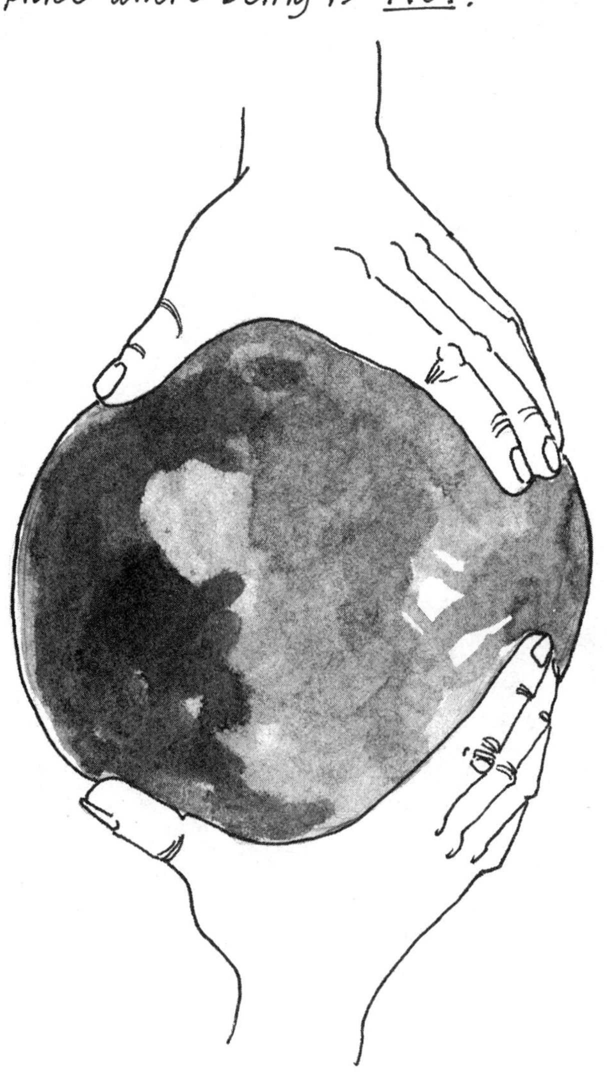

From this it follows that motion is impossible, because motion would involve Being going from where Being is to where Being isn't (but there can't BE any such place as the place where Being isn't).

In a series of famous Paradoxes, Parmenides' disciple, the sly old fox ZENO of Elea (c. 490 – ?), "proved" the impossibility of motion using a method known as "reductio ad absurdum."

In this form of argumentation you begin by accepting your opponent's premises and you demonstrate that they lead logically to an absurdity or a contradiction.

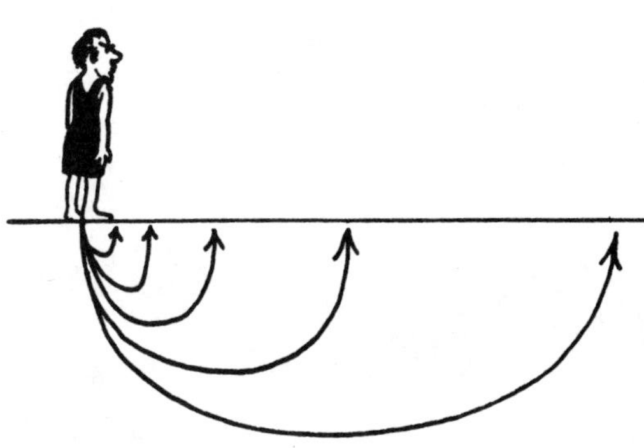

Zeno argued that, even granting motion, one could never arrive anywhere, not even to such a simple goal as a door. Before you can get to the door, you must go halfway, but before you can go halfway, you must go halfway of the remaining halfway, but before you can do that, you must go halfway of halfway, but before you can go halfway, you must go halfway. When does this argument end? Never! It goes on to infinity. Therefore, motion would be impossible even if it were possible.

In yet another of his paradoxes, Zeno demonstrated that in a race between Achilles and a tortoise, if Achilles gave the tortoise a head-start (as would only be fair), the swift runner could never overtake the lumbering reptile. This is because, before Achilles can pass the tortoise, he must arrive at the point where the tortoise used to be, but given the hypothesis of motion, the tortoise will never still be there. He will have moved on. This will forever be the case. When Achilles arrives at a point where the tortoise was, the tortoise will have progressed. Achilles can never catch him.

Parmenides and Zeno caused a crisis in Greek philosophy. First, they forced the distinction between information based on the five senses, and that based on pure reason (a distinction which will later develop into two schools of philosophy: Empiricism and Rationalism); second, they forced a re-evaluation of the monistic presupposition accepted by all Greeks heretofore (namely, the view that reality is composed of ONE THING), because thinkers came to realize that such a view led directly to Parmenides' untenable conclusions.

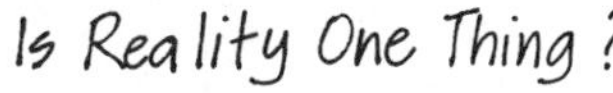
Is Reality One Thing?

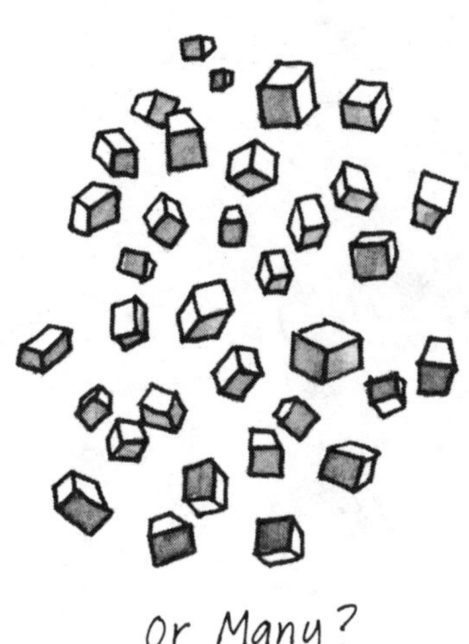
Or Many?

The next group of philosophers are known as PLURALISTS, precisely because they believed that ultimate reality is composed of a plurality of things rather than of only one kind of thing.

The first of this group was EMPEDOCLES (?–c.440), who believed that everything was composed of the simplest parts of the four elements, fire, air, earth and water. He called these elements "the four roots."

But in the face of Zeno's critique of motion, Empedocles believed he needed to posit two forces to explain change and movement. These he called LOVE and STRIFE. Love is the force of unity, bringing together unrelated items to produce new creations, and strife is the force of destruction, breaking down old unities into fragments.

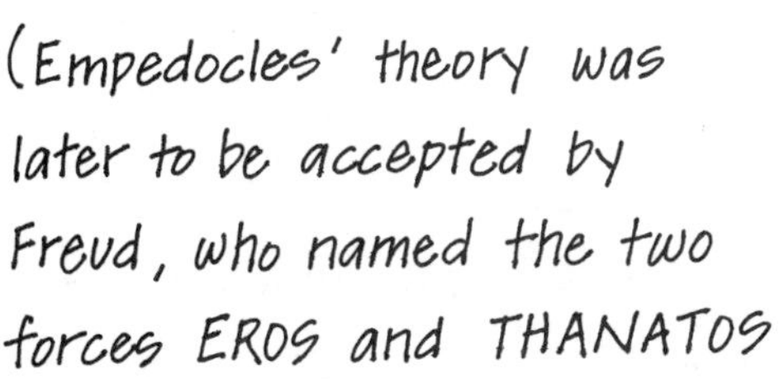

(Empedocles' theory was later to be accepted by Freud, who named the two forces EROS and THANATOS [the life instinct and the death instinct]. Freud agreed with Empedocles that these forces formed the bases of all organic matter.)

The first theory of evolution developed out of Empedocles' system. Love brings together certain kinds of monsters. "... many heads grew up without necks, and arms were wandering about naked, bereft of shoulders, and eyes roamed about alone with no foreheads."

And those that could survive, did survive.

(Aristotle later criticized this view as "leaving too much to chance.")

The next pluralist, ANAXAGORAS (c. 500 – c. 428), found Empedocles' theory too simplistic. He replaced the "four roots" with "infinite seeds." Each of these "seeds" is something like an "element" in today's chemistry, so in some ways, this all sounds very modern. Every object in the world contains seeds of all elements, and in each object, the seeds of one element predominate.

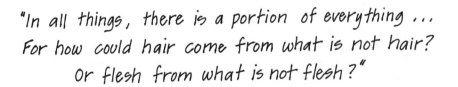

"In all things, there is a portion of everything ... For how could hair come from what is not hair? Or flesh from what is not flesh?"

Anaxagoras replaced Empedocles' all too mythical figures of Love and Strife with one force, a mental one, which he called "NOUS," or Mind. This means that the universe is organized according to an intelligent, rational order.

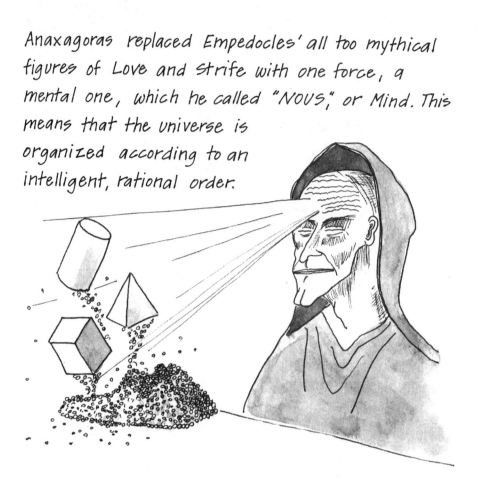

Anaxagoras' "NOUS" is almost like a god who creates objects out of the "seeds," or elements.

Therefore this view was still too mythical for Anaxagoras' successors, a group of philosophers led by LEUCIPPUS (c. 460–?) and DEMOCRITUS (c. 460–c. 370) known as "the atomists."

They saw the world as composed of material bodies, which themselves were composed of groups of "atoms." The Greek word ἄτομος means "indivisible," that which cannot be split. Democritus made each atom a little piece of "Parmenidean Being" (uncreated, indestructible, eternal, indivisible, containing no "holes") and set them moving through empty space (which, contrary to Parmenides, was now real) traversing absolutely necessary paths which were determined by rigid natural laws. Thus, by the year 370 B.C., Greek philosophy had been led to a thoroughgoing materialism and a rigorous determinism. There was nothing in the world but material bodies, and there was no freedom, only necessity.

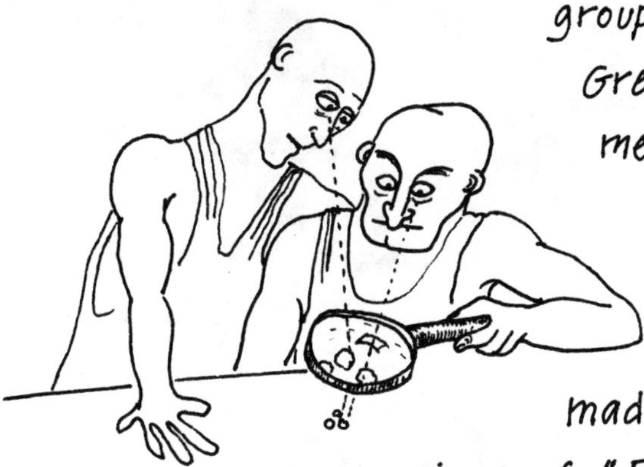

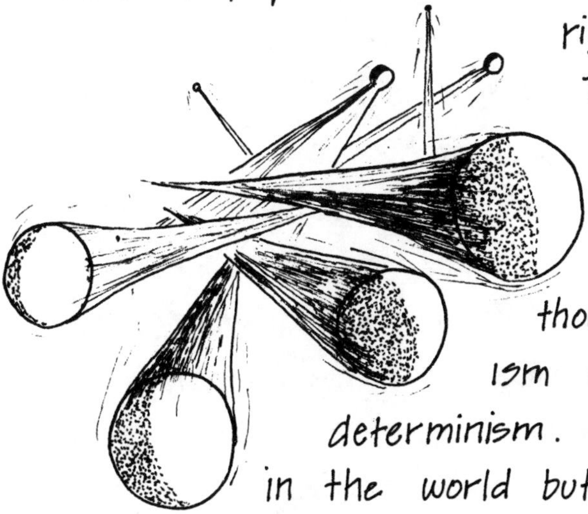

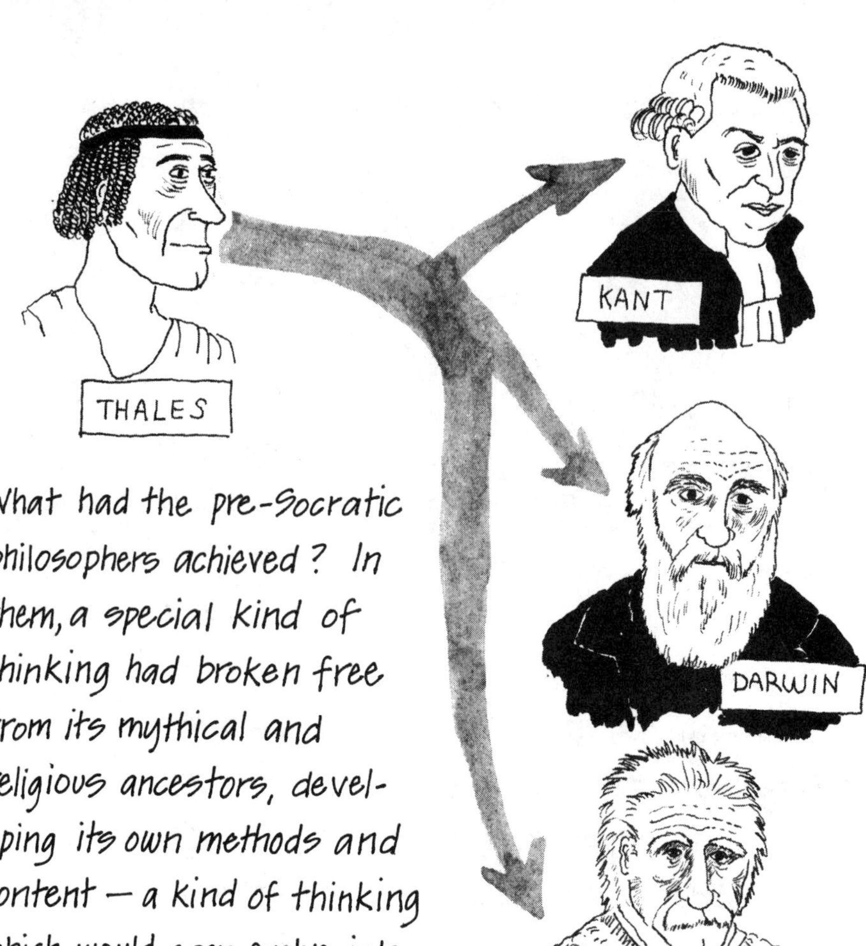

What had the pre-Socratic philosophers achieved? In them, a special kind of thinking had broken free from its mythical and religious ancestors, developing its own methods and content — a kind of thinking which would soon evolve into what today we know as science and philosophy. Looking back at the pre-Socratics <u>WE</u> see a direct lineage between them and the great thinkers of our own time: the dichotomy between reason and the senses which Kant was to resolve in the 18th century was first made clear by the pre-Socratics; the first attempt to formulate a theory of evolution was made by them; and the first effort to solve the riddle of how mathematical numbers hold sway over the flux of reality —

all this we see as a more or less unbroken genealogy from their time to ours.

But to the Greeks of the fifth century, the presocratic philosophers had left a legacy of confusion.

The only thing the philosophers had succeeded in doing was to undermine the traditional religious and moral values, leaving nothing substantial in their place. (As Aristophanes said, "When Zeus is toppled, Chaos succeeds him, and Whirlwind rules.")

Besides, "the times they were a' changin'," socially and politically as well as intellectually. The old aristocracy, dedicated to the noble values of the Homeric legends, was losing ground to a new mercantile class, which was no longer interested in the virtues of Honor, Courage and Fidelity, but in Power and Success. How to achieve these in an incipient democracy? Through politics. And the access to political power was then, as it is today, through the study of rhetoric (read "law")— the art of swaying the masses with eloquent, though not necessarily truthful, argumentation.

II. THE ATHENIAN PERIOD

No surprise, then, that the next group of "philosophers" were not really philosophers as such, but were rhetoricians who became known as SOPHISTS ("wise guys"). They travelled from city to city, charging admission to their lectures — lectures not on the nature of reality or truth, but on the nature of power and persuasion. Not just skepticism, but cynicism, became the rule of the day.

Perhaps the most famous (and least cynical) of the Sophists was PROTAGORAS (ca. 490-ca. 422). He taught that the way to achieve success was through a careful and prudent acceptance of traditional customs — not because they were true, but because an understanding and manipulation of them is expedient. Far from being "true," for Protagoras all customs were relative, not absolute. In fact everything is relative to human subjectivity. Protagoras' famous claim is "HOMO MENSURA" — Man is the measure.

Man is the measure of all things, of things that are, that they are, and of things that are not, that they are not.

Protagoras' emphasis on subjectivity, relativism and expediency is the backbone of all Sophism.

According to some stories, Protagoras was indicted for blasphemy, and his book on the gods was burned publicly in Athens — yet one of the few remaining fragments of his concerning religion states...

I do not know about the gods.

Another famous Sophist was GORGIAS (ca. 483–375). He seems to have wanted to de-throne philosophy and replace it with rhetoric. In his lectures, and in a book he wrote, he "proved" the following theses:

(1) There is nothing.

(2) If there were anything, no one could know it.

(3) If anyone did know it, no one could communicate it.

The point, of course, is that if you can "prove" these absurdities, you can "prove" anything.

Yet another Sophist was THRASYMACHUS, who is known for the claim, "Justice is in the interest of the stronger." That is to say, MIGHT MAKES RIGHT. According to him, all disputation about morality is empty, except insofar as it is reducible to a struggle for power.

According to the accounts handed down to us, two of the most cynical Sophists were CALLICLES and CRITIAS.

Callicles claimed that traditional morality is just a clever way for the weak masses to shackle the strong individual. He taught that the strong should throw off these shackles, and that doing so would be somehow "naturally right." What matters is POWER, not justice. But why is power good? Because it is conducive to SURVIVAL. And why is survival good? Because it allows us to seek PLEASURE — pleasure in food, drink and sex. This is what the enlightened man aims at, qualitatively and quantitatively. The traditional Greek virtue of <u>moderation</u> is for the simple and the feeble.

Critias (who was to become the cruelest of the Thirty Tyrants, who overturned the democracy and temporarily established an oligarchical dictatorship) taught that the clever ruler controls his subjects by encouraging their fear of non-existent gods.

So we see that the essence of Sophism is comprised of subjectivism, skepticism and nihilism. Everything the pre-Socratics stood for is devalued. There is no objective reality, and if there were, the human mind could not fathom it. What matters is not truth, but manipulation and expediency. No wonder Socrates was so offended by Sophism.

Yet we must say a few kind words about Sophism in spite of its negativism. First, many of the Sophists were skilled politicians who actually contributed to the history of democracy. Second, history's animosity toward them is based mostly on reports we have of them from Socrates and Plato, who were enemies of the Sophists. Third, and most importantly, Sophism had the positive effect of making the human being self-conscious. In pre-Socratic philosophy, there was no special consideration of the human. Suddenly, with Protagoras' "Man is the Measure," the human becomes interested in himself.

The Sophists, who were professional teachers, met their match in a man who was possibly the greatest teacher of all time, SOCRATES (469-399 B.C.). In spite of his overall disagreement with them, Socrates followed the Sophists' lead in turning away from the study of the cosmos and concentrating on the case of the human. But unlike the way the Sophists discoursed about the human being, Socrates wanted to base all argumentation on objectively valid definitions. To say, "Man is the measure," is saying very little if one does not know what "man" is.

"I am surprised that Protagoras did not say that a pig, or a dog-faced baboon, is the measure of all things."

Socrates' discourse moved in two directions — outward, to objective definitions, and inward, to discover the inner person, the soul, which, for Socrates, was the source of all truth. Such a search was not to be conducted at a weekend lecture, but was the quest of a life time.

[Truth (trōōth): verity, conformity with fact. Honesty, integrity.]

The questions which Socrates asked, he was hardly ever able to answer. Nevertheless, the query had to continue, for, as we know from his famous dictum ...

"The unexamined life is not worth living."

Socrates spent much of his time in the streets and marketplace of Athens, querying every man he met as to whether that man knew anything. Socrates said that, if there was an afterlife, he would pose the same question to the shades in Hades.

Ironically, Socrates himself professed to know nothing. The oracle at Delphi said that therefore Socrates was the wisest of all men. Socrates at least knew that he knew nothing, while the others falsely believed themselves to know something.

Socrates himself wrote no books, but his conversations were remembered by his disciple, Plato, and later published by him as dialogues. The typical Socratic dialogue has three divisions:

How wonderful that you know what virtue is — and to think, you're only 20 years old!

(1) A problem is posed (e.g., the problem of what virtue is, or justice, or truth, or beauty), Socrates becomes excited and enthusiastic to find someone who claims to know something.

SOCRATES! What have you done to me?

(2) Socrates finds "minor flaws" in his companion's definition, and slowly begins to unravel it, forcing his partner to admit his ignorance. (In one dialogue, Socrates' target actually ends up in tears.)

(3) An agreement is reached by the two admittedly ignorant men to pursue the truth seriously. Almost all of the dialogues end inconclusively. Of course, they must do so. Socrates cannot give his disciple the truth. Each of us must find it out for ourselves.

In his quest for truth, Socrates managed to offend many of the powerful and pompous figures of Athens. His enemies conspired against him, getting him indicted for teaching false doctrines, for impiety, and for corrupting the youth. They brought him to trial hoping to humiliate him by forcing him to grovel and beg for mercy.

Far from groveling, at his trial Socrates humbled his prosecutors and angered the unruly jury of 500 by lecturing to them about their ignorance. Furthermore, when asked to suggest his own punishment, Socrates recommended that the Athenians build a statue in his honor and place it in the main square. The enraged jury condemned him to death by a vote of 280 to 220.

Ashamed of their act, and embarrassed that they were about to put to death their most eminent citizen, the Athenians were prepared to look the other way when Socrates' prison guard was bribed to allow Socrates to escape.

THE DEATH OF SOCRATES
(Vaguely After Jacques-Louis David, 1787)

In spite of the pleas of his friends, Socrates refused to do so, saying that if he broke the law by escaping, he would be declaring himself an enemy of all laws. So he drank the hemlock, and philosophized with his friends to the last moment. In death, he became the universal symbol of martyrdom for the Truth.

The most important of Socrates' young disciples was PLATO (427-347 B.C.), who was one of the most powerful thinkers in history. He is also the founder of the first university, "the Academy," where students read as exercises the Socratic dialogues which he had written.

PLATO

Because of his authorship, it is often dificult to distinguish between the thought of Socrates and that of Plato. In general, we can say that Plato's philosophy was more metaphysical, more systematic, and more "other-worldly" than Socrates' philosophy.

Plato's philosophy is introduced allegorically in the "Myth of the Cave," which appears in his most important work, The Republic. There he has Socrates conceive the following vision: Imagine prisoners chained in such a way that they face the back wall of a cave. There they have been for life, and can see nothing of themselves or of each other. They see only shadows on the wall of the cave.

These shadows are cast by a fire which burns on a ledge above and behind them. Between the fire and the prisoners there is a wall-lined path along which people walk carrying vases, statues, and other artifacts on their heads. The prisoners hear the echoes of voices and see the shadows of the artifacts, and they mistake these echoes and shadows for reality.

Plato has Socrates imagine that one of the prisoners is unchained, turned around, and forced to look at the true source of the shadows. But the fire pains his eyes. He prefers the pleasant deception of the shadows.

Behind and above the fire is the mouth of the cave, and outside in the bright sunlight (only a little of which trickles into the cave) are trees, rivers, mountains and sky.

Now the former prisoner is forced "up the steep and rugged ascent" (Plato's allegory of education), and brought to the sunlit exterior world. But the light blinds him. He must first look at the shadows of the trees (he is used to shadows), then at the trees and mountains. Then finally he is able to see the sun itself (the allegory of enlightenment).

Plato suggests that if this enlightened man were to return to the cave, he would appear ridiculous, because he would see sunspots everywhere, and not be able to penetrate the darkness.

And if he tried to liberate his fellow prisoners they would be so angry at him for disturbing their illusions that they would set upon him and kill him — a clear allusion to the death of Socrates.

	EPISTEMOLOGY	ONTOLOGY		
KNOWLEDGE	Pure Reason	the Forms	The INTELLIGIBLE WORLD	THE GOOD
	Understanding	Concepts		
OPINION	Belief	Particular objects	The VISIBLE WORLD	THE SUN
	Conjecture	Images		

The allegory of the liberation of the slave from darkness, deceit and untruth, and the hard journey into the light and warmth of the Truth, has inspired many philosophers and social leaders. But Plato meant it as more than just a poetic vision. He also gave it a precise technical application, seen in his "Simile of the Line," also found in The Republic. On the left side of the line we have an epistemology (theory of knowledge), on the right side, an ontology (theory of being). In addition we have an implicit ethics (moral theory) and aesthetics (theory of beauty). The totality constitutes Plato's metaphysics (general world view).

For each state of being (right side of the Line) there is a corresponding state of awareness (left side). The lowest state of awareness is that of "conjecture," which has as its object "images," such as shadows and reflections (or images on the TV screen and video games).

The person in a state of conjecture mistakes an image for reality. This corresponds to the situation of the cave-bound prisoners watching the shadows.

The next level, that of "Belief," has as its object a particular thing — a particular horse, or a particular act of justice. Like Conjecture, Belief still does not comprise knowledge, but remains in the sphere of Opinion. This is because it is not yet conceptual, but is grounded in the uncertainties of sense perception. (The person in a state of belief is like a prisoner who sees the artifact held above the wall inside the cave.)

"Opinion," and the objects of which it is aware, are all sustained by the Sun. Without the Sun, there could be no horse, and no image of a horse, nor could we be aware of them in the absence of light.

In order for Opinion to become Knowledge, the particular object must be raised to the level of theory. (This stage, called "Understanding" by Plato, corresponds to the status of the released prisoner looking at the shadows of the trees in the world above the cave.)

A horse is a domesticable quadruped with closed hoofs and 32 pairs of chromosomes; and that creature is such an entity. Ergo it is a horse!
How do you know it's a horse
He Knows!
Actually it's a zebra.

But according to Plato, theories and definitions are not empirical generalizations dependent on particular cases and abstracted from them. To the contrary, rather than coming from "below" on the Line, theories are themselves "images" of something higher — what Plato calls the "Forms." (In the same way that shadows and reflections are merely images of particular things, so theories or concepts are the "shadows" of the Forms.) When one beholds the Forms, one exercises Pure Reason, and one is like the liberated prisoner who gazed upon the trees and mountains in the sunlit upper world.

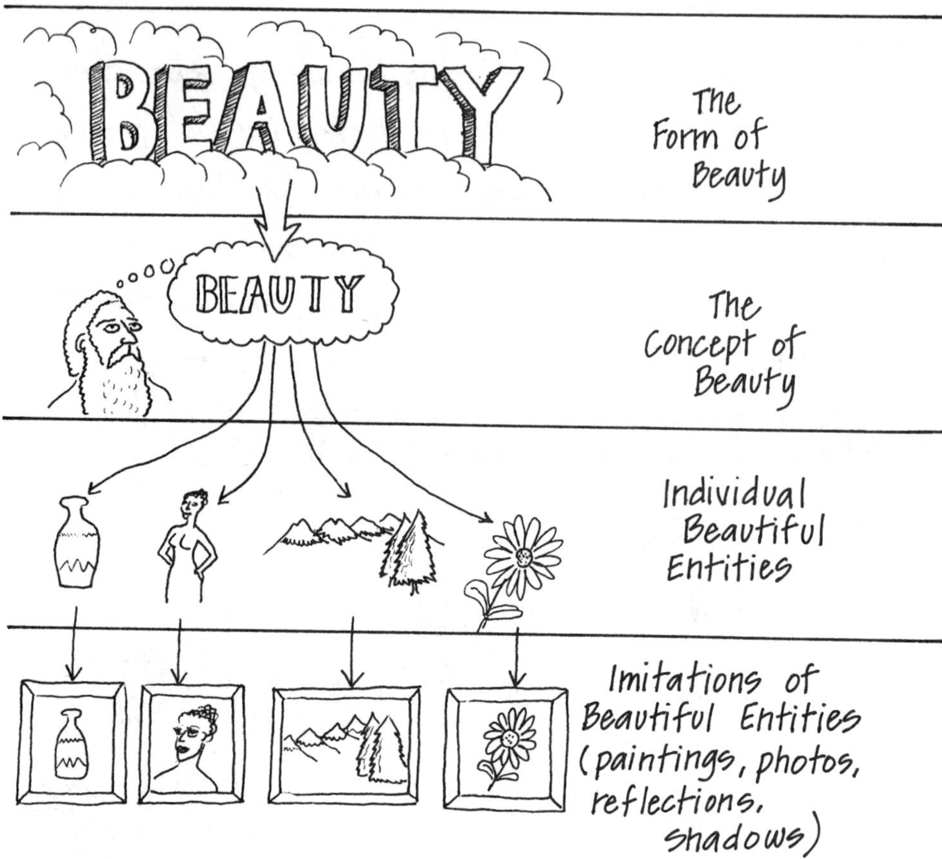

Plato's conception of the Forms is very complicated, but we can simplify it by saying that they are the eternal truths which are the source of all Reality. Take, for example, the concept of beauty. Things in the sensible world are beautiful to the extent that they "imitate" or "participate" in Beauty. However, these beautiful things will break, grow old, or die. But Beauty itself (the Form) is eternal. It will always be. The same can be said of Truth and Justice. (Also, more embarrassingly, of Horseness or of Toothpickness.)

Furthermore, just as the sensible world and awareness of it are dependent on the Sun, so are the Forms and knowledge of them dependent on the Good, which is a Super-Form, or the Form of all Forms. The state of beholding the Good is represented in the myth of the cave by the released prisoner beholding the Sun itself. Plato's theory is such that the whole of Reality is founded upon the Good, which is Reality's source of being. And all Knowledge is ultimately knowledge of the Good.

Moreover, Plato optimistically holds that if one ever comes to know the Good, one becomes good. Ignorance is the only sin. No one would willingly do wrong.

How can we learn the Truth? Where can we find the Forms and the Good? Who can teach us? Plato had curious answers to these questions. In the dialogue called <u>Meno</u>, Plato had an unschooled slaveboy solve a difficult mathematical problem by answering affirmatively or negatively a series of simple questions posed by Socrates. Plato concluded from this episode that the slaveboy always knew the answer, but didn't know that he knew. All truth comes from within—from the soul. Our immortal soul is born with the truth, having beheld the Forms in their purity before its embodiment. Birth, or the embodiment of the soul, is so traumatic that one forgets what one knows, and must spend the rest of life plumbing the depths of the soul to recover what one already knows. Hence Plato's strange doctrine that all knowledge is recollection. Now we see Socrates' rôle as that of helping his student to remember, just as does the psychoanalyst with his patient today. (Plato's theory of recollection is the source of the Freudian conception of the unconscious.)

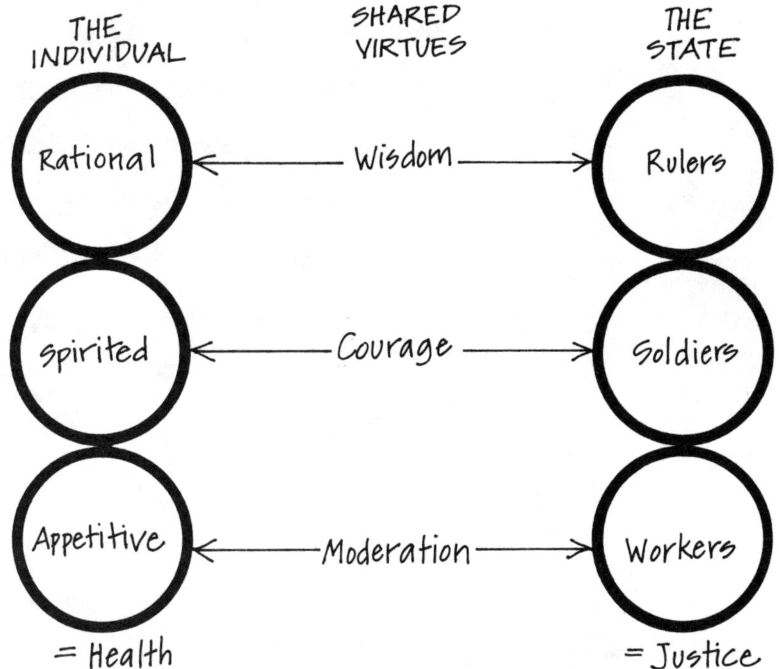

The Republic is well-known not only for its epistemology, but also for its social philosophy. The latter for Plato is a combination of psychology and political science. He said that the City (the "Republic") is the individual writ large. Just as the individual's psyche has three aspects — (a) the appetitive, animal side, (b) the spirited source of action, and (c) the rational aspect — so does the ideal City have three classes — (a) the workers and the artisans, (b) the soldiers, and (c) the rulers. In the psyche, the rational part must convince the spirited part to help it control the appetitive. Otherwise, there will be an unbalanced soul and neurosis will ensue.

Similarly, in the City, the rulers must be philosophers who have beheld the Forms, hence who know what is good. They must train the military caste to help control the naturally unruly peasants. The latter will be allowed to use money, own property, and wear decorations in moderation, but the members of the top two classes, who understand the corrupting effect of greed, will live in an austere, absolute communism, sleeping and eating together, owning no property, receiving no salary, and having sexual relations on a pre-arranged schedule with partners shared by all. These rules will guarantee that the City will not be frenzied and anarchic — a strange beginning for the discipline of Political Science (one from which it has still not recovered)!

The members of the ideal city will be allowed to play simple lyres and pipes and sing patriotic, uplifting songs, but most artists will be drummed out of the Republic. This is for four reasons: (1) Ontological: since art deals with images (the lowest rung in the Simile of the Line), art is an imitation of an imitation of an imitation. (Art is "thrice removed from the throne.") (2) Epistemological: the artist is at the conjectural stage. He knows nothing but <u>claims</u> to know something. (3) Aesthetical: Art expresses itself in sensual images, hence distracts us from Beauty itself, which is purely spiritual. (4) Moral: Art is created by and appeals to the appetitive side of the soul (Freud's "ID"). Art is either erotic or violent, or both, hence it is an incitement to anarchy. Even Homer must be censored.

(The whole enterprise of <u>The Republic</u> can be viewed as a plea that philosophy take over the rôle which art had hitherto played in Greek culture.)

Plato did not live to see the inauguration of his ideal state, nor to see the installation of a Philosopher King who would Know the Good, but the legacy which Plato left is still very much with us, for better or for worse. The eminent British-American philosopher Alfred North Whitehead once said that the history of philosophy is merely a series of footnotes to Plato.

Plato's influence is clearly seen in the thought of one of his best students, ARISTOTLE (384-322 B.C.). Aristotle, born in Stagira, spent 20 years at Plato's academy. Soon after the death of the master, Aristotle left the school because of disagreements with its new chiefs, and he founded an academy of his own, the Lyceum. In Aristotle's school, Platonic philosophy was taught, but it was also criticized.

The main thrust of Aristotle's dispute with his mentor concerned the latter's "other-worldliness." For Plato, there are two worlds: the unspeakably lofty world of Forms, and the world of mere "things," which is but a poor imitation of the former. Aristotle contradicted this view, asserting that there is only ONE world, and that we are right smack in the middle of it. In criticizing Plato, Aristotle asked: If Forms are essences of things, how can they exist separated from things? If they are the cause of things, how can they exist in a different world? And a most telling criticism has to do with the problem of CHANGE AND MOTION, which the early Greeks had tried to solve.

They thought that either stability was an illusion (the view of Heraclitus, for example), or that motion was an illusion (the view of Parmenides). Plato had tried to resolve the dilemma by acknowledging the insights of both Heraclitus and Parmenides. The former's world is the unstable and transient realm of the visible. The latter's world is the immutable realm of the intelligible composed of the eternally unchanging Forms, which themselves are poorly reflected in the transitory world of the Visible. But did Plato's compromise really solve the problem of motion and change? Is it really comprehensible to explain "changing things" by saying that they are bad imitations of unchanging things?

Aristotle thought not.

In offering his own solution to the problem, Aristotle employed some of the same terminology as Plato. He said that a distinction must be drawn between FORM and MATTER, but that these two features of reality can be distinguished only in thought,

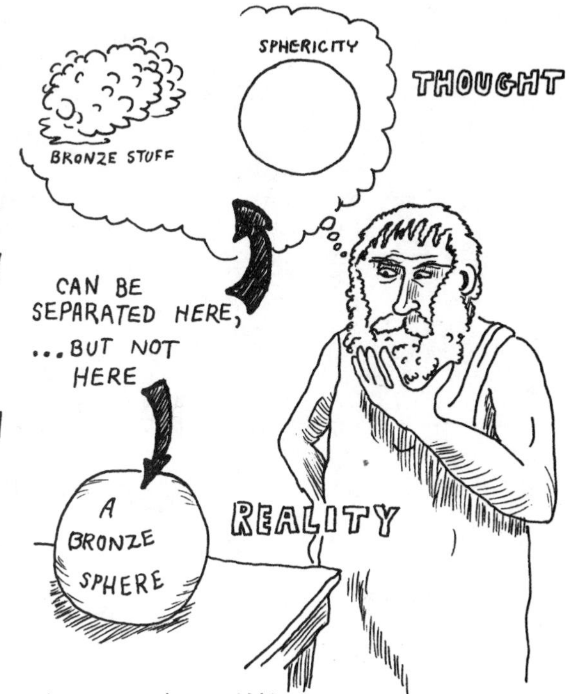

not in fact. Forms are not separate entities. They are embedded in particular things. They are IN the world. To think otherwise is an intellectual confusion. A particular object, to count as an object at all, must have both form and matter. Form, as Plato had said, is UNIVERSAL, in the sense that many particulars can have the same form. Aristotle called an object's form its "whatness." That is, when you say <u>what something is</u> (it's a tree, it's a book), you are naming its form. The form is a thing's "essence" or "nature." It is related to the thing's FUNCTION (a wheel, a knife, a brick, etc.).

An object's MATTER is what is unique to that object. Aristotle called it the object's "THISNESS." All wheels or trees have the same form (or function), but no two have the same matter. Matter is "the principle of individuation." An object with both form and matter is what Aristotle called a SUBSTANCE. His anti-Platonic metaphysics holds that reality is composed of a plurality of substances. It is not composed of an upper tier of eternal Forms and a lower tier of matter which unsuccessfully attempts to imitate those Forms. This is Aristotle's PLURALISM as opposed to Plato's DUALISM (a dualism which verges on IDEALISM, because for Plato the most "real" tier of reality is the non-material). How does Aristotle's pluralism solve the problem of motion and change, a problem which was unsuccessfully addressed by his predecessors? It does so by reinterpreting MATTER and FORM as POTENTIALITY and ACTUALITY, and turning these concepts into a

theory of change. Any object in the world can be analyzed in terms of these categories. Aristotle's famous example is that of an acorn. The acorn's matter contains the potentiality of becoming an oak tree, which is the acorn's actuality. The acorn is the potentiality of there being an oak tree. The oak tree is the actuality of the acorn. So, for Aristotle, "form" is an operating cause. Each individual substance is a self-contained teleological (i.e., goal-oriented) system.

In fact, Aristotle analyzed all substances in terms of four causes: the material cause is the "stuff" out of which something is made (e.g., a chunk of marble which is to become a statue). The formal cause is the form, or essence, of the statue, that which it strives to be. (This exists both in the mind of the artist, and potentially in the marble itself.) The efficient cause is the actual force which brings about the change (the sculptor's chipping the block of stone). The <u>final cause</u> is the ultimate purpose of the object (the beautification of the Parthenon).

Nature, then, is a teleological system in which each substance is striving for self-actualization and for whatever perfection is possible within the limitations allowed it by its particular essence. As in Plato's theory, everything is striving unconsciously toward "the Good." Aristotle believed that for such a system to work, some concrete perfection must actually exist as the TELOS (or goal) toward which all things are striving.

This entity Aristotle called "the Prime Mover." It serves as a kind of God in Aristotle's metaphysics, but unlike the traditional gods of Greece, and unlike the God of Western religion, the Prime Mover is almost completely nonanthropomorphic. It is the cause of the universe, not in the Judeo-Christian sense of creating it out of nothing, but in the sense of a Final Cause; everything "moves" toward it in the way a runner moves toward a goal. The Prime Mover is the only thing in the universe with no potentiality because, being perfect, it cannot change. It is pure actuality, which is to say, pure activity. What activity?

The activity of pure thought. And what does it think about? Perfection! That is to say, about itself. The Prime Mover's knowledge is immediate, complete self-consciousness.

— What we seem to have here is an absolutely divine case of narcissism.

Aristotle's moral philosophy, as it appears in his manuscript now called *The Nicomachean Ethics*, reflects his teleological metaphysics. The notion of *goal*, or *purpose*, is the overriding one in his moral theory. Aristotle noted that every act is performed for some *purpose*, which he defined as the "good" of that act. (We perform an act because we find its purpose to be worthwhile.) *Either* the totality of our acts is an infinitely circular series (we get up in order to eat breakfast, we eat breakfast in order to go to work, we go to work in order to get money, we get money so we can buy food in order to be able to eat breakfast, etc., etc., etc.), in which case life would be a pretty meaningless endeavor, *or* there is some ultimate good toward which the purposes of all acts are directed. If there is such a good, we should try to come to know it so that we can adjust all our acts toward it, in order to avoid that saddest of all tragedies — the wasted life.

According to Aristotle, there is general verbal agreement that the end toward which all human acts are directed is _happiness_, and that therefore happiness is the human good, since we seek happiness for its own sake, not for the sake of something else. But unless we philosophize about happiness and get to know exactly what it is and how to achieve it, it will be platitudinous simply to _say_ that happiness is the ultimate good. In order to determine the nature of happiness, Aristotle turned to his metaphysical schema and asked, "What is the function of the human?" (in the same way he would ask about the function of a knife or an acorn). He came to the conclusion that man's function is to engage in "an activity of the soul which is in accordance with virtue and which follows a rational principle." Before grasping this complicated definition we must determine what "virtue" is, and what kinds of virtues there are. But first, as an aside, it must be mentioned that Aristotle believed that certain material conditions must hold before happiness can be achieved.

This list of conditions will reveal Aristotle's elitism:

We need good friends, riches, and political power. We need a good birth, good children, and good looks ("... for the man who is very ugly in appearance ... is not very likely to be happy"). We must not be very short. Furthermore, we must be free from the need of performing manual labor. ("No man can practice virtue who is living the life of a mechanic or laborer.") — It should be noted that Aristotle's moral theory would be left substantially intact if his elitist bias were deleted.

Now, as to virtues, there are two kinds: INTELLECTUAL and MORAL. Intellectual virtues are acquired through a combination of inheritance and education, moral virtues through imitation,

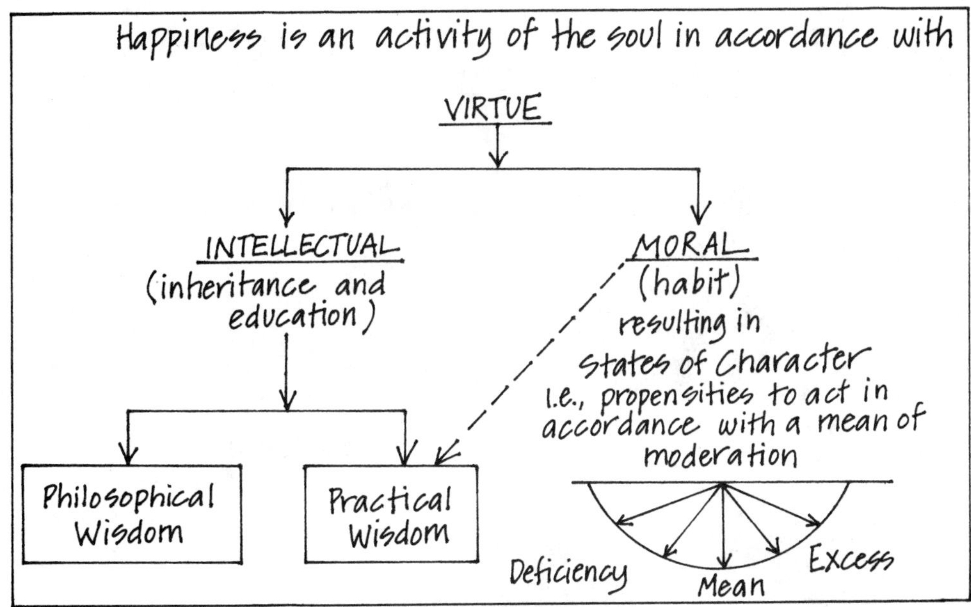

practice and habit. The habits which we develop result in "states of character," that is, in dispositions to act certain ways, and these states of character are "virtuous" for Aristotle if they result in acts which are in accordance with a "golden mean" of moderation. For example, when it comes to facing danger, one can act with excess, i.e., show too much fear. (This is cowardice.) Or one can act deficiently by showing too little fear. (This is foolhardiness.) Or one can act with moderation, and hence virtuously, by showing

the right amount of fear. (This is courage.) Aristotle realized that the choices we must make if we are to learn moral virtue cannot be made mathematically; rather, they are always context-bound and must be approached through trial and error.

Returning to the intellectual virtues of practical and philosophical wisdom, the former is the wisdom necessary to make judgments consistent with one's under-

standing of the good life. It is therefore related to moral virtue (as in the diagram). Philosophical wisdom is scientific, disinterested and contemplative. It is associated with pure reason, and, for Aristotle, the capacity for reason is that which is most human; therefore philosophical wisdom is the highest virtue. So, when Aristotle defined happiness as "an activity of the soul in accordance with virtue," the activity referred to is philosophical activity. The human being can only be happy by leading a contemplative life, but not a monastic one. We are not only philosophical animals, but social ones as well. We are engaged in a world where decisions concerning practical matters are forced upon us constantly. Happiness (hence the good life) requires excellence in both spheres.

Not only did Aristotle make major contributions to metaphysics and ethics, he also wrote important treatises on aesthetics and politics. Furthermore, he singlehandedly founded the science of logic, that is, the science of valid inference. Symbolic logic has developed a long way since Aristotle's time, but it is indebted to him as its founder, and it has made more additions than corrections to his work.

Some of Aristotle's empirical claims about the world leave something to be desired (for instance, his claim that falling rocks accelerate because they are happy to be getting home, or his claim that snakes have no testicles because they have no legs). Nevertheless, Aristotle's metaphysics, his ethics, his logic, and his aesthetics remain permanent monuments to the greatness of human thought.

«»

III. The Hellenistic Period

After the death of Aristotle, Greek civilization entered what historians call the Hellenistic era. It is a period of cultural decline. The Greek city states, unable to solve the problem of political unity, were decimated by the Peloponnesian War, and ravaged by the plague. First they fell under Macedonian rule, then, after the death of Alexander the Great, eventually were absorbed into the newly emerging Roman Empire. Many of the philosophies of this "decadent" period began in Greece but received their greatest exposure in Rome. This is true of the two major philosophies of the period, Epicureanism and Stoicism.

The philosophy of Epicurus (341–270 B.C.) is known (not surprisingly) as EPICUREANISM. If today the term hints of gluttony, debauchery and bacchanalian orgies, that is not Epicurus' fault, but the fault of some of his Roman interpreters, because Epicurus himself led a life of sobriety and simplicity, eating bread, cheese and olives, drinking a bit of wine, napping in his hammock, and enjoying conversation with his friends while strolling through his garden. He died with dignity and courage after a painful, protracted disease.

Epicureanism was grounded in the atomic theory of Democritus, but in fact, Epicurus, like all post-Alexandrian philosophers, does not seem to have been really interested in science, but in finding out about the good life. However, since Aristotle's time, the notion of "the good life" had suffered a set-back. It no longer made sense to advocate being active, influential, political and responsible as a way of self-improvement. Reality seemed to be unmoved by personal initiative, and the individual himself was developing a feeling of powerlessness as he was about to be absorbed into the massive, impersonal bureaucracy of the Roman Empire. Like Aristotle, Epicurus believed that the goal of life was happiness, but happiness he equated simply with PLEASURE. No act should be undertaken except for the pleasure in which it results, and no act should be rejected except for the pain which it produces. This provoked Epicurus to analyze the different kinds of pleasure. There are two kinds of desires, hence two kinds of pleasure as a result of gratifying those

The individual in the Roman Empire

desires: NATURAL DESIRE (which has two subclasses), and VAIN DESIRE.

I. Natural desire
   A. Necessary (e.g., desire for food and sleep).
   B. Unnecessary (e.g., desire for sex).

II. Vain desire (e.g., the desire for decorative clothing or exotic food).

Natural necessary desires <u>must</u> be satisfied, and are easy to satisfy. They result in a good deal of pleasure and in very few painful consequences. Vain desires do not need to be satisfied, and are not easy to satisfy. Because there are no natural limits to them, they tend to become obsessive and lead to very painful consequences.

The pursuit of Vain Pleasure

The desire for sex is natural, but usually can be overcome, and when it can be it should be, because satisfaction of the sexual drive gives intense pleasure, but involves one in relationships which are usually ultimately more painful than pleasant, and are often extremely painful.

One of the natural and necessary desires to which Epicurus pays a great deal of attention is the desire for <u>repose</u>. This is to be understood both physically and psychically. The truly good person (that is, the one who experiences the most pleasure) is the one who, having overcome all unnecessary desires, gratifies his necessary desires in the most moderate way possible, leaves plenty of time for physical and mental repose, and is free from worry.

cashier, Do You Mind!!
sshh! She's Reposing!

We will notice that Epicurus' definition of pleasure is <u>negative</u>, that is, pleasure is the absence of pain. It is this negative definition which prevents Epicurus from falling into a crass sensualism. The trouble with this definition is that, taken to its logical extremity, the <u>absence</u> of life is better than any life at all (as Freud discovered in his <u>Beyond the Pleasure Principle</u>, where he claimed that behind

Beyond the Pleasure Principle

the "pleasure principle" is THANATOS, the Death instinct).

This is a bit ironic, since Epicurus himself had claimed that his philosophy dispelled the fear of death. Democritus' atomism led Epicurus to believe that death was merely the absence of sensation and consciousness; therefore, there could be no sensation or consciousness of death to fear. "Where death is, we are not. Where we are, death is not."

Some of Epicurus' Roman followers interpreted "pleasure" quite differently, defining it as a positive titillation. It is because of these extremists that today Epicureanism is often associated with sensualistic hedonism. Sickly Epicurus, swinging in his hammock, would have disapproved. (Though not too harshly. Polemics cause agitation, which is painful.) Epicurus' theory never constituted a major philosophical movement, but he had disciples in both Greece and Rome for a number of centuries. His most famous follower was the Roman LUCRETIUS, who, in the first century B.C., wrote a long poem, On the Nature of Things, expounding the philosophy of his master. It is through Lucretius' poem that many have been introduced to the thought of Epicurus.

Zeno at the Stoa

STOICISM was another important Hellenistic philosophy which was transported to Rome. It was founded in Greece by ZENO of CYPRUS (334-262 B.C.), who used to preach to his students from a portico, or "stoa" (hence the term, "stoicism", literally, "Porchism"). Like Epicureanism, stoicism had its roots in pre-Socratic materialism, but stoicism too, especially in its Roman form, became disinterested in physics and peculiarly concerned with the problem of human conduct. The three most interesting of the Roman Stoics were SENECA (4-65 A.D.), a dramatist and high-ranking statesman, EPICTETUS (late first century A.D.), a slave who earned his freedom, and MARCUS AURELIUS (121-180 A.D.), a Roman emperor. (It's quite striking that a slave and an emperor could share the same philosophy of resignation, though probably this was easier for the emperor than for the slave!) The Stoics accepted the

I'm resigned to my fate

Yes (sigh!), I too.

Socratic equation, "virtue = knowledge." There is a cognitive state which, once achieved, guarantees complete well-being. One should strive throughout one's life to acquire this wisdom. Human excellence is attained instantaneously once one has gained the enlightenment.

The duration of such a life of perfection is indifferent (which fact leads to the Stoic advocacy of suicide under certain circumstances). In order to achieve this state of blessedness, one must free oneself from all worldly demands, particularly those of the emotions and of pleasure-seeking. The Stoic wise man is an ascete. He has transcended the passions which create a disorderly condition in the soul. The Stoic has no interest in all those objects which excite the passions of grief, joy, hope or fear in normal human beings.

What is the content of Stoic wisdom? It is similar to the Aristotelian notion that the good consists of acting in accordance with one's nature. The Stoic addition to this idea is that to so act requires acting in accordance with Nature itself, that is, with the totality of reality (which the Stoics take to be divine). Considered as a whole, reality is perfect. Humans will also become perfect if they learn to live in accordance with the divine plan of reality. This requires that one make one's desires identical with the overall providential plan for the universe. In fact, a person can do nothing but conform to the grand design, and Stoic wisdom consists in recognizing this truth. Fools are those who try to impose their own selfish desires on reality. This results in unhappiness and unfreedom. If freedom is the unity of will and ability (that is, being able to do what one wants), then the only way to be free is to want what the universe wants. We shouldn't wish that we could get what we desire, rather we should desire what we get. If we could learn to equate what we want with what's the case, then we would always be free and happy, since we'd always get just what we want. This is Stoic wisdom.

Don't try to get what you want, — rather want what you get.

The Stoics realized that if one ever achieved this lofty state, the apparent harshness of reality might jeopardize one's inner equilibrium, and one might back-slide into pain and anxiety. For this reason, and because the Stoics believed that the amount of time one spent in the enlightened state was indifferent, the Stoics advocated suicide under certain conditions. Epictetus said of suicide, "Tis smokey and I go away." Seneca said, "The dirtiest death is preferable to the daintiest slavery," and, "To die well is to escape the danger of living badly." In fact, on the advice of the Emperor Nero, Seneca did step into the bath and open his veins.

During the period when Stoicism was exercising its greatest influence, a new social and religious form of thought was coming to the fore: Christianity. And although the Christians had not learned to defend their new religion with a systematic philosophy as they would in the Middle Ages, their doctrine was in competition with the philosophies of the day for the hearts and minds of men and women. All such thought-systems were responding to the same problems, so it is no surprise that there are some similarities between Christianity and a philosophy like Stoicism; for example, both philosophies share the doctrine of resignation, the disdain for attachment to earthly things, and the concern with conforming to the will of divine Providence. (The differences cannot be overlooked, however, such as the discrepancy between Stoic and Christian teachings on suicide. Also, Stoicism was inclined to be quietistic and acquiescent to political authority, while in its inception Christianity tended to be activistic and resistant to political domination.

Epictetus said, "Take no oath, or . . . take only as many as you must." This attitude contrasts greatly with that of many Christians who refused to swear an oath on the divinity of the emperor, and were martyred for that refusal.)

After the death of the Stoic Marcus Aurelius ("the last good emperor"), a long period of upheaval and disorder ensued. The helplessness which people felt in the face of the decadence of the crumbling Empire was responded to by a religious revival. The most prominent philosophical religious competitor with Christianity during the third century A.D. was a mystical form of Platonism Known today as NEO-PLATONISM, espoused by PLOTINUS (204-270). We have already seen a deepseated propensity toward other-worldliness in Plato, which Aristotle had criticized. Plato's claim of superiority for the other world fit in well with the world-weariness of the third century.

For Plotinus, as for Plato before him, absolute truth and certainty cannot be found in this world. Plato had taught a purely rational method for transcending the flux of the world and achieving truth and certainty, but Plotinus preached that such a vision can only be achieved extra-rationally, through a kind of ecstatic union with the

One. The One was for Plotinus the Absolute, or God. Nothing can be truly known about the One in any rational sense, nor can any characterization of the One be strictly correct. If we review Plato's Simile of the Line from a Plotinian perspective, we will see that language, and therefore thought, function by drawing distinctions (we say "this is a pen," meaning it is not the desk, etc.), but in the One, no distinctions exist, hence nothing can be thought or said about it. A person can know the One only by uniting with it. That can be done in this life in moments of mystical rapture, but in the long run the goal can only be achieved in death.

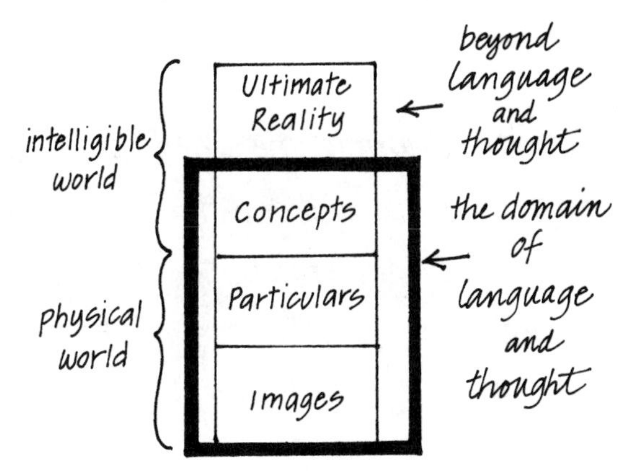

One can prepare for the ultimate union through an ascetic program of virtuous living. Plotinus' own version of "the Line" is based on his idea that God, or the Absolute, does not perform acts of creation (that would sully God's unchangeableness), rather God "emanates." That is to say, God is reflected onto lower planes, and these reflections represent kinds of imitations of God's perfection in

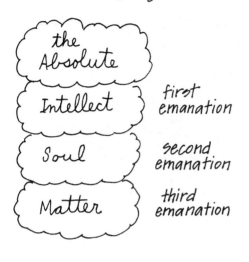

descending degrees of fragmentation. (What we have here is a kind of "gooey" Simile of the Line.) This metaphysics borders on pantheism – the view that reality and God are the same.

the Absolute

Intellect — first emanation

Soul — second emanation

Matter — third emanation

Because the philosophy of Plotinus and his followers was the last philosophy of the classical period, his version of Platonism was the one which was handed down to the Medieval world, and because of this fact we will see that the problem of pantheism crops up again in the Middle Ages, this time not to haunt the death scene of Classicism, but the birth scene of Christian philosophy.

IV. MEDIEVAL PHILOSOPHY

In the year 313 A.D. the Roman Emperor Constantine was converted to Christianity, and, even though only one in ten citizens of the Empire was a Christian, Christianity became the official religion of the realm. During the next couple of centuries the early Church Fathers turned to the prevailing neo-Platonic philosophical tradition in their search for intellectual foundations for their still relatively new religion. The first truly important philosopher in this Christian Platonic tradition was AUGUSTINE OF HIPPO (354-430). He had one foot squarely planted in the Classical world, and one in the Medieval world, and he straddled the abyss which separated these two worlds.

As a young student of rhetoric in Rome, acutely aware of

his own sensual nature, Augustine was concerned with the problem of good and evil. He became attracted to Manicheanism, (founded by Mani of Persia in the third century), which, combining certain Christian and Persian elements, was a philosophy which understood reality in terms of an eternal struggle between the Principle of Light (Good) and the Principle of Darkness (Evil). The strife between these two principles manifested itself as the world. The soul represented the good and the body represented evil. As a Manichee, Augustine could attribute his many sins to a principle somehow outside himself.

The Devil made me do it!
F.P.O.
M-108

But Augustine soon became dissatisfied with this "solution" to the problem of evil, and he became attracted to Neo-Platonism and its conception of an <u>immaterial</u> <u>reality</u>. It was from Neo-Platonism that Augustine got his idea of evil not as a real feature of reality, but as a LACK, an incompleteness, a privation. (Recall

Woe is me. I'm a sinkhole of nothingness.

the Simile of the Line: the more goodness a thing has, the more real it is. Conversely, the less reality it has, the worse it is. Just as a dental cavity is a lack of calcium [a hole is not a thing, it is an absence of being], so is a sin not a thing, but an absence of goodness.) In 388, after a minor mystical experience, Augustine converted to Christianity, and never again vacillated in his intellectual commitment. In 391 he was ordained priest, and in 396 became the Bishop of Hippo, on the North African coast. During this period, Christianity was still seeking to achieve focus on its own identity, and Augustine spent an enormous amount of energy combatting a series of heresies: Donatism, Priscillianism, Arianism, and of course, that of his former persuasion, Manicheanism. But at the same time he had to combat a new and especially difficult heresy, that of Pelagianism. Pelagius' heresy was that of over-accentuating the rôle of free will in salvation, and minimizing the rôle of God's grace. Much to Augustine's embarrassment, Pelagius had been using Augustine's book on free will to defend his own view.

Does God's Foreknowledge Determine Our Actions?

So Augustine found himself walking a tightrope. He had to attack the Manichees for minimizing free will, and attack the Pelagians for over-emphasizing it. This problem occupied him in some very subtle philosophical reasoning.

THE PROBLEM: If God is all-wise (omniscient) then he knows the future. If he knows the future, then the future must unfold exactly in accordance with his knowledge (otherwise, he does not know the future). If the events in the future must occur according to God's foreknowledge of them, then they are necessary and there is no freedom. If there is no freedom, then humans are not responsible for their acts, in which case it would be immoral to punish people for their sins. (If God knew millions of years before Judas was born that he would betray Jesus, how could God send Judas to hell for his sin?) So the conclusion seems to be: either God is omniscient but immoral, or he is benevolent but ignorant. How can Augustine avoid this unpalatable dilemma? He does so with a number of sophisticated arguments. One is that, for God, there is no past or future, only an eternal present. For him, everything happens at once. To say, "God knew millions of years before Judas' birth that he would betray Jesus," is to make the human error of believing that God is in time. In fact, God is outside of time. (That's what it means to say

Judas

God Is Not In Time

that God is eternal.) Another tack of Augustine's is to admit that God's knowledge of the world entails necessity, but to deny that necessity is incompatible with freedom. Like the Stoics, Augustine believed that freedom is the capacity of doing what one wants, and one can do what one wants even if God (or anyone else) already knows what that person wants. Augustine pointed out that God's foreknowledge of a decision doesn't *cause* the decision, any more than my own acts are caused by my knowledge of what I'm going to do.

This is a sample of Augustinian thought. His philosophy is a profound meditation on the relation between God and the human being. It was addressed to a troubled and expiring world. The old order was crumbling. In fact, on the same day Augustine succumbed to the infirmities of old age in the cathedral at Hippo, the barbaric Vandals were burning the city. Even though they left the cathedral standing out of respect for him, the fires that consumed Hippo were the same ones which consumed the Roman Empire. The Classical Period was over, and that long night which some call the Dark Ages had commenced.

At the death of Augustine, Western philosophy fell into a state of deterioration which was to last for 400 years. This period, the advent of the Medieval world, truly was the Dark Night of the Western soul. The Roman legions could no longer control the frontiers of the Empire and the Teutonic tribes from the eastern forest swarmed over the old Empire.

Rome was sacked twice within a 35-year period. The new "Barbarian" emperors no longer bore Latin names but Germanic ones. They were not interested in culture as it had been known in Classical times. Philosophy as the Greeks and Romans had understood it was in danger of perishing.

During this long dark night philosophy flickered only as individual candle flames at distant corners of the old dead Empire. Certain isolated monasteries in Italy, Spain Britain, and on the rocky crags of islands in the Irish Sea produced what are known as the ENCYCLOPEDIASTS, who systematically compiled and conserved whatever remnants of Classical wisdom they could lay their hands on. The three salient figures in this tradition are BOETHIUS (480-525) in Italy, ISIDORE (570-636) in Spain, and THE VENERABLE BEDE (674-735) in England. (St. Isidore's encyclopedia is particularly revealing. Under the letter "A" we find both an entry on the Atomic theory, and an entry on the Antipodes, a people who were supposed to inhabit the rocky plains of southern Africa, and who, Isidore believed, had their big toes on the outside of the feet, thereby allowing them more maneuverability among the rocky fields where they dwelt!)

An Antipode Showing Off In Rocky Terrain

Isidore's hodge-podge is emblematic of the state of philosophy during the Dark Ages.

Suddenly, after four centuries of relative silence, philosophy blossomed forth in the work of the first great metaphysical system-builder of the Middle Ages, the redundantly named JOHN SCOTUS ERIGENA ("John the Irishman, the Irishman" [ca. 810 - ca. 877]). John had been called from Ireland to the Palatine school of King Charles the Bald to translate the Greek document known today as "the Pseudo-Dionysius" (a work falsely believed to have been written by St. Paul's Christian convert, St. Dionysius, but believed today to have been written by a neo-Platonic philosopher unsympathetic to Christianity). Erigena's own book, <u>On the Divisions of Nature</u>, was greatly influenced by his reading of the "Pseudo-Dionysius," and is a confusing combination of Christian dogma and neo-Platonic pantheism. Through his book and his influential translation, Platonism gained an even greater foothold in Christianity.

John's goal was the categorization and understanding of the totality of reality (what he calls "Nature"). The first categorical distinction he drew was between

THINGS THAT ARE and THINGS THAT ARE NOT

John Scotus Divides Up Nature

This distinction involves the Platonic supposition that there is a hierarchy of being, that some things are more real than other things. "Things-that-are-not" are those entities which on a neo-Platonic scale contained a lesser degree of reality. For example, a particular tree or horse contains less being than the Form "Tree," or the Form "Horse," hence particulars are subsumed under this negative category. So are all "lacks" or "deprivations," such as sinful acts or acts of forgetting. The most surprising thing we find in this category is what John called "super-reality" — that which cannot be grasped by the human intellect, that which on the eo-Platonic scale is "beyond being." Apparently John was talking about God.

What is left? What can be called "The-things-that-are"? Only those entities which can be comprehended by pure human intellect, namely, the Platonic Forms! All else is other than being.

So we find this Christian scholar in the apparently awkward position of claiming that God is among those things classified as non-existent — in the same class where you would expect to find mountains made of gold, centaurs, griffins and round squares. So why doesn't this end all discussion of God once and for all? Because John's method of the "vias affirmativa and negativa" (borrowed from the "Pseudo-Dionysius") allowed him to make sense of the nothingness of a being-beyond-being.

VIA AFFIRMATIVA	VIA NEGATIVA
We affirm: "<u>God is wise.</u>" ↑ This affirmation is true only as metaphor. "Wisdom" is a word which gets its meaning from <u>human</u> discourse. We can apply it to God only analogically to give us a hint of his nature.	We deny the affirmation: "<u>God is not wise</u>." ↑ This negation is literal. Because "wisdom" gets its meaning from human discourse, it cannot literally apply to God.

This affirmation and its negation do not lead to a self-contradiction, rather they serve as thesis and antithesis, and are dialectically reconciled in a (Hegelian-like) synthesis which will lead us to realize that God is somehow super-wise. The same method will show us why John said that God does not exist, but that he [super-] Exists.

There is yet another way in which John Scotus Erigena divided Nature:

(1) Nature that creates and is uncreated.
(2) Nature that creates and is created.
(3) Nature that is created and does not create.
(4) Nature that is not created and does not create.

#1 = God
#2 = the Platonic Forms
#3 = the physical world
#4 = God

(Remember, in this neo-Platonic schema, to say that something "x" <u>creates</u> is to say that there is something below x in the hierarchy of reality which is dependent upon x. Conversely, to say that something "y" <u>is created</u> is to say that y is dependent on something above it for its existence.)

In this system, God is both Alpha and Omega, beginning and end, creator and goal of creation. God issues out into the world and comes back to himself. All this looks suspiciously like Plotinus' pantheistic system of emanations, and though many attempts were made to defend <u>The Divisions of Nature</u> against the charge of heresy, eventually it was condemned as heterodoxical in 1225 by Pope Honorius III.

ALPHA and OMEGA

After John Scotus Erigena, there were no great system-makers again for the next 350 years. From the ninth to the thirteenth century, philosophy would be done in a more piecemeal manner than it was done by Augustine or John Scotus, or than it would be in the thirteenth century by Thomas Aquinas. It was confined to a kind of philosophical grammar of theological terms. However, this does not mean that it was always unimpressive. One of the most striking pieces of philosophical logic produced in the Medieval period is the proof of God's existence created by ANSELM of CANTERBURY (1033-1109), later Saint Anselm.

Anselm's argument began with a reference to the fool (of Psalms 53:1) who "says in his heart, 'There is no God'." But, said Anselm, even the fool "is convinced that something exists in the understanding, at least, than which nothing greater can be conceived. For when he hears of this he understands it.... And assuredly that than which nothing greater can be conceived, cannot exist in the

PSALMS 53:1

understanding alone. For suppose it exists in the understanding alone: then it can be conceived to exist in reality, which is greater.... Hence, there is no doubt that there exists a being than which nothing greater can be conceived, and it exists both in the understanding and in reality.... and this being thou art, O Lord, our God."

Try out Anselm's argument. Conceive in your mind the most perfect being you can think of. (Anselm believed it will look very much like the conception of the traditional Christian God – a being which is all good, all knowing, all powerful, eternal and unchangeable.) Now ask yourself, does the entity you conceived exist <u>only</u> in your mind? If it is even possible that it exists only

One that exists
only here is less
perfect than one
which exists
out here.

there, then it is NOT the most perfect entity conceivable, because such an entity which existed both in your mind and EXTRA-mentally would be even more perfect. Therefore, if it's possible even to conceive of a most perfect being, such a being necessarily exists.

This is a slippery argument, and it immediately found detractors. A contemporary of Anselm's, GAUNILON, monk by profession, made the following objections on behalf of the fool. (1) It is in fact impossible to conceive of "a being than which nothing greater can be conceived." The very project boggles the mind. (2) If Anselm's argument were valid, then it would follow that the mere ability to conceive of a perfect tropical island would logically entail the existence of such an island.

Gaunilon's Objections

Anselm's response was as simple as Gaunilon's rebuttle: (1) If you understand the phrase "most perfect being," then you already have conceived of such a being.

(2) There is nothing in the definition of a tropical island which entails perfection, but the very definition of God entails that he be all-perfect, so it is impossible to conceive of God as lacking a perfection, and since it is obviously more perfect to be than not to be, the bare conception of God entails his existence.

This argument is both more difficult and more ingenious than it may appear to you. It is in fact a very good argument (which is not to say that it is flawless). Its genius is its demonstration that the sentence, "God does not exist," is a self-contradictory sentence. That is why only a fool could utter it.

Take note of how very Platonic Anselm's argument is. First, it is purely a priori — that is, it makes no appeal whatsoever to sensorial observation; it appeals exclusively to pure reason. Secondly, it makes explicit the Platonic view that the "most perfect" equals "the most real." (Recall the Simile of the Line.)

The ontological proof has had a long and chequered history. We shall see it again more than once before our narration ends. Many think that Immanuel Kant finally put it to rest in the 18th century (by showing that the flaw in the argument was not one of logic, but of grammar), but even today, 900 years after it was written, the argument has astute defenders.

Two problems which plagued the philosophers of the Middle Ages were THE PROBLEM OF FAITH vs. REASON, and THE PROBLEM OF THE UNIVERSALS. These received their best Medieval solution at the hands of Thomas Aquinas in the 13th century. The first problem concerned the question of whether to emphasize the claims of divine revelation or the claims of philosophy in one's conception of reality, and there were extremists in both camps. We've seen that philosophers like John Scotus Erigena had purely conceptual schemes in which there seemed to be no room for mere religious belief. Even St. Anselm's God seemed purely philosophical, and a far cry from the Stern Father and Vengeful Judge of the Old Testament. On the other end of the spectrum was the anti-philosopher, TERTULLIAN (169-220), whose famous cry was, "Credo quia absurdum"— "I believe that which is absurd"— with the implica-

Credo Quia Absurdum

tion that he believed it <u>because</u> it was absurd.

The debate between these two groups reached a high pitch and produced a number of startling claims, such as the view of the group called "the Latin Averröists," who, thinking they were following the lead of the great Arab philosopher Averröes, produced the "Doctrine of the Double Truth." This was the view that on many issues there were two mutually contradictory truths, one produced by faith and one by reason, but both valid from their respective points of view. So, for example, from the anatomical perspective the human being was a compilation of organs which, when they ceased to function, brought about the termination of the person, but from the theological perspective the human being was a soul which was, through God's grace, immortal.

This theory, though logically unsatisfactory, did for a short time play the historically positive rôle of allowing science to develop without having to conceive of itself in theological terms.

The other vexing problem of the day, the "problem of the universals," was the question concerning the status of the referents of words. The problem was introduced into the Middle Ages by Boethius, who had translated from the Greek an essay about Aristotle by the neo-Platonic author Porphyry (232-304). The latter had queried the ontological status of genera and species. We know that there exist individual things which we call "whales," but does the <u>genus</u> "Balaenoptera," or the <u>species</u> "Balaenoptera physalis" (Fin whale), or the <u>species</u> "Balaenoptera musculus" (Blue whale) exist in nature, or are they only artificial categories existing merely in the mind? (The same problem appears in sentences like, "This dog is brown." Do the words "dog" and "brown" only name the individual, or the <u>classes</u> of canines and brown things, and are those classes real or artificial?)

Whales exist only in the mind.

The debate which ensued was, of course, similar to the debate between Plato and Aristotle over the status of the Forms, but the original works of the Greeks were lost to the philosophers of the early Middle Ages, and it took them 900 years to arrive at the point which Aristotle had gained in one generation. The issue reached such a state of confusion that John of Salisbury (ca. 1115–ca. 1180) claimed that in his day there were as many ideas on the subject as there were heads. The extremes in this debate were represented, on one side, by the strict Platonists (today called "exaggerated realists"). They held that classes were not only real, but more real than individuals. Anselm himself was a representative of this view. The other extreme, represented by ROSCELIN (ca. 1050–1120) and WILLIAM OF OCKHAM (ca. 1280–ca. 1349), was the doctrine known as "nominalism" from the latin word for "name"—nom. According to this view, which was eventually found unacceptable by the Church, only particulars are real, and words denoting classes are merely names. According to the nominalists, the system of names creates differences and similarities, which exist only in the mind of the speaker, or in the system

of language itself.

You and I may smile when we are told by anthropologists that an Amazonian tribe includes in the same class toads, palm-leaves and arm pits (namely, the class of entities which are warm and dry on top and damp and dark underneath), but the nominalist asks us if this classification is any more arbitrary than our claim that whales and moles are members of the same class (namely, the class of entities with mammary glands)?

As was mentioned earlier, it was THOMAS AQUINAS (1225-1274) who is generally credited with working out the best Medieval solution both to the problem of Faith vs. Reason, and the problem of the Universals.

Prima mangiare, poi filosofare!

Thomas was an Italian nobleman who ran away from his family's castle to join the Dominican Order (where, by the way, he was so well-fed that a niche eventually had to be carved out of the dinner table to accommodate his ample girth). Before we talk about his philosophy, let's say something about the world he inhabited, 13th century Europe.

More than 100 years had elapsed between Anselm's death and Thomas' birth. In that century European scholars were becoming more and more acquainted with the "lost" works of the classical age through Christendom's extended contact with the Arab and Jewish philosophers of Moslem Spain. Not only were the works of Aristotle rediscovered, but magnificent commentaries on his philosophy were provided by the Spanish metaphysicians MAIMONIDES (1135-1204), a Jew, and AVERRÖES (1126-1198), an Arab. Though the theories of Aristotle were found to be shocking by some, his philosophy was actually more compatible with the new this-worldly attitude of the 13th century than was the now somewhat stale other-worldliness of Platonic thought. The human race had survived the millennium. The year 1000 had passed without the world ending, as many had expected.

The old apocalyptic prophecies faded further into the future, and, as Europe emerged from the darkest moments of the Dark Ages, interest in the world of here and now was revived. Aristotle surfaced as the champion of these new interests. It fell to Thomas Aquinas to 'Christianize" him — no easy task considering that Aristotle held such unChristian views as:

(A) The earth is eternal. (There never was a creation.)
(B) God is indifferent to human affairs. (He doesn't even know we exist.)
(C) The soul is not immortal.
(D) The goal of life is happiness.
(E) Pride is a virtue and humility a vice.

No surprise that Aristotle's works were banned by the University of Paris in 1210. (Indeed, Thomas' works themselves were condemned at Paris and at Oxford just after his death.)

Thomas Aquinas wrote over 40 volumes. His leading works are two encyclopedic projects, the _Summa theologica_ and the _Summa contra gentiles_. These tremendously systematic works comprise a whole

structure which has often been compared to the Gothic cathedrals, which were the new architectural style of his day. Like them, Thomas' work is a mirror held up to late Medieval society, but also a beacon unto it.

Thomas' main job was that of <u>reconciliation</u>, not only the reconciliation of Aristotle with Christendom, but also that of Reason with Faith, and of the warring sides in the debate over the status of Universals. Concerning the latter, Thomas was able to take advantage of the Aristotelian solution: Universals are neither autonomous Forms nor mere mental states. They are "imbedded" in particular objects as their "whatness." The human mind has the power of <u>abstraction</u> based on its ability to recognize real similarities which exist in nature. These abstractions become <u>concepts</u>. This solution came to be known as MODERATE REALISM. (It had been anticipated 120 years earlier by PETER ABELARD [1079–1142], whose view is called CONCEPTUALISM.)

Concerning the problem of Reason vs. Faith, Thomas began by distinguishing between <u>philosophy</u> and <u>theology</u>. The philosopher uses <u>human reason</u> alone. The theologian accepts <u>revelation</u> as his authority.

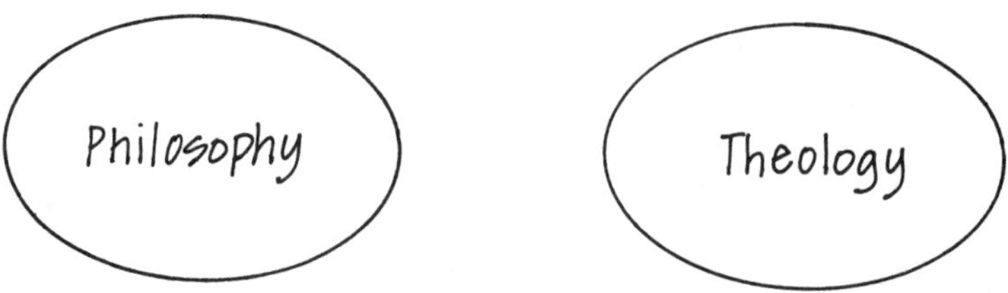

Then Thomas distinguished between REVEALED THEOLOGY (accepted purely on faith) and NATURAL

THEOLOGY (susceptible of the proof of reason). That is, he showed where philosophy and theology overlap.

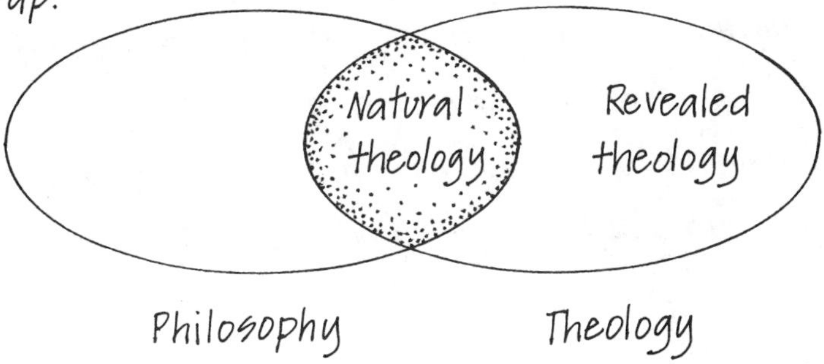

Natural theology

Revealed theology

Philosophy

Theology

When reason cannot establish the claims of faith, Thomas admitted this, and left those claims to the theologians and to personal belief (e.g., the claim that the universe has a beginning in time).

Most of Thomas' system is concerned with natural theology. Typical of this sphere are Thomas' proofs of God's existence. He provided five such proofs. Three of the "five ways" are very similar. We will select the second of the five as representative of Thomas' natural theology.

> "In the world of sense we find there is an order of efficient causes. There is no case known (neither is it, indeed, possible) in which a thing is found to be the efficient cause of itself; for so it would be prior to itself, which is impossible. Now in efficient causes it is not possible to go on to infinity.... Now to take away the cause is to take away the effect. Therefore if there be no first cause among efficient causes, there will be no ultimate, nor any intermediate cause.... Therefore it

is necessary to admit a first efficient cause, to which everyone gives the name of God."

In the most superficial reading of his proof, Thomas was giving us a domino theory and simply saying that, if there is a series of causes and effects, such a series must be caused by a being which is itself uncaused, otherwise we will have an infinite regress, which Thomas

finds intellectually repugnant. This version of the argument was submitted to careful scrutiny (for instance, by David Hume in the 18th century). Thomas' alleged knowledge of an order of causes was challenged, as well as the claim that an infinite series of causes is impossible. However, Thomistic scholars have demonstrated that the "second Way" is more complicated than it appears to be, involving a horizontal system of causes (in which an infinite series cannot be disproved), and a hierarchical system of dependencies (which, according to Thomas, cannot admit of an infinite regress).

Whatever its validity, there are some historically notable features about this and the four other Thomistic proofs. Unlike the ontological proof of Anselm, they all begin with an a posteriori claim, that is, with an appeal to observation. This is one of the Aristotelian characteristics of the argument, and in its commitment to the reality of the observable world, it contrasts greatly with the Platonism of Anselm's *a priori* proof. Still, there are vestiges of Platonism in the "Five Ways," including whatever appeal there is to a *hierarchy* of causes.

Like Aristotle's Philosophy, all of Thomas' thought, is teleological. This is especially true in his ethics. Human activity is viewed as a means-end structure. We choose desired goals, then choose among acts which lead to those goals. The acts are relative to the ends, but the ends (health, beauty, duty) are themselves relative to some absolute ends which give meaning to the relative ends; otherwise every series of actions would lead to an infinite regress.

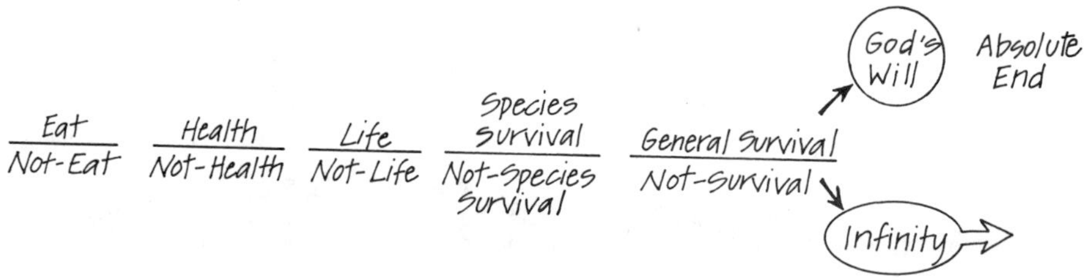

God's Will
Absolute End
Eat / Not-Eat
Health / Not-Health
Life / Not-Life
Species Survival / Not-Species Survival
General Survival / Not-Survival
Infinity

(Notice this is the same kind of argument which led Thomas to posit God as an uncaused cause.) If we want to make correct choices, we must know what the ultimate goal is. Aristotle said it was happiness. Thomas agreed, but thought he now knew what the Greeks did not—that happiness itself must be eternal to be an absolute. Our happiness, hence our correct choices and acts, depends on knowledge of God—not just on philosophical knowledge of God, but on the expectation of that full and final knowledge, the Beatific Vision.

Thomas himself seems to have experienced some kind of ecstatic realization two years before his death (a prefiguring of the Beatific Vision?) which caused him to cease writing. He said that in the face of that experience, all his words were like mere straw.

The work of St. Thomas Aquinas represents the apogee of scholastic philosophy. But at the very moment when scholasticism was being articulated as the most excellent statement of the high Medieval mind, there were already currents developing which would begin to undermine the scholastic synthesis, foreshadowing as they did the birth of a new, more secularly oriented world. These were the voices of men who, intentionally or unintentionally, separated the theological from the philosophical in ways which prepared the path for the "new science" of the Renaissance. Such was the thought of ROGER BACON (ca. 1212 - ca. 1292), whose disdain for speculative metaphysics, and whose curiosity about the natural world, influenced others to move along the new path — people like JOHN DUNS SCOTUS (ca. 1265 - ca. 1307), WILLIAM of OCKHAM (ca. 1280 - ca. 1349), JOHN BURIDAN (ca. 1300 - ca. 1358), and NICHOLAS of ORESME (1320-1382). And these anti-scholastic philosophers prepared the way for a new brand of thinkers in the next two centuries who would be neither theologians nor philosophers as we have come to know them, but scientists — men like NIKOLAUS COPERNICUS (1473-1543), TYCHO BRAHE (1546-1601), JOHANNES KEPLER (1571-1630), GALILEO GALILEI (1564-1642) and WILLIAM HARVEY (1578-1657). It would be they, along with artists and politicians, and not the metaphysicians who would set the tone of the new age.

V. THE 17th AND 18th CENTURIES

Though there were a number of lesser philosophers during the Renaissance, the first truly magnificent philosophical system of the modern period was that of the Frenchman...

RENÉ DESCARTES (1596–1650)

Descartes may not have been very good looking, but he was SMART!

Descartes first carved a niche for himself in the pantheon of intellectual giants by discovering

ANALYTICAL GEOMETRY,

thereby fulfilling the old Pythagorean dream of demonstrating the relation between plane geometry and pure algebra.

Having made his contribution to math, Descartes was about to publish his manuscript on physics, but when, in 1633, he heard that Galileo Galilei had been arrested by the Inquisition for teaching views about the physical world which were very close to Descartes' own

views, Descartes ran, did not walk, to his publisher to withdraw his manuscript.

Galileo's crime had been to peer through his newly invented telescope and discover that the planet Jupiter had three moons.

Why should anybody care? Least of all, why should the Brothers of the Inquisition care?

Because the Renaissance mind had inherited from the Medieval world the view that the Garden of Eden was the belly-button of the universe, and that God had

created the rest of the cosmos in concentric layers around the stage of the human drama.

Of course there had been rumors floating around that the Sun and not the Earth was the center of the planetary system, but the scientific evidence against that

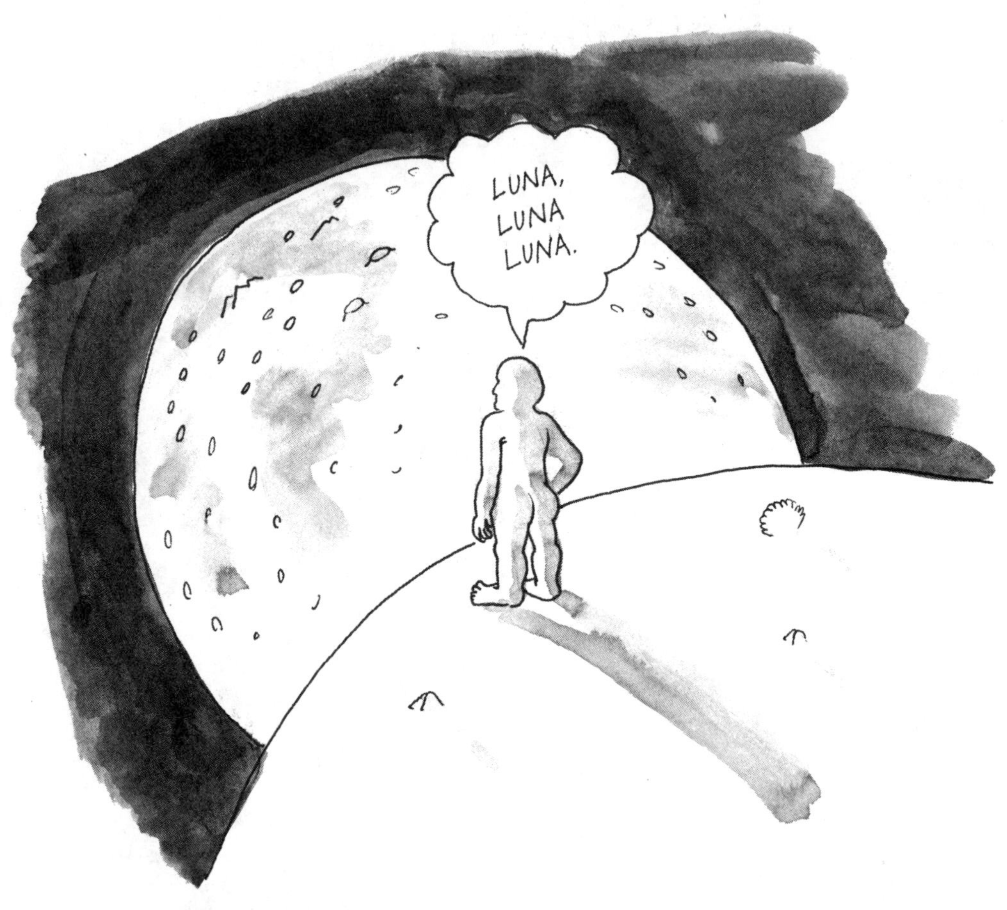

view was the undisputed fact that the Moon orbits the Earth. If the Sun is the center of everything, then why doesn't the Moon orbit the Sun instead of the Earth?

So, if Galileo proved that Jupiter has three moons which orbit it, then he had pulled the last strut out from under the geocentric theory of the universe. As Freud was to say later, this was the first of the three major blows against the human's conception of his own self-importance.

(The other two were Darwin's revelation that we are only animals, and Freud's discovery that we are SICK animals.)

It was too much for the Brothers of the Inquisition, so off went Galileo to jail.

Descartes was a good Catholic, but a modern Catholic. He believed the Church had made a big mistake in the Galileo episode. He correctly saw that if Religion tried to stem the tide of Science, Religion would be swept away. But Descartes did not want to have to go to jail to prove it.

So he decided to ease his ideas about physics onto an unsuspecting religious establishment by smuggling them into a book of philosophy, called Meditations, which, in a grovelling and self-effacing manner, he dedicated to "the Most Wise and Illustrious Doctors of the Sacred Faculty of Theology in Paris."

Meanwhile, to his friend he wrote, ". . . the six Meditations contain all the fundamental ideas of my physics. But please keep this quiet." Descartes hoped that the theologians would be convinced by his arguments before they realized that their own views had been refuted.

In his Meditations on First Philosophy, Descartes announced a massive intellectual project. He related his intention to tear down the edifice of Knowledge and rebuild it from the foundations up.

In order to discover a firm foundation of absolute certainty upon which to build his objective system of knowledge, Descartes chose a method of "radical doubt," whose motto was "De omnibus dubitandum,"—everything is to be doubted. So Descartes would doubt away anything which could possibly be doubted, no matter how weak the grounds were for doubting, until he could discover a proposition which was logically indubitable. This proposition, if it existed, would be the absolutely certain foundation of all knowledge.

Descartes began his philosophical journal while sitting at his desk in front of the fire. He wrote, "Everything that I have hitherto accepted has been learned from the senses." But the senses are known deceivers, and it is not prudent ever to trust a known liar.

Descartes' point is clear. We all know about optical illusions (the "bent oar" in the pond, the "water" on the road, the tracks which "meet at the horizon"), as well as illusions associated

with the other senses. So in one fell swoop, radical doubt had deprived Descartes of all sensory information.

But Descartes immediately felt he had gone too far. Only a madman could stare at his hands and wonder if they really were his hands. It seemed that in one step, radical doubt had led not to philosophy but to lunacy.

But then Descartes recalled that on other occasions he had believed he was sitting before the fire, looking at his hands, only to awaken later to discover that it all was a dream. Much to his amazement, Descartes realized that there is no test to prove with absolute certainty that at any given moment one is not dreaming. (Any test you can *think*, you can *dream*, so it's no test at all.)

Therefore, consistent with radical doubt, Descartes assumed that it was always possible that he *was* dreaming. This totally undermined the possibility that the senses could provide us with certain knowledge.

What about mathematics? Perhaps it can be a candidate for absolute certainty. Descartes said, "Whether I am asleep or awake, 2 and 3 are 5, and a square has no more than four sides." But radical doubt required Descartes to suspect even the simplest propositions of arithmetic if there was <u>any</u> reason for doing so. Well, what if the Creator of the universe was not the benevolent God of Catholicism, but an Evil Genius, a malevolent demon whose sole purpose was that of Deception, ...

2+3=5

so that even the most simple mathematical judgment would always be false? Could Descartes know for sure that such a demon did not exist?

No! There existed the logical possibility that Descartes' mind was being controlled externally by a malevolent force. So Descartes assumed that all the world was nothing but the dream of the Evil Genius. Descartes asked, under these conditions could _anything_ be certain?

Descartes concluded that there was one, and only one, thing which was absolutely certain — that he existed! His assertion, "I THINK, THEREFORE I AM," was true whether he was dreaming, whether the senses deceived, and whether there was an Evil Genius.

Having discovered certainty in selfhood, and having established that his self was his consciousness, Descartes must now find a way of escaping the confines of his own subjectivity and establishing the existence of an external world. To do so, he analyzed the contents of his mind and discovered it

contained certain innate ideas (shades of Plato), including these:

Using a version of St. Anselm's "ontological argument" (remember, it was _a priori_, making no appeal to the external world –

a world which for Descartes did not yet exist), he "proved" God's existence, thereby disposing of the Evil Genius. (A perfect, omnipotent, omnibenevolent God would not allow such a Deceiver to exist.)

Thereby, Descartes recovered math into his system (the only objection to math was the Evil Genius hypothesis), and by applying math to his innate idea of corporeal substance, Descartes came up with what he took to be the correct account of reality — the world as known by mathematical physics. Descartes had pulled it off. He showed that you can have both God and Galileo!

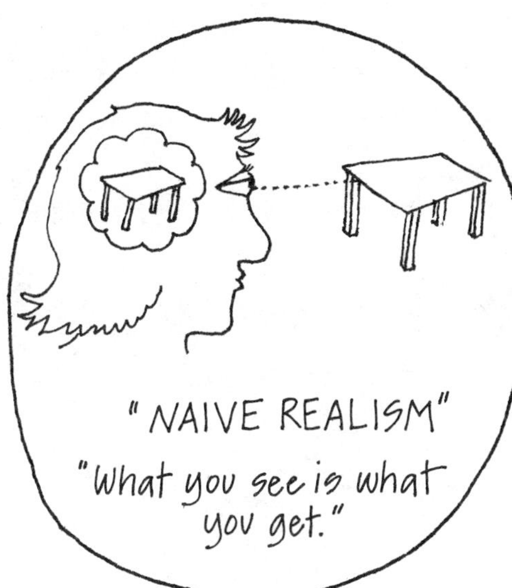
"NAIVE REALISM"
"What you see is what you get."

However, Descartes did leave himself with a few problems. First of all, he had replaced the common sense view of the relation between self and world (what philosophers call "naive realism"), ...

but he replaced it with a most circuitous route, indeed. Second, he assigned all perceivable qualities ("red," "blue," "sweet," "warm," "melodious") to the mind, and left only mathematically measurable quantities in the external world — a cold, colorless, odorless, soundless, tasteless world of matter in motion.

GOD
MATH
CARTESIAN REALISM
"what you see is not what you get

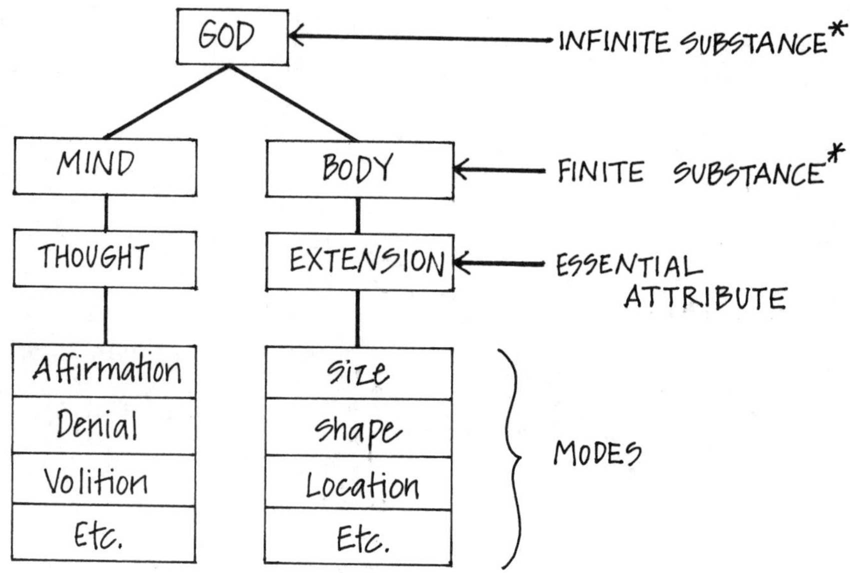

Furthermore, Descartes' picture of the world was hopelessly divided into substances that were defined in ways which mutually excluded each other. How could the mental world (a non-spatial, purely spiritual sphere) have any effect on the physical world of crass matter, and vice-versa, in this radically dualistic scheme of things? Descartes tried to solve the problem by claiming that MIND meets BODY at the center of the brain, in the pineal gland. (It should have been obvious that this solution would not work.)

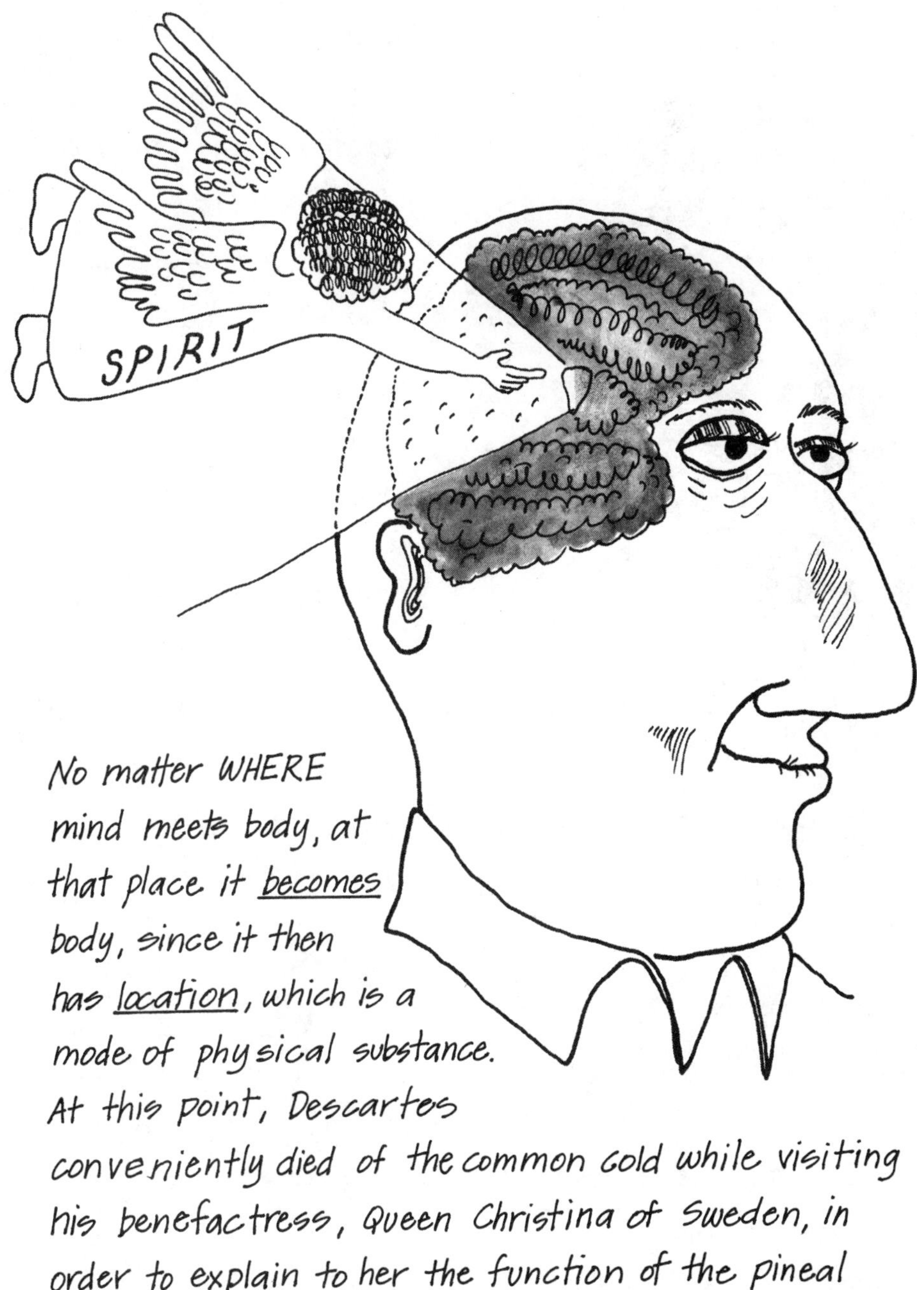

No matter WHERE mind meets body, at that place it becomes body, since it then has location, which is a mode of physical substance. At this point, Descartes conveniently died of the common cold while visiting his benefactress, Queen Christina of Sweden, in order to explain to her the function of the pineal gland. Thereby, he left to his followers the legacy of his radical dualism.

THOMAS HOBBES
Squares the Circle

Meanwhile, across the Channel, THOMAS HOBBES (1588-1679) was dealing with problems similar to those addressed by his contemporary, René Descartes. Hobbes was a contentious old codger who dabbled in everything. (His experiments in math led him to claim that he had squared the circle and cubed the sphere.) At one point or another he managed to antagonize every political party in Britain, and had to flee to France.

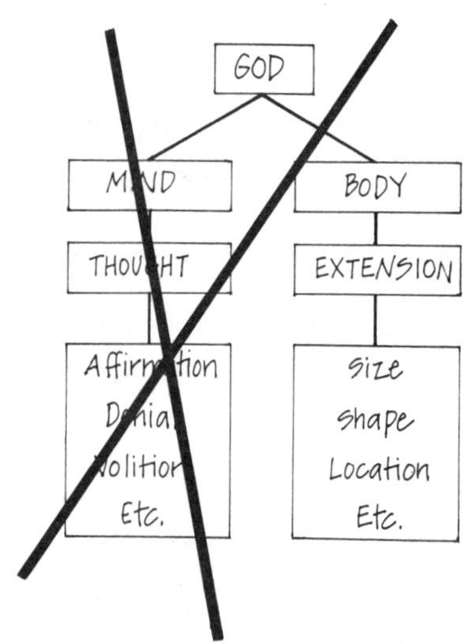

Hobbes solved Descartes' dualistic dilemma simply by dismantling dualism. He loudly proclaimed a form of mechanistic materialism reminiscent of Democritus' atomism, thereby rejecting one side of Descartes' diagram; and Hobbes' thinly disguised atheism rejected Descartes' "infinite substance" as well. For Hobbes, the only things which existed in reality were bodies in motion. In spite of his claim that "there exist everywhere only bodies," Hobbes did not actually deny the existence of thoughts. He simply held them to be "phantasms," shadows of brain activity, mere epi-phenomena which had no practical effect on the physical system. Similarly, though he was a determinist, he was, like the Stoics and St. Augustine, a "soft determinist." (A soft determinist believes that freedom and determinism are compatible.) It was OK to talk about freedom as long as all one meant by it was "unimpeded movement." (Water flows down a channel both necessarily and freely.)

Hobbes' psychology is very pessimistic. Every living organism obeys laws of individual survival; therefore, all human acts are motivated by self-interest and the quest for power. Altruism is not just a bad idea; it is impossible. Far from being immoral, egoism is the only show in town. ... "of the voluntary acts of every man, the object is some good to himself."

Hobbes is best known for his political philosophy, which is influenced by his egoistic theory of motivation. He recognized the state as an artificial monster ("the Leviathan") which restricts what little freedom there is in nature and flaunts its power over the individual, but Hobbes justified the existence of the political state by contrasting it to the notorious "state of

nature," dominated by scarcity and fear, where "every man is enemy to every man," and where life is "solitary, poor, nasty, brutish and short." In the state of nature there is no law, no morality, no property, and only one "natural right"— the right to protect oneself using any means at one's disposal, including violence and slaughter. If two people are on a desert island, and there isn't an abundance of coconuts to eat, then neither dares turn his back nor sleep lest the other bash him with a rock in order to get all the coconuts for himself. However, if both are rational they will realize that the most likely way of surviving is to agree with each other to forswear violence and share the coconuts. The trouble is, given the selfish

nature which Hobbes attributes to all of us, there is no reason at all for either party to keep the agreement if they can figure a way to break it with impunity. So there is every reason for them to distrust each other. In spite of their "agreement," neither dares yet to sleep a wink.

The solution requires that a third party be found. The first two parties give to the third party all the rocks (and perhaps an army), and they give up their right to violence. In exchange, she promises to use her absolute power to guarantee that the first two parties honor their agreement with each other. ("She" may be either a monarch or a parliament — in either case

THE SOVEREIGN

she is the source of all authority.)

This is Hobbes' famous "social contract." He realized that there is nothing to prevent the new sovereign from abusing her power (indeed, given her egoistic nature and innate lust for power, it is almost inevitable that she would do so), but he believed that the state, even with its necessary abuse of power, was better than the alternative — the horrors of anarchy in "the state of nature."

(It should be mentioned that, typically, Hobbes' political theory managed to please no one in Britain. The parliamentarians didn't like it because of its absolutist implications, the King didn't like it because of its denial of the divine right of monarchs.)

Back on the Continent, the Dutch-born Jewish philosopher, BARUCH SPINOZA (1634-1677), was trying to resolve the dilemmas of Descartes' legacy while remaining within the rationalistic tradition which Descartes exemplified. (Rationalists believe that the true source of Knowledge is Reason, not the senses, and that the correct philosophical model

BARUCH SPINOZA

must be an <u>a priori</u> one, not one based on empirical generalizations.) Spinoza was, according to Bertrand Russell, "the noblest and most lovable of the great philosophers." This is because he, more than any other philosopher, <u>lived</u> his philosophy, even though he realized that doing so would result in his alienation from both the Jewish and the Christian community alike. Spinoza accepted his ex-communication from Synagogue, Church and society without rancor, and he never sought fame nor riches, nor even a professorship, living out his life philosophizing and grinding lenses in order to earn a meager living. He accepted as his reward the state of tranquility afforded to him by his philosophy, and his motto could well have been his own epigram, "All excellent things are as difficult as they are rare."

Spinoza tried to submit Cartesian metaphysics to a geometrical method even more rigorous than that used by Descartes himself. Like Descartes', Spinoza's philosophy is centered on a definition of SUBSTANCE, but Spinoza had detected a contradiction in Descartes' account. Descartes had said, "By substance we can conceive nothing else than a thing which exists in such a way as to stand in need of nothing beyond itself." Then Descartes had gone on to say, "And in truth, there can be conceived but one substance which is absolutely independent, and that is God," which he called "infinite substance." In spite of this admission that by definition there could exist only one kind of being which was absolutely independent, Descartes (in a contradictory manner, according to Spinoza) proceeded to distinguish between "infinite substance" and "finite substances" — the latter were called corporeal substance (body) and mental substance (mind). This radical dualism led Descartes to his notorious mind/body problem and his universally scorned pineal gland solution.

Spinoza avoided this embarrassment by accepting Descartes' definition of substance (as that which is absolutely independent) and taking deadly seriously the inference that there could be only ONE such substance. (If there were two they would limit each other's independence.)

FIRST SUBSTANCE
THERE AIN'T ROOM ENOUGH IN THIS COSMOS FOR BOTH OF US!
2nd SUBSTANCE

Furthermore, because finiteness would constitute a limitation on God's absolute independence, Spinoza defined God as having infinite attributes. So once again one arrives at the conclusion that there can be but one substance, because any substance other than God would have to possess attributes which have already been defined as belonging to God.

Let's look at a schematized comparison of the systems of Descartes and Spinoza:

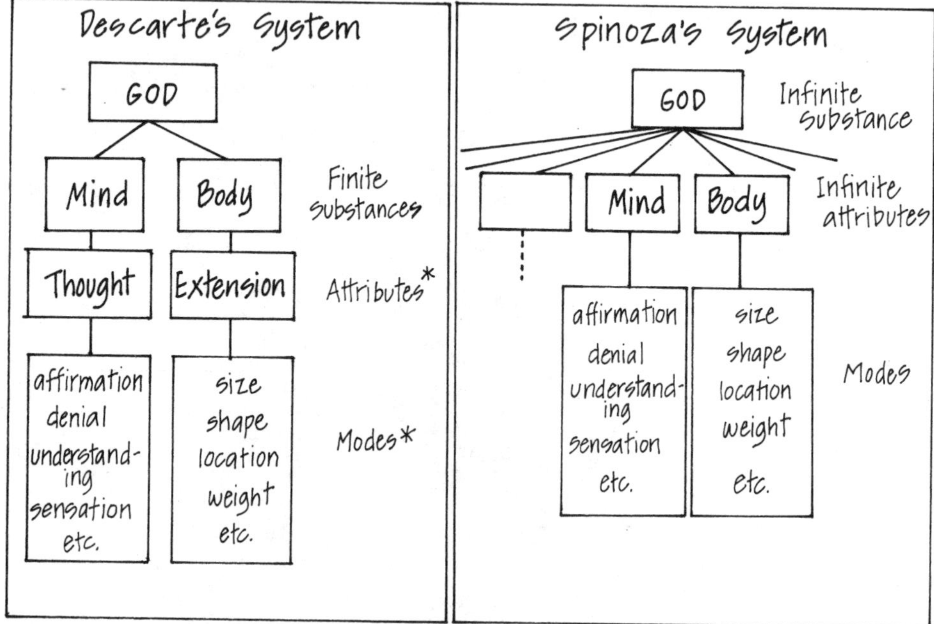

*(An <u>attribute</u>, for Descartes, is a characteristic which is the <u>essence</u> of a substance [i.e., that which is essential to it]. For Spinoza, an attribute is a characteristic which to the human intellect <u>seems</u> to be an essence. A <u>mode</u> is a specific modification of an attribute [i.e., a characteristic of a characteristic].)

Like Descartes, Spinoza equated "infinite substance" with God, but he also equated it with "Nature." The equation "Nature = God" makes him a pantheist. (It is also this equation which got him into trouble with both the Jewish and Christian theologians.) There are two human perspectives on reality (i.e., on God): one viewed through the attribute of mind (resulting in IDEALISM, the claim that only mind exists), and one viewed through the attribute of body (resulting in MATERIALISM, the view that only matter exists). In theory, there is an infinite number of other perspectives on reality, but only these two are open to the human intellect. A completely consistent idealistic or materialistic account of reality can be given, but no consistent dualism is possible. Dualism involves a confusion of perspectives. (So much for Descartes' pineal gland.)

Mais Monsieur Descartes, est-ce que vous avez mal à la glande pinéale?
I'm sure it's due to substance abuse

The true philosopher attempts to transcend the purely human perspective and view reality <u>sub specie aeternitatis</u>, that is, from the perspective of reality itself. From this perspective one comes to realize that the human has no privileged position in the cosmos, the human has no more and no less dignity than anything else in nature. One must come to love everything, which is to say, to love God (because one must either love everything, or nothing at all). The <u>love of God</u> is tantamount to the <u>knowledge of God</u>, which is to say, a philosophical knowledge of reality. This difficult intellectual love of God is, like that of Platonism, a form of rationalism tainted with mysticism. It also contains a Stoic component, insofar as knowledge of reality leads one to realize that everything which happens, happens of necessity. There is no randomness and no freedom of the will. But the realization that there is no such thing as free will, neither for God nor for humans, can itself be a liberating realization because one is thereby freed from the demands of desire and passion, both of

The Unrequited Love of Nature

which were seen by Spinoza as murky emotions which manage to control us only because of our failure to grasp the rational structure of reality. With knowledge, these emotions can be transformed into clear and distinct ideas leading to a kind of blessedness and joy. Spinoza wrote: "There cannot be too much joy: it is always good: but melancholy is always bad."

The third of the great Continental rationalists was the German, GOTTFRIED LEIBNIZ (1646-1716). He was a universal genius who made significant advances in symbolic logic, and who created a plan for the invasion of Egypt which may have been used by Napoleon 120 years later. He also invented a calculating machine which could add, subtract and do square roots. Furthermore, he discovered infinitesimal calculus simultaneously

GOTTFRIED LEIBNIZ

"Leibniz was one of the supreme intellects of all time, but as a human being he was not admirable."

Bertrand Russell

with Sir Isaac Newton (and got into a squabble with him concerning who had stolen the idea from whom).

Like Spinoza, Leibniz wished to correct the errors of Cartesian metaphysics without rejecting its main structure; but Leibniz was not satisfied with Spinoza's pantheistic monism, nor with his naturalism (i.e., his view that all is nature, and that the human being has no special status in reality). Leibniz wanted a return to a Cartesian system with real individuals and a transcendent God. Leibniz's system, as set forth in his <u>Monadology</u> and <u>Essays in Theodicy</u>, can be summarized in terms of three principles: "the Principle of Identity," "the Principle of Sufficient Reason," and "the Principle of Internal Harmony."

(1) THE PRINCIPLE OF IDENTITY: Leibniz divided all propositions into two types, which later philosophers would call ANALYTIC propositions and SYNTHETIC propositions. Take a look at the following table:

ANALYTIC	SYNTHETIC
A) TRUE BY DEFINITION: (true merely by virtue of the meanings of the words in the sentences.) B) NECESSARY: (their opposites are self-contradictions. They <u>cannot</u> be false.) C) A PRIORI: (their truth is known independently of observation.)	A) NOT TRUE BY DEFINITION: (their truth or falsity depends not on <u>meanings</u> but on facts in the world.) B) NOT NECESSARY, RATHER CONTINGENT: (<u>could</u> be false if facts were different.) C) A POSTERIORI: (their truth or falsity is known by observation.)

Following are some examples of <u>analytic</u> <u>sentences</u>:

(a) "All bachelors are men."

(b) "2+3 = 5"

(c) "Either A or not-A"

This category includes definitions and parts of definitions (a), and arithmetic and the principles of logic [(b) and (c)]. These were said by Leibniz to be based on the Principle of Identity in the sense that this principle is the positive counterpart of the Principle of Non-Contradiction (which says that it cannot be the case that A and not-A at the same time) in that the negation of every analytical sentence is a self-contradiction. (E.g., "<u>Not</u> all bachelors are men" implies the contradictory assertion, "Some men are not men" [because the definition of "bachelor" is "unmarried man"].)

Following are some examples of <u>synthetic</u> <u>sentences</u>:

(a) "The cat is on the mat."

(b) "Caesar crossed the Rubicon in 49 B.C."

Now, having drawn what many philosophers believe to be a very important distinction, Leibniz made the surprising move of claiming that all synthetic sentences are really analytic. <u>Sub specie aeternitatis</u>, that is to say, from God's point of view, it is the case that all true sentences are <u>necessarily</u>

true, even though it doesn't seem to be the case to us humans. For Leibniz, Tuffy the cat's characteristic of " being on the mat at time T^1 " is a characteristic necessary to that specific cat in the same way that "being a feline" is necessary to it.

You see, I couldn't not be on the mat!

(2) This brings us to THE PRINCIPLE OF SUFFICIENT REASON. According to Leibniz, for anything which exists, there is some reason why it exists, and why it exists exactly as it does exist. Leibniz claimed that this is the main principle of rationality, and that anyone who rejects this principle is irrational. If the cat is on the mat, then there must be some reason why the cat exists at all, and why it is on the mat and not,

e.g., in the dishwasher. Both of these reasons should be open to human scientific inquiry, though perhaps only God can know why the cat exists necessarily, and is necessarily on the mat.

What is true of the cat is true of the whole cosmos, said Leibniz. There must be a reason why the universe exists at all, and this reason ought to be open to rational human inquiry. Leibniz asked, "Why is there something rather than nothing?" Like St. Thomas, he concluded that the only possible answer would be in terms of an uncaused cause, an all-perfect God whose being was itself necessary. — So if Leibniz was right, we can derive the proof of the existence of God from the bare notion of rationality.

(3) Which takes us to THE PRINCIPLE OF INTERNAL HARMONY. If there is a God, God must be both rational and good. Such a divinity, Leibniz told us, must desire, and be capable of creating, the maximum amount of existence possible ("metaphysical perfection") and the maximum amount of activity possible ("moral perfection"). Therefore, at the moment of creation, God entertained all possibilities. He actualized only those possibilities which would guarantee the maximum amount of metaphysical and moral perfection. For example, God not only considered

the individual "Caesar" in all of Caesar's ramifications (would write _The Gallic Wars_, would cross the Rubicon in 49 B.C., would die on the Ides of March) before actualizing him. Perhaps he considered actualizing (i.e., creating) "Gaesar" and "Creasar" in Caesar's place, who, as potential actualizations, were identical to Caesar in all respects except that Gaesar would cross _not_ the Rubicon but the Delaware River in 49 B.C., and Creasar would cross the Love Canal. God saw that _only_ Caesar was compatible with the rest of the possibilities which he would activate, and therefore he actualized him and not the others. A similar thought experiment could be performed with God's creation of BRUTUS (as opposed, perhaps, to "Brautus" and "Brutos"). So the relation between Caesar and Brutus is not a causal one, but one of _internal harmony_. And the same holds true of the relations among all substances. God activates only substances which will necessarily harmonize with each other to the greatest extent possible. This now explains why all true sentences are analytic. If Tuffy is on the mat at 8PM, that is because _this_ cat _must_ be on the mat at 8PM (otherwise it is not Tuffy, but another cat). It also explains Leibniz's notorious claim that "this is the best of all possible worlds." The world may appear very imperfect to _you_, but if you knew

Candide Inspects the Ruins of Lisbon After the Earthquake of 1755

what the alternative was, you would be very grateful indeed to God. (It is this feature of Leibniz's philosophy which was to be lampooned by Voltaire in Candide.)

Every philosopher in the 250 year period after the publication of Descartes' Meditations conceived of reality in terms of SUBSTANCES. Leibniz called these substances MONADS, which he defined as "units of psychic force." They are simple (that is, they have no parts), and each is "pregnant" with all of its future states. Each monad is a mirror of the entire universe (God actualized only those monads which <u>would</u> mirror the rest of the universe), but they perceive the rest of reality only as features of their own inner states. "The monads have no windows." All monads have a psychic life, but some have a higher degree of psychic life than others. These monads (or communities of monads clustered around a "dominant monad") are conscious. Some conscious clusters of monads are also free, and these are human beings. (Of course, as in the theory of St. Augustine, God already knows how they will spend their freedom.)

Perhaps it can be said that Leibniz's philosophy solves the problems of Descartes' dualism, but it does so at the expense of common sense, and seems to be fraught with as many problems as Descartes' theory. It should come as no surprise that a philosopher would soon rise to the defense of common sense and of observation, reacting against the speculative flights of fancy of a Spinoza or a Leibniz. Such a philosopher was John Locke.

After A Philosophy Lecture Three Students Actually Find A Monad Behind A Pile of Old Socks

JOHN LOCKE (1632-1704) was the first of the classical British empiricists. (Empiricists believed that all knowledge derives from experience.) These philosophers were hostile to rationalistic metaphysics, and particularly to its unbridled use of speculation, its grandiose claims, and its epistemology grounded in

JOHN LOCKE

innate ideas.) In his *Essay Concerning Human Understanding*, Locke began his attack on Descartes' "innate ideas" by threatening them with Occam's Razor. ("Occam's Razor" is a principle of simplification derived from William of Occam. It cautions, "Do not multiply entities beyond necessity." Given two theories, each of which adequately accounts for all the observable data, the simpler theory is the correct theory.) If Locke could account for all human knowledge without making reference to innate ideas, then his theory would be simpler, hence better, than that of Descartes. He wrote, "Let us then suppose the mind to be, as we say, white paper, void of all characters, without any ideas: How comes it to be furnished? To this I answer, in one word, from EXPERIENCE." So the mind at birth is a *tabula rasa*, a blank slate, and is informed only by "experience," that is by sense

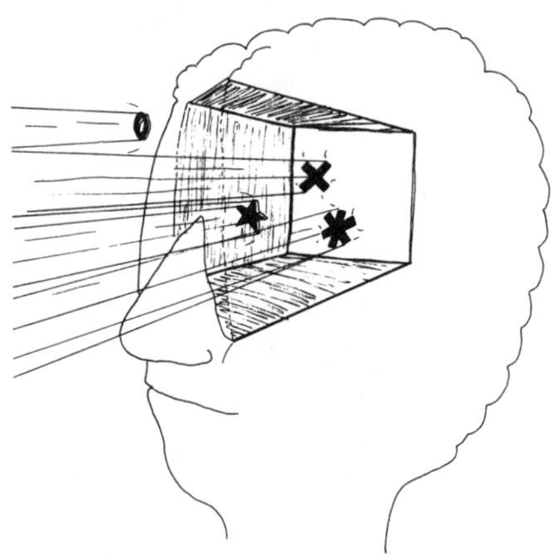

The *TABULA RASA* Being Marked by Experience

experience and acts of reflection. Locke built from this an epistemology beginning with a pair of distinctions: one between SIMPLE and COMPLEX ideas, and another between PRIMARY and SECONDARY qualities.

Simple ideas originate in any one sense (though some of them, like "motion," can derive either from the sense of sight or the sense of touch). These ideas are "simple" in the sense that they cannot be further broken down into yet simpler entities. (If a person does not understand the idea of "yellow," you can't explain it to him. All you can do is point to a sample and say, "yellow.") These simple ideas are Locke's primary data, his psychological atoms. All knowledge is in one way or another built up out of them.

THE PROBLEM: To Construct Knowledge From Simple Ideas

"Complex ideas" are, for example, combinations of simple ideas. These result in our knowledge of particular things (e.g., "an apple" — derived from the simple ideas "red-spherical-sweet"), comparisons ("darker than"), relations ("north of") and abstractions ("gratitude"). Even abstractions, or "general ideas," are nevertheless particular ideas which stand for collections. (This doctrine places Locke close to the theory known in the Medieval world as "nominalism." All the empiricists share with the nominalists the anti-Platonic thesis that only particulars exist.)

Locke's distinction between "primary" and "secondary" qualities is one that he borrowed from Descartes and Galileo, who had in turn borrowed them from Democritus. Primary qualities are characteristics of external objects. These qualities really do inhere in those objects. (Extension, size, shape and location are examples of primary qualities.) Secondary qualities are characteristics which we often attribute to external objects, but which in fact exist only in the mind, yet are caused by real features of external objects. (Examples of secondary qualities are colors, sounds and tastes.) This view of the mind has come to be known as REPRESENTATIVE REALISM. According to it, the mind represents the external world but does not duplicate it. (The view that the mind literally duplicates external reality is called "naive realism.") The mind is something like a photograph in that there are features of a photo which very accurately represent the world (e.g., a good picture of three people correctly depicts the fact that there <u>are</u> three people, and that each of them has two eyes, one nose and one mouth), and there are features of the photograph which belong exclusively to the photo (its glossiness, its two-dimensionality, the white border around its content). So, as in Descartes' system, there is a real world out there, and it has certain real qualities — the primary qualities. Now, these qualities – what are they qualities <u>of</u>? In answering this question, Locke never abandoned the basic Cartesian metaphysics of substance.

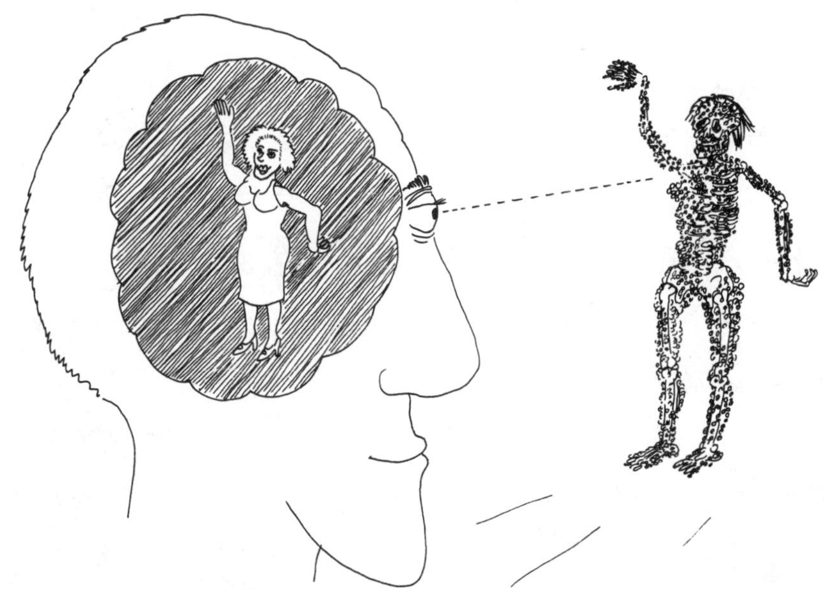

What Appears To Be Out There What Is Out There

A real quality must be a quality of a real <u>thing</u>, and real things are <u>SUBSTANCES</u>. (Once again, given anything in the world, it is either a substance, or a characteristic of a substance.) Well then, what is the status of this pivotal idea of "substance" in Locke's theory? Recall that Descartes had claimed that one could not derive the idea of substance from observation precisely because perception could only generate qualities. For this very reason it was necessary to posit the idea of substance as an <u>innate</u> idea. But Locke was committed to the rejection of innate ideas and to the claim that all knowledge comes in through the senses. So what did he say about the idea of substance? Rather amazingly, he said the following: "So that if anyone will examine himself concerning his notion of pure substance in general, he will find he has no other idea of it at all, but only a supposition of he knows not what <u>support</u> of such qualities which are capable of producing simple ideas in us."

So, having claimed that he could account for all knowledge purely in terms of "experience," and having arrived at the concept which had dominated philosophy for the last several generations, Locke proclaimed it a mystery, and even joked about it. (He compared the philosopher trying to explain substance to the Indian who explained that the world was supported by a great elephant, which in turn was supported by a tortoise, which in turn was supported by—"*something, he knew not what*.") This is a bit embarrassing, and either a rather inauspicious beginning for empiricism, or it is the beginning of the end of the metaphysics of substance. (We shall soon see that it is the latter.)

John Locke concerned himself not only with epistemology, but with politics as well. In his theory, developed in *Two Treatises on Government*, Locke, like Hobbes, drew a distinction between "the state of nature" and "the political state." However, what he meant by "state of nature" was very different indeed from what Hobbes meant by it. Far from being a condition in which there is "no justice nor injustice, no right nor wrong, no mine and thine distinct," Locke's

THE STATE OF NATURE
According to Hobbes

"state of nature" is a <u>moral</u> state – the state into which we are all born as humans, where we are all bestowed with certain <u>God-given</u> natural rights, the right to "life, health, liberty and possessions." Recall that for Hobbes, there was only one natural right, the right to try to preserve one's life. Hobbes seems to have believed that a kind of instinct for survival authorized that right. Locke's theory contains several natural rights, all of which are moral rather than instinctual,

THE STATE OF NATURE
According to Locke

and they derive their authority from God. Hobbes purposely left God out of his theory because he was trying to escape medievalism, where all philosophy presupposed God's existence. Hobbes was particularly insistent that there was no such thing as a "natural right to property," since in nature there is no property, only possession ("... only that to be every man's, that he can get; and for so long as he can keep it"). Locke, to the contrary, claimed we have a natural right to whatever part of nature we have "mixed our labor with." So if I till the soil, or cut down a tree and make a house from it, then this garden and that house are <u>mine</u> (and will be my children's when they inherit them from me). Locke did put qualifications on this natural right to property. One can accumulate as much "natural property" as one can use, as long as:

a) it does not spoil in its accumulation,

b) enough has been left for others,

c) its accumulation is not harmful to others. Locke's wealthy friends were probably glad to hear that "gold and silver may be hoarded up without injury to anyone."

(It is noteworthy that Locke's theory presupposes a state of abundance in nature, while Hobbes' presupposes a state of scarcity. It may well be true that human nature would express itself very differently in these vastly dissimilar "states of nature.")

According to Locke, individual political states are to be evaluated in terms of how well they protect the natural rights of the individuals living in those states. A good state is one which guarantees and maximizes those rights; a bad state is one which does not guarantee them; and an evil state is one which itself assaults the natural rights. Locke's version of "the social contract" is that all citizens consent to be ruled by a government elected by a majority for just as long as that government protects the natural rights. But a tyrannical government is illegitimate and <u>ought</u> to be revolted against. — Note that, unlike Hobbes, Locke is able to distinguish between a legitimate and an illegitimate government, and provides a theory of justifiable revolution. It is clear that the "Founding Fathers" used Locke's theory to justify the American revolution, and they incorporated his ideas into our Declaration of Independence and Constitution. Perhaps what is best in the American system derives from what is best in Locke's theory, and some social critics claim that what is worst in the American system is derived from what is worst in Locke's theory. America can be seen as a great Lockean experiment.

The second of the British empiricists was the Irishman, GEORGE BERKELEY (1685-1753), a teacher at Trinity College in Dublin who eventually became the Anglican Bishop of Cloyne. As a philosopher he was very impressed by Locke's work, and wanted to correct what he took to be its errors and inconsisten-

GEORGE BERKELEY

cies while remaining true to the basic platform of empiricism ("blank slate" theory, psychological atomism, nominalism, commitment to Occam's Razor). In fact, he applied Occam's Razor to the idea of material substance so scrupulously that he shaved it clean away and was left with a type of SUBJECTIVE IDEALISM - the view that only minds and ideas exist.

Early in his Principles of Human Knowledge, Berkeley attacked Locke's distinction between Primary and secondary qualities. It will be recalled that the former were said to inhere in material substance which existed independently of the mind, while the latter existed only in the mind (or, as Berkeley put it, their ESSE IS PERCIPI — their "being" is "to be perceived"). Now, Berkeley pointed out that our only access to so-called primary qualities is through secondary qualities.— The only way we can know the size, shape, location or dimensionality of an object is by feeling it or seeing it (i.e., through the secondary qualities of tactile or visual sensation). Berkeley concluded from this that descriptions of "primary qualities" are really only interpretations of secondary qualities - different ways of talking about colors, sounds, tastes, odors and tactile sensations. Therefore "primary qualities" too exist only in the mind. Their esse is also percipi.

To explain how this translation of secondary qualities into primary qualities was possible, Berkeley drew a distinction between DIRECT PERCEPTION and INDIRECT PERCEPTION. Direct (or "immediate") perception is the passive reception of basic sense-data (Locke's "secondary qualities" and "simple ideas"). Indirect (or "mediate") perception is the interpretation of those sense-data. Consider the process of learning to read. The small child confronts a written page and sees only black "squigglies" on a white background.

(This is direct perception.) Through a process of acculturation the child eventually learns to see these markings as words, loaded with meanings. (This is indirect perception.) It is an interesting fact that once we've learned to read, it is very difficult to recover the child's "innocent eye" and see the words again as mere "squigglies." This explained to Berkeley why we adults perceive the world as groupings of THINGS rather than as sense-data. Nevertheless, claimed Berkeley, the "things" we see in the so-called external world are really only "collections of ideas," philosophically analyzable into their component sense-data. Said Berkeley, "As several of these [sense-data] are observed to accompany each other, they come to be marked by one name, and so to be reputed as one <u>thing</u>. Thus, for example, a certain color, taste, smell, figure and consistence having been observed to go together, are accounted one distinct thing, signified by the name apple; other collections of ideas constitute a stone, a tree, a book, and the like sensible things." What's true of the component parts of a stone is true of the whole stone. Its <u>esse</u> is also <u>percipi</u>.

Notice that the notion of "material substance" (Locke's "something, I know not what") has simply disappeared in Berkeley's system. And the rôle played by the rationalists' "innate idea of substance" in explaining how we come to know the world as a concatenation of individual physical objects has been taken over by LANGUAGE. We teach our children <u>words</u> which organize the ideas in their minds into "things." Berkeley's subjective idealism holds that each of us lives in his or her own subjective world composed of the sense-data of the five senses. This is the same world we entered into as infants. But we were taught a language, which is to say, taught to "read" our sense-data. Language is also the cement of INTER-subjectivity. I am able to bridge the gap between my private world and yours through the shared use of conventional symbols. Without language I would be stuck solipsistically in the echo chamber of my own mind.

Berkeley believed that with these two categories (sense-data and language) he could account for all possible human knowledge – all except the knowledge of GOD. (Berkeley was a bishop, after all, so don't be surprised to find God playing a key rôle in Berkeley's philosophy, even if it was a bit embarrassing to him that God's *esse* is not *percipi*.) God's existence can be deduced from the regularity and predictability of sense-data. If the so-called physical world's "being" is to "be perceived," and hence is dependent on the mind, then why is it that when I return to an empty room which I had vacated earlier, everything is just as I left it? Why didn't the room disappear when I stopped perceiving

When I said that ESSE IS PERCIPI, of course I didn't mean that YOURS was!

Why Doesn't the Room Disappear When We Leave It?

it? Because God was perceiving it while I was out. God is the guarantor of the laws of nature. When it says in the Bible that God created the world, that means that he created sense-data and minds (spirits, selves) to perceive them. God did not cause there to be some unperceivable, mysterious stuff—"material substance"—which in turn causes ideas. Believing that there was such a "stuff" was the error of Locke's Rep.esentative Realism. Locke failed to see that the representation is the reality. Berkeley has merely eliminated the "middle man." His theory

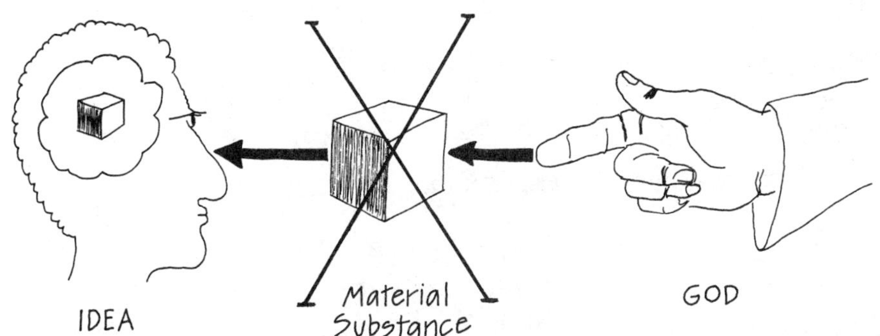

Berkeley Eliminates the Middle Man

explains everything that Locke's does, but is more economical; hence, according to Occam's Razor, it is better than Locke's. So Berkeley believed.

The third of the "Holy Trinity" of British empiricism is the Scot, DAVID HUME (1711-1776). He published his first book, A Treatise of Human Nature, when he was twenty-seven and he hoped to achieve fame and fortune from it, but, by his own reckoning, it "fell dead-born from the press." Ten years later he rewrote it and published it as An Enquiry Concerning the Human Understanding.

DAVID HUME

This book was considerably more successful than its predecessor, possibly because it was a bit more moderate. Today Hume is recognized as the most acute, if the most perplexing, of the British empiricists.

Hume's philosophy began with a revival of Leibniz's analytic/synthetic distinction (see p. 170), or in Hume's words, a distinction between "relations of ideas" and "matters of fact." It will be recalled that analytic propositions are expressed by sentences

a) whose negation leads to a self-contradiction,
b) which are a priori,
c) which are true by definition, and therefore
d) are necessarily true.

Synthetic propositions are expressed by sentences which are the opposite of sentences expressing analytic propositions; that is, they are sentences

a) whose negation does not lead to a self-contradiction,
b) which are a posteriori,
c) which are not true by definition, and
d) when they are true, they are not necessarily true (they can be false).

Now, in accepting this distinction Hume was admitting that there are such things as a priori necessary truths. It would seem that any empiricist who accepted this was jeopardizing the program of empiricism by recognizing the legitimacy of the rationalists' dream, but Hume defused this situation by adding one more characteristic to the list of features of "relations of ideas." He said that they are all TAUTOLOGICAL, that is, they are all redundant, repetitive, merely verbal truths which provide no new information about the world, only information about the meaning of words. Thus, given the conventions of the English language, it is certainly true that "all sisters are siblings," but saying this tells one nothing about any particular sister that wasn't already known by calling her a sister in the first place. Similarly, anybody who really understands the concept "five" and the concepts "three," "two" and "plus" already knows that "3+2=5." So the rationalistic dream of a complete description of reality which is *a priori* and necessarily true is a will-o'-the-wisp, because *a priori* truths aren't descriptions of *anything*, according to Hume. Only synthetic claims — "matters of fact" — can correctly describe

Mommy! Today I learned that all brothers are siblings. It is not the case that it is raining and not raining at the same time. All red things are members of the class of red things.
Yes but *is* the cat on the mat?

reality, and these claims are necessarily <u>a posteriori</u>. Therefore, all true knowledge about the world must be based on observation. This is, of course, the central thesis of all empiricism.

What Hume was claiming was that there are basically only three categories of analysis. Given any proposition whatsoever, that proposition is either ANALYTIC, SYNTHETIC, or NONSENSE. Hume said: "When we run over libraries, persuaded of these principles, what havoc must we make? If we take in our hand any volume — of divinity or school metaphysics, for instance — let us ask, <u>Does it contain any abstract reasoning concerning quantity or number</u> [i.e., analytical truths]? No. <u>Does it contain any experimental reasoning concerning matter of fact and existence</u> [i.e., synthetic truths]? No. Commit it then to the flames, for it can contain nothing but sophistry and illusion." (No wonder

DAVID HUME - LIBRARIAN

Hume lost his job as a librarian.)

There is, then, very clearly a "Humean method" of philosophizing. One takes any claim which one would like to test, and asks a series of questions about that claim:

1) IS IT ANALYTIC?

(This is determined by negating the sentence in which the claim is expressed. If the resultant negative sentence is a self-contradiction, then the original sentence is analytic.)

☐ YES. (If the answer is YES, the claim is true, but philosophically trivial.)

☐ NO. (If the answer is NO, go to the next question.)

2) IS IT SYNTHETIC?

This question is posed by Hume in the following way: "When we entertain... any suspicion that a philosophical term is employed without any meaning or idea (as is but too frequent), we need but inquire, from what impression is that supposed idea derived? And if it be impossible to assign any, this will serve to confirm our suspicion."

In other words, question #2 can be answered affirmatively only if it is possible to trace its ideas back to sense-data ("impressions"). For example, all the ideas in the sentence, "This stone is heavy," can be traced back to sense-data, hence it passes the empirical criterion of meaning.

☑ YES.

But what if, in a particular case, the answer to question #2 is negative?

☑ NO.

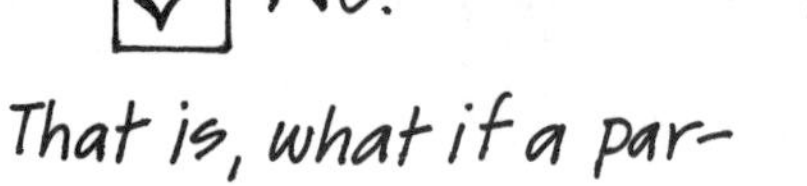

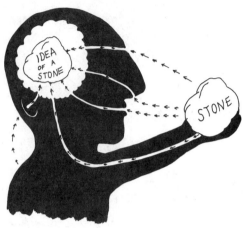

That is, what if a par-

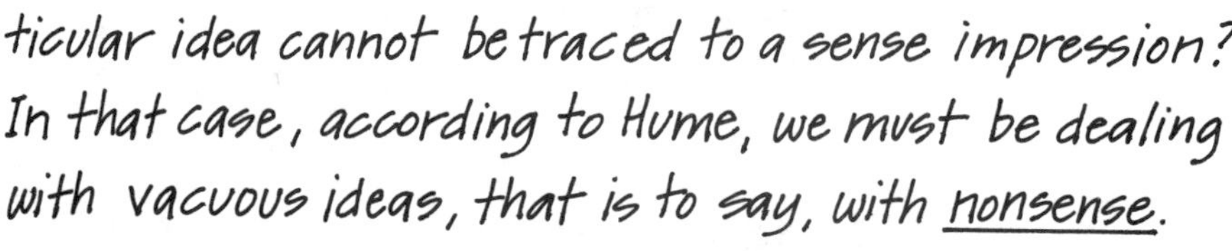

ticular idea cannot be traced to a sense impression? In that case, according to Hume, we must be dealing with vacuous ideas, that is to say, with <u>nonsense</u>.

Now, with Hume's method in hand, if we turn to some of the traditional philosophical topics, like GOD, WORLD and SELF, we arrive at some pretty startling conclusions. Let's start with the sentence, "God exists."

1) Is this proposition analytic?

That is to ask, is its negation ("God does not exist") a self-contradiction? Most people would answer "No." Of course, there are some who would answer "Yes"—namely all those defenders of the "Ontological proof of God's existence" (e.g., Anselm, Descartes, Spinoza), but Hume would respond to them by saying that if the sentence "God exists" is analytical, then it is tautological and tells us nothing about reality. The true sentence, "A necessary being necessarily exists," still doesn't tell us whether there _is_ a necessary being.

☑ NO

So if we assume that "God exists" is not analytical, the next question is,

2) Is this proposition synthetic?

Hume believed it was impossible to trace the idea of God back to sense-data. He said, "Our ideas reach no further than our experience. We have no experience of divine attributes and operations. I need not conclude my syllogism. You can draw the inference yourself." So, although Hume didn't actually say so, his method seems to imply that the idea of God is vacuous, and that statements about God are literally non-_sense_.

So much for God in Hume's system. What about the world? Berkeley, using Occam's Razor, had already eliminated "material substance" from empiricism. This was _one_ of the key concepts philosophers had used to explain the world. Hume now turned to another, one that was employed not only by philosophers, but by scientists, and by ordinary people of common sense — that of CAUSALITY.

Let's take the sentence, "X causes Y," where "X" and "Y" are both events. (We'll use Hume's example: "X" is the event of billiard ball "A" striking billiard ball "B," and "Y" is the event of billiard ball "B" moving after being struck.)

1) Is the sentence "X causes Y" analytic? (That is to say, is the sentence, "X does not cause Y," a self-contradiction?) Obviously not, because it is perfectly possible to conceive of "A" striking "B" and "B" <u>not</u> moving.)

☑ NO

2) Is the sentence "X causes Y" synthetic? Now, it seems that the answer will be affirmative, because there should be no difficulty in tracing back the idea of "cause" to sense-data. But Hume <u>found</u> a difficulty. When he analyzed the concept, he broke it down into three components: a) priority, b) contiguity, and c) necessary connection. "Priority" (the fact that X precedes Y) can be traced to sense-data. So can "contiguity" (the fact that X touches Y). But no matter how many times Hume observed ball A strike ball B,

he could not find any <u>necessary connection</u> (the fact that if X happens, Y <u>must</u> happen), yet this was exactly what needed to be found if the concept of causality was to be sensible.

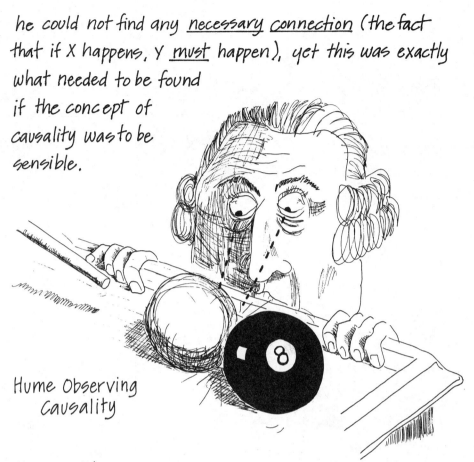

Hume Observing Causality

So "causality" proved to have the same status as "material substance" and "God". This embarrassment has far-reaching consequences. It means that whenever we say that one thing A causes another B, we are really only reporting our own <u>expectation</u> that A will be followed by B in the future. This is a psychological fact about us, and not a fact about the world. But if we try to show the rational grounding of our expectation, we cannot do so. Even if A was followed by B innumerable times in the past, that does not justify our claim to know that it will do so again in the future.

Hume's discovery has come to be known as THE PROBLEM OF INDUCTION. What makes us so certain that the future will behave like the past? If we answer, "because it has always done so in the past," we are begging the question, because the real question is, <u>must</u> it do so in the future just because it has always done so in the past? Nor can we appeal to "the Laws of Nature", because then the question is, what guarantees that the "Laws of Nature" will hold tomorrow? And there is no analytic nor synthetic guarantee of this. Hume concluded from all this that THERE ARE NO NECESSARY CONNECTIONS BETWEEN ANY TWO EVENTS IN THE UNIVERSE. This idea leads to what one philosopher has called "dustbowl empiricism," — the view that, on close inspection, reality, like a dust cloud, proves to be composed of discrete, unrelated entities casually (not causally) associated with each other in a tenuous and ephemeral manner.

"Hume's fork" (the analytic/synthetic distinction) has equally disastrous results for the concept of SELF. There is no sense-datum to which the concept can be traced. Far from finding the self to be the simple, indubitable, absolutely certain, eternal soul which

Descartes had claimed it to be, Hume found, according to his method, that "there is no such idea" as "self." The so-called self proves to be "a bundle or collection of different perceptions [... heat or cold, light or shade, love or hatred, pain or pleasure ...] which succeed each other with an inconceivable rapidity, and are in a perpetual flux and movement."

Hume Discovers The Self—Such As It Is

David Hume had consistently and vigorously followed the program of empiricism to its logical conclusion. The results were disastrous for the philosophical enterprise. The sphere of rationality was found to be very small indeed, reduced as it was to verbal truths and descriptions of sense-data; yet nearly everything that interested people as philosophers or non-philosophers fell beyond those limits. Hume believed he had shown that human life was incompatible with rationality and that human endeavors always had to be extra-rational, hence irrational. (Rationally, I can never know that the loaf of bread which nourished me yesterday will nourish me today, hence I can never be rationally motivated to eat.) But Hume knew perfectly well that the human being could not be sustained by the meager fruits of philosophy. Even while writing his philosophical manuscript he knew that, once he put down his pen, he too would revert to the normal, illogical beliefs of humanity — namely, beliefs in self, world and causality (if not in God). He even suggested, maybe with tongue in cheek, that perhaps we should abandon philosophy and take to tending sheep instead.

David Hume — Shepherd

It would be fair to say that the history of philosophy should have ended with Hume if his views had prevailed. To survive Hume's attack, philosophy would need a powerful, subtle and original mind to come to its defense. It found such a protector in the German, IMMANUEL KANT (1724-1804). Kant spent the whole of his life in the old Hanseatic city of Königsberg in the northeastern corner of Prussia (today, the U.S.S.R.) where, at least until his fiftieth year, he passed his days complacently in the bourgeois life of a respected professor of the university. This old bachelor, whose personal life was so methodical that his neighbors used to set their clocks by his afternoon walks, had been trained in the rationalistic metaphysics of Christian von Wolff, an undistinguished disciple of Leibniz, and Kant had found no reason to doubt any of its tenets — that is, not until one fine day in his late middle-age when a copy of Hume's Enquiry crossed his desk. Kant's reading of it "awakened him from his dogmatic slumber," as he later reported. He realized that Hume's powerful argument undermined everything Kant had believed, and that no honest progress in philosophy could be made until Hume's skeptical arguments had been refuted.

Herr Professor Immanuel Kant On His Daily Walk

Kant's response to Hume, and his attempt to synthesize what he took to be the best of Hume's philosophy with the best of what was left of rationalism after Hume's full-scale frontal assault on it, is found in *The Critique of Pure Reason*. There Kant accepted Hume's analytic/synthetic distinction as the key philosophical tool of analysis. Kant agreed with Hume that all analytic propositions are *a priori*, and that all *a posteriori* propositions are synthetic, but he disagreed with Hume's claim that all synthetic propositions are *a posteriori*, and that all *a priori* propositions are analytic (hence tautological). That is to say, according to Kant there is such a thing as a SYNTHETIC *A PRIORI* TRUTH, a meaningful statement about reality whose truth is known independently of observation.

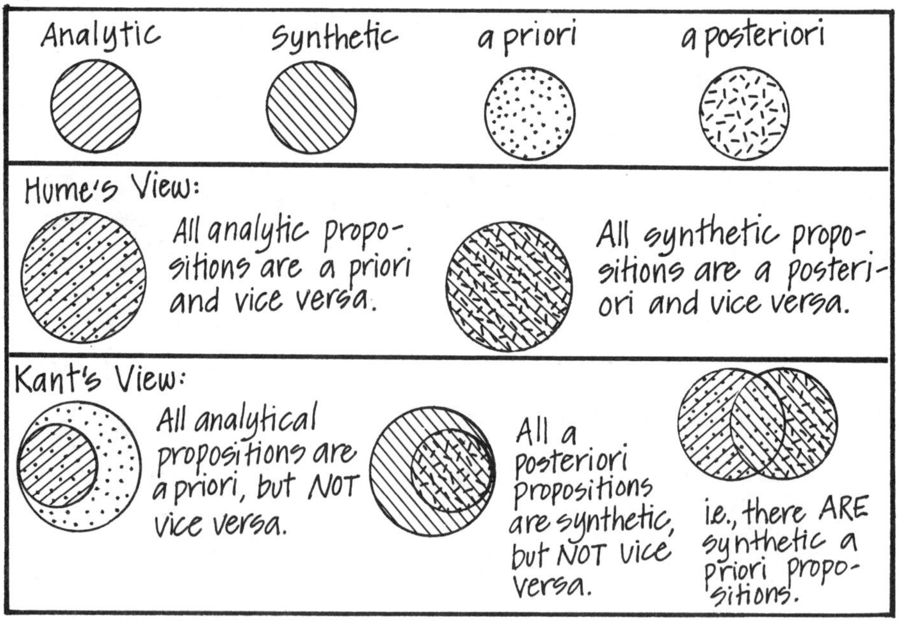

Analytic Synthetic a priori a posteriori

Hume's View:

All analytic propositions are a priori and vice versa.

All synthetic propositions are a posteriori and vice versa.

Kant's View:

All analytical propositions are a priori, but NOT vice versa.

All a posteriori propositions are synthetic, but NOT vice versa.

i.e., there ARE synthetic a priori propositions.

Kant believed that only by demonstrating the existence of such truths could Hume be refuted and philosophy, science and common sense (and perhaps religion) be made respectable again. This would be done by showing that the knowledge which Hume denied was in fact grounded in synthetic _a priori_ truth, as were the very arguments which Hume had mustered against such claims of Knowledge. Kant began by dividing the mind into three "faculties" – intuition (i.e., perception), understanding and reason — and then performing what he called a "transcendental" analysis of each faculty.

Kant first dealt with THE FACULTY OF INTUITION. Here the primary question which concerned Kant was not "What is perception?" nor "Is perception possible?", rather it was "_How_ is perception possible?" That is, he began with the common sense view that we _do_ perceive the world, and asked what conditions must hold for that to be possible. For example, he wanted to know how it was possible that we are able to utter true sentences about the height of the Matterhorn, if the empiricists were right to say we never perceive SPACE, only sense-data. And he wanted to know how it was possible that we are able to utter true sentences about the amount of time it takes to get to

Berlin if the empiricists were correct to say we never perceive TIME, only sense-data. Kant's solution was to demonstrate that SPACE and TIME are the synthetic *a priori* foundations of the faculty of perception. An *a posteriori* sentence like "The cat is on the mat" *presupposes* the truth of the sentence, "objects exist in space and time." According to Kant, we sometimes know the first sentence to be true, yet *it* cannot be true unless the second is also true. The latter is not analytic and it is not *a posteriori* (there is no sense-datum of space or time – Hume was right about that), so it must be a synthetic *a priori* truth.

Kant called this method of analysis a "transcendental deduction," because it "transcends" direct observation, or better, gets behind and underneath it to discover its necessary conditions. This analysis led Kant to conclude that SPACE and TIME were not features of external reality. Rather they were features of the *structure of the mind*. The human mind analyzes the data it receives in terms of space and time. Space and time are the "irremovable goggles" through which we perceive the world.

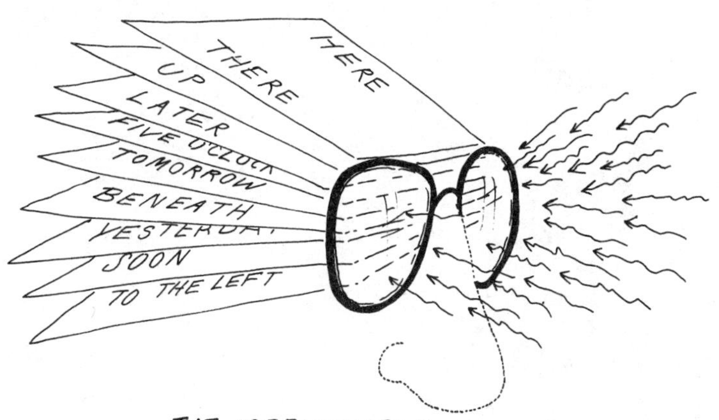

THE IRREMOVABLE GOGGLES

They are not like pieces on a chess board (things in the world), rather they are like the rules according to which we play chess and in whose absence chess would not exist.

Having discovered the synthetic a priori foundations of the faculty of intuition, Kant then turned to the FACULTY OF UNDERSTANDING. This is the faculty which enables us to understand facts about the world (... that Mt. Whitney is higher than Death Valley, ... that the cat is on the mat). Once again, Kant began not by asking, "Can there be knowledge of the world?" Instead, he began with the common-sense assumption that we do have such knowledge, and asked how such knowledge was possible. He found that it was grounded in the synthetic a priori foundations of the faculty of the understanding which he called "the categories of the Understanding." These categories included those of UNITY/PLURALITY/TOTALITY, CAUSALITY and SUBSTANTIALITY. These concepts are not deduced by the mind from reality; on the contrary, the mind brings them to reality. This is why Hume had been unable to find them "out there" when he looked for them. A sentence such as "Every event is caused" (which to Hume, was neither empirical, nor true by definition) is, according to Kant, a synthetic _a priori_ truth.

Obviously this theory is reminiscent of the Platonic-Cartesian doctrine of innate ideas, but there is a major difference. Kant did not claim that we are born with a group of _ideas_, but that the mind is structured in such a way that it analyzes its data in terms of a particular set of synthetic _a priori_ _rules_, which are like a permanent program in a computer and which produce ideas when fed information by the senses. If you are a human being, then you make sense of the world in terms of such concepts as time/space/substantiality/causality. The

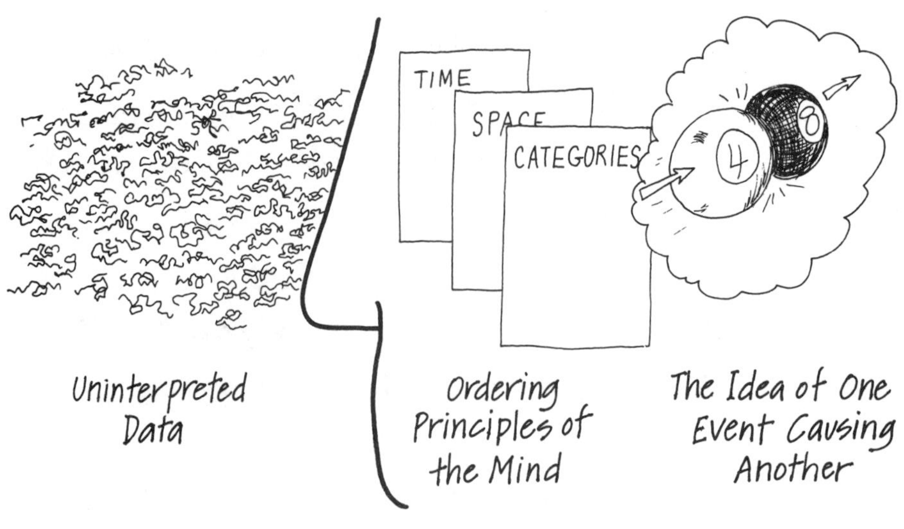

mind _must_ order the world in terms of "thingness," though there is nothing "out there" called SUBSTANCE. The mind _must_ understand the world in terms of causal series even though there is nothing out there which is _the_ cause of any event.

Kant's position was meant to represent a compromise between the warring rationalists and empiricists. His famous assertion, "thoughts without content are empty, intuitions without concepts are blind," was meant to grant to the rationalists that sense-data alone could not provide knowledge, and to grant to the empiricists that there could be no knowledge in the absence of sensorial contribution. Kant's solution seemed to many to be successful; however it had the consequence of putting him in the disconcerting position of admitting that there does exist some kind of ultimate reality (what he called "the noumenal world," or "the thing-in-itself" [_das Ding-an-sich_]), but that the human mind is incapable of knowing it. Rather, we humans are limited to knowledge of what Kant called "the phenomenal world"— the world as perceived, conceived, imagined, interpreted, analyzed and theorized about by the human mind. That is, we can only know a world which has passed through the human mind, through the gridwork of space and time and the categories of the understanding. Contrary to

Kant Peers Beyond the Curtain of the Phenomenal World and Sees Nothing

Hume's conclusion, for Kant common sense and science are valid, but only insofar as their claims are about the phenomenal world. But nothing positive can be said about ultimate reality, other than that it exists. This meant that traditional metaphysics of the type attempted by philosophers from Plato through Leibniz was impossible. Kant deduced this conclusion from his "transcendental" analysis of the faculty of reason.

THE FACULTY OF REASON was supposed by Kant to be the faculty which produced the "pure" concepts (i.e., concepts uncontaminated by the senses) such as "God" and "soul." Were there any synthetic a priori foundations for this faculty? (which is another way of asking, can we hope to know any "higher truths" about ultimate reality?). Kant's notorious answer — which was so scandalous to the metaphysicians and theologians —was, NO! Traditional metaphysics was impossible because it was always the result of illegitimately applying notions of space, time and causality to the noumenal world when in fact these concepts can only be applied to the observable world. This is why all proofs of God's existence

The House of Metaphysics Before and After "THE CRITIQUE OF PURE REASON"

must fail, along with all attempts to describe ultimate reality in terms of that mysterious category, "substance." We humans must therefore despair of ever knowing of God, Justice, immortality or freedom, since all of these ideas overreach the human capacity for knowledge.

If Kant had concluded The Critique of Pure Reason at this point, he would have satisfied the Humean critics of metaphysics and theology while at the same time pleasing the defenders of common sense and science, but he would not have satisfied those impulses in the human heart toward higher sentiments. To these stirrings Kant addressed the rest of his Critique. There he claimed the following: there is no logical necessity to conceive of the world in terms of God, Immortality, Justice and Freedom (in the way that there is a logical necessity of conceiving the world in terms of time, space and causality); nevertheless, without such inspirational concepts, many humans would lose their enthusiasm for life. If one could not believe, for example, that the human soul is free and that ultimately justice will triumph, then one might well lose the motivation required for the engagement in the day-to-day world. Therefore, according to Kant, one has the

No God, No immortality, No justice. I can't stand it! Barkeep, bring me another.

right to _believe_ (but not to claim to know) that God, soul, immortality, justice and freedom exist, not as _metaphysical_ necessities, but as _practical_ (i.e., moral) necessities. We have the right to treat these topics _as if_ they were synthetic _a priori_ truths if doing so will make us better, more successful human beings.

Kant's attempt to distinguish knowledge from belief, yet ground belief in moral necessity, was acceptable to many who were tired of the extravagant claims made by metaphysicians and theologians but who were also looking for a legitimate rôle for _belief_ in the modern world. Kant's critics, however, accused him of merely "kicking God out the front door in order to let him in through the back door."

After _The Critique of Pure Reason_, Kant wrote a number of other important philosophical works, including _The Critique of Practical Reason_, and _The Foundations of the Metaphysics of Morals_, both of which addressed specifically the problem of ethics. In its emphasis on intention and duty, Kant's theory demonstrated Christianity's influence on him, and in its attempts to ground duty in reason, Kant's theory showed him to be a thinker of the Enlightenment. By positing freedom _as if_ it were grounded in a synthetical _a priori_ truth (for without freedom there can be no moral acts), one can derive an ethical code from its foundations in reason. Being a rule-guided activity, reasoning itself is based on a respect for rules and laws. From such respect, Kant deduced a moral command, which he called the CATEGORICAL IMPERATIVE: "So act that the maxim of your action could be willed as a universal law." All moral acts can be derived from principles which may be universalized without contradiction. Kant thought that, as creatures of reason, we are duty-bound to obey such principles. Here, we will oversimplify this idea a bit to see what Kant was talking about.

Let's suppose that you owe a friend five dollars, and to your annoyance, he pressures you to repay. So you say to yourself, "If I kill him, I won't have to repay the debt." But as a true Kantian, you first check to see if you could universalize the principle governing the proposed action. You ask yourself, what if everyone accomplished his goals by killing someone? Could there exist a universal law, "EVERYONE OUGHT TO KILL SOMEONE"? This would be an impossible law because if everyone complied with it, there would be no one left to comply

LAW OF THE LAND
Everyone must kill someone

with it. Therefore we are duty-bound not to kill as a way of solving problems. OK, then what if you lie to your friend, telling him that you already repaid the debt? Can the principle behind this proposal be universalized? Could there be a general law, "EVERYONE OUGHT ALWAYS TO LIE"? Obviously not, because it would be impossible

even to state the law without breaking it. Therefore we are duty-bound not to lie. — Well, what if you repay the five dollars, then steal them back? Can the principle behind this act be universalized? Imagine a general law saying, "EVERYONE OUGHT ALWAYS TO STEAL."

Where Theft is the Law of the Land

But this too is an impossible law, because the concept of stealing is parasitical upon the concept of <u>property</u>, but if everyone always steals, there can be no property; there can be only temporary possession, that is, stuff passing from person to person. — So we are also duty-bound to refrain from stealing. (If you are a true Kantian, it's beginning to look as though you will have to pay your debt!)

Kant formulated the Categorical Imperative in a number of ways, not just in terms of the principle of universalizability. One such formulation was this: "So act as to treat humanity, whether in thine own person or in that of any other, in every case as an end withal, never as a means only." By saying we should treat people as ends, and not merely as means, Kant was of course admonishing us against <u>using</u> other people as a means to our own ends. He thought that morality entailed the recognition of the <u>dignity</u> of each person as a person. This side of his ethics has widespread practical implications for such issues as sexual relationships, discrimination, informed consent, and death with dignity.

If one dwelt solely on the first formulation of the Categorical Imperative (the one based on universalizability), Kant's ethics might seem quite bloodless;

but this second formulation adds some warmth to his moral doctrine. Nevertheless, there is a bit of coldness at the heart of his view. He was so intent on making morality a question of DUTY, that he refused to grant any worth to INCLINATION. According to him, if a person who was motivated by feelings of empathy toward humanity rendered assistance to a helpless, needy person, this act would be of less moral value than would be the same act performed by someone who actually loathed humanity, but who was motivated purely by a sense of duty.

Kant's ethical conclusions, like his metaphysical conclusions, were essentially conservative in nature. His theory rationalized all the virtues which his Lutheran upbringing had extolled. (Lutherans had always known that the human's relation to God was one of belief, not of knowledge; and they had always known that they were duty-bound not to murder, lie or steal.) Nevertheless, it is striking that Kant derived his principles from Reason and not from divine commandment. Here he was more of an Enlightenment figure than a Lutheran. And many believe that in saying that certain kinds of metaphysical speculation are a waste of time, Kant revealed something essential about the limits of human reasoning, and in saying that morality requires acts to be viewed from a perspective other than that of self-interest, he revealed something essential about ethics.

«»

VI. The 19th Century

If Kant believed that his "critical philosophy" would spell the end of speculative metaphysics, he was sorely mistaken. Even during his lifetime there was emerging a generation of metaphysicians, some of whom, ironically, were using Kantian principles to advance their speculations well beyond the limits which Kant lay down in his Critique. Kant was especially embarrassed by the use of his ideas and terminology by philosophers who were calling themselves Kantians while creating a kind of highly metaphysical idealism of the type Kant had repudiated. But it must be said that he himself was somewhat responsible for this turn of events. After all, he had defined non-human reality as a noumenal thing-in-itself, then announced that it was inaccessible to human thought, with the consequence that human thought had access only to itself. As that earlier idealist, George Berkeley, would have pointed out, an inaccessible noumenal world is hardly better than no noumenal world at all, and indeed, this new generation of German philosophers derived their idealism from their dissatisfaction with Kant's claim that there existed a non-mental world that was unknowable.

G.W.F. HEGEL

Primary among the ranks of the German Idealists were JOHANN GOTTLIEB FICHTE (1762-1814), FRIEDRICH WILHELM JOSEPH von SCHELLING (1775-1854), and GEORG WILHELM FRIEDRICH HEGEL (1770-1831). Of these, it was Hegel who achieved the greatest prominence, and it will be he who will represent German Idealism for us.

Kant had argued that the appearances of ultimate reality are processed by the human mind, which thereby creates a world for us humans to inhabit. Hegel went further and claimed that the mind did not merely <u>structure</u> and <u>regulate</u> reality, but that it

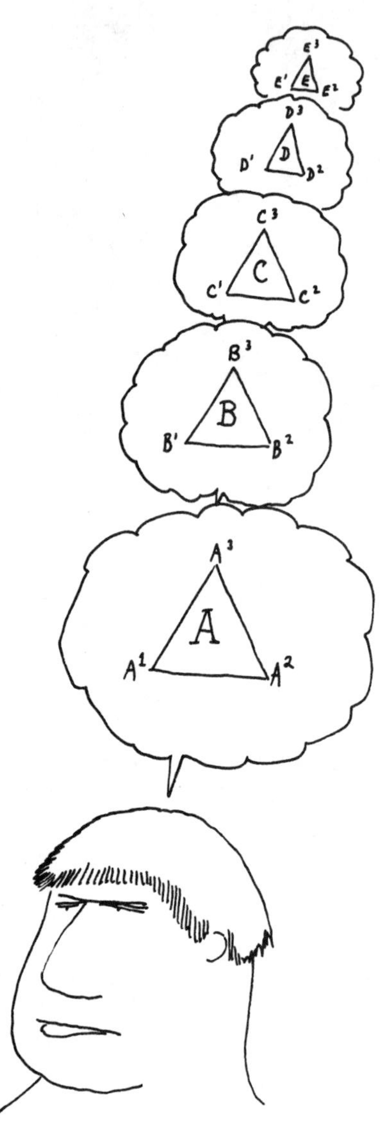

The Evolution of the Mind

generated it and *constituted* it. That is to say, reality is simply mind or spirit (*Geist* in German). This left Hegel with a philosophy which he himself called "Absolute Idealism." It is *absolute* idealism not only in the sense that absolutely nothing but ideas exist, but also because ultimately Hegel equated "mind" with "divine mind," or "Absolute mind." This meant that if MIND = REALITY, then REALITY = GOD. This view, in some ways similar to Spinoza's, made Hegel a pantheist. Furthermore, besides equating *Geist* with reality and God, Hegel also equated it with HISTORY. Kant had seen the mind as structurally identical from individual to individual, culture to culture, and historical period to historical period. Hegel criticized Kant's view as static and ahistorical. According to Hegel, even though the mind does have a universal, abstract structure, its content changes evolutionarily from period to period. There exists a mode of philosophical introspection which reveals the general structure of Mind and even allows us to reconstruct history in an *a priori* manner. In our attempt as philosophers to investigate the nature of the mind, we can reconstruct the *logical* (not chronological) beginnings of creation. It goes something like this:

In the beginning, God, pure Mind, and hence, pure Being, attempted to *think himself*. But the thought of pure Being is an impossible thought, therefore when God attempted to think Being, he thought *nothing*. That is, he thought the opposite of Being.

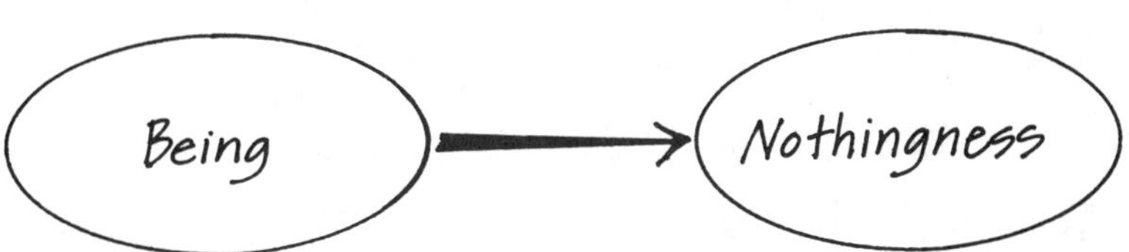

But remember, in the unusual system being suggested here, God *is* God's thought, therefore in his failure to think pure Being, God has distanced himself from his own essence. This is what Hegel calls God's SELF-ALIENATION. The "truth" of Hegel's insight can be seen in Biblical symbolism in the relation between God and Satan. Satan is a fallen angel. He has "fallen away" from divinity. He is, in Hegel's way

Satan Falls Away From God
— Divine Self-Alienation —

of thinking, divinity self-alienated.—Another Biblical indication of Hegel's "truth" can be seen in God's answer to Moses when God spoke to him through the burning bush. When the shrub burst into flame, Moses had asked it, "Who art thou?" and God had answered, "I am that which is" (or, in ungrammatical Hebrew, "I am that what am"). Here we see that God cannot say himself without dividing his essence into a subject-object relationship. ("I am ..." [= subject] ☞ "that which is" [= object]. If the subject is the object, then it is not itself as subject.) Hegel's God then is in a kind of identity crisis. But if God experiences an identity crisis, so does the human, because the human mind is nothing but a manifestation of the divine mind. The history of an individual's mind, like history itself, is the process of self-awareness and self-recovery.

God's Identity Crisis

Returning to the dichotomy BEING ⟷ NOTHINGNESS — can there be any reconciliation between the two? Well, these two impossible thoughts (neither pure being nor pure nothingness can truly be thought) represent the absolute limitation of all thinking and all reality. That is, all thought and all reality must fall somewhere between these two extremes. Hegel's term for anything occurring between these polar opposites is "Becoming." So we can call "Being" a THESIS (positive, +), "Nothingness" an ANTITHESIS (negative, –), and "Becoming" a SYNTHESIS (combination of positive and negative +/–). This universal structure of all thought and reality Hegel calls THE DIALECTIC.

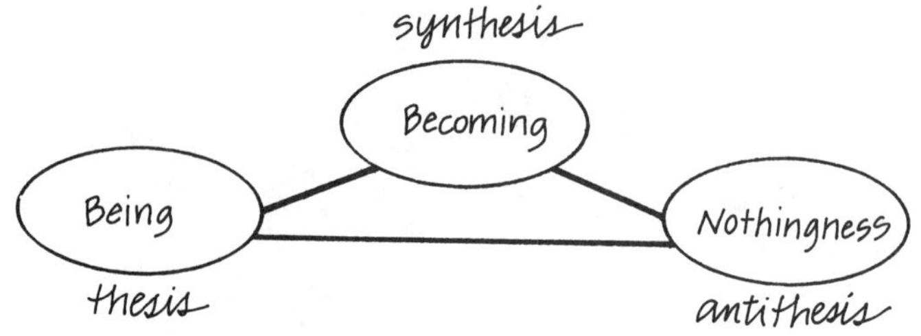

Therefore, given anything in the world – a table, for instance – it is in fact a <u>process</u> synthesizing a positivity and a negativity. It <u>is</u> the table by <u>not</u> being the chair or the floor. This is the nature of thought, language and reality. They are systems of positivities created by negativities, and vice-versa. Every thought, word and thing exists only as a part of a system of exclusions. Again, a thing is what it is by <u>not</u> being its Other, yet that "otherness" is what defines it as a being. This now explains why the thoughts of Pure Being and Pure Nothingness are impossible. Thought and language only function in a system of contrasts, yet Pure Being encompasses all, hence there is nothing to contrast with it, <u>except</u> Nothingness, which is nothing. (Are you following this dizzying "logic"?) Furthermore, it can be deduced from all this that every SYNTHESIS must become a new THESIS, and, defined as it is by its opposite, this new thesis must spawn its own ANTITHESIS. So history is an eternal process of the Dialectic, with each historical moment being a concatenation of contradictions

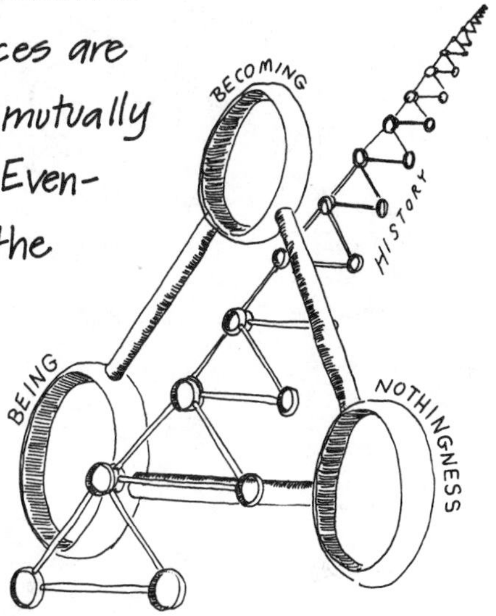

— the tension between the positive and the negative. These forces are opposed to each other, yet mutually dependent upon each other. Eventually the tension between the thesis and the antithesis destroys the historical moment, but out of its ashes a new historical moment is born, one which brings forward the best of the old moment. — Here is Hegel's optimism; there is progress built into history. And if we individuals think we see regression and backsliding at specific times in history, this is because we are blind to "the cunning of Reason," which uses apparent retrograde movements to make hidden progress. Such is the nature of Reason's (i.e., God's) process of self-recovery. Consider, for example, the period of Graeco-Roman democracy. On the one hand, there existed among the Greek and Roman democrats the commitment to self-determination, freedom and human dignity (as seen, for example, in Pericles' "funeral speech"). On the other hand, during their democratic periods, both Greece and Rome were imperialistic, slave-holding states. These two essential features

of the society in question were contradictory but, ironically, were mutually dependent upon one another. The slaves existed for the pleasure of the new democratic class; but, without slavery and the booty from plundering, there never would have been a class of men liberated from toil who could dedicate their time, skills and intellect to the creation of a democratic state. Yet eventually the conceptual contradiction between freedom and unfreedom, the two pillars of Graeco-Roman democracy, tore the society apart, and prepared the way for a new kind of society, Medieval feudalism.

Now, feudalism might not seem to you and me like a

progression over earlier democratic societies, and in fact it might seem like a retrogression. But from Hegel's point of view Medieval society represents an advance in freedom over Greece and Rome because in feudalism there were no slaves. Even the most humble serf had legal rights.

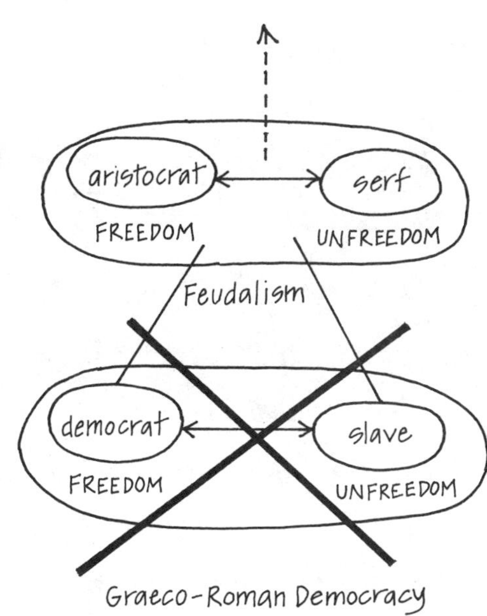

What happened in history also happens individually. Each of us passes through various stages in our conceptions of our self and our freedom. There is the stage at which we believe we can be free only by escaping the domination of others and by dominating them. Then we come to realize that in dominating them we ourselves are dominated because we become dependent upon those we dominate, both materially and in terms of self-identity. (Who am I? I am the Lord. But only as long as I am recognized as such by the bondsman. Without his recognition I would be nobody. Hence in effect he is the Lord and I am the bondsman.) Only by acknowledging that neither Lord nor bondsman is free can one transcend the unfreedom of relationships of domination, and discover higher forms of freedom — which is to say, discover the path of Reason and Divinity.

This is a sample of Hegelian thinking. From it we get an inkling of the psychological, sociological, historical and theological dimensions of Hegel's thought. What we miss in this sampling is the absolute systematization of his philosophy. An outline of one of his several proposals for such a system follows:

THE SYSTEM

I. The Idea-in-itself (= LOGIC) [This we've just discussed. See pp. 225–227.]
   A. Being.
   B. Nothingness.
   C. Becoming.

II The Idea-outside-itself (= NATURE) [Nature, i.e., the material world qua <u>material</u> is the opposite of spirit, but must be <u>potentially</u> spirit. The <u>goal</u> of inanimate matter is spirit.]

III. The Idea-for-itself (= SPIRIT) [The Idea recovered from its loss into its opposite.]
   A. Subjective spirit. [Mind as self-conscious and introverted.]
   B. Objective spirit. [Mind projecting its own laws outward, creating a human world.]
      1. Law. [Exterior - comes to the individual from without.

2. Morality. [Interior - comes from within the individual.]

3. Ethics. [Synthesis of the Law exteriorized and interiorized.]

a. Family.

b. Society.

c. State.

C. Absolute spirit

1. Art.

2. Religion.

3. Philosophy.

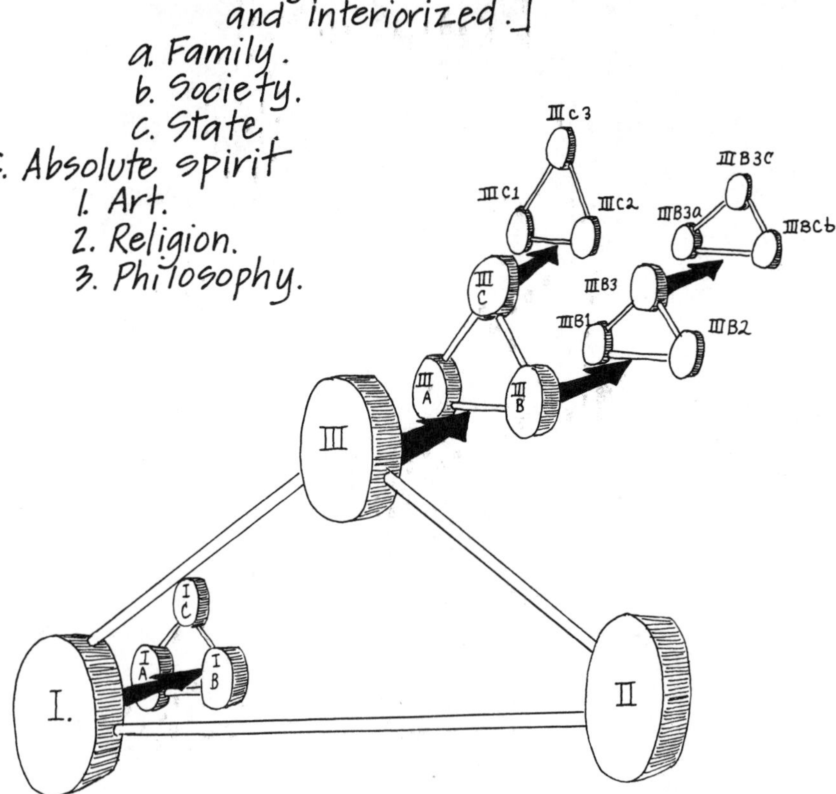

The System

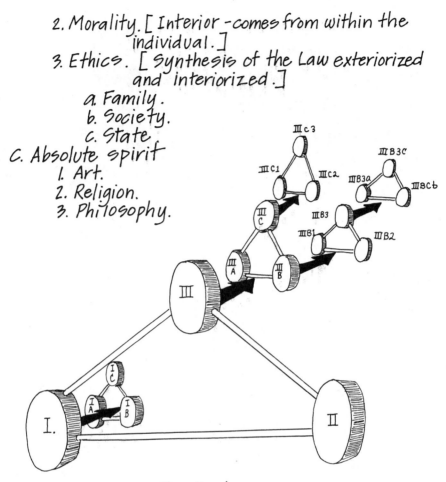

Notice that this whole system is structured in terms of interrelating triads of THESES - ANTITHESES - SYNTHESES (even though Hegel rarely used those terms), and that THE STATE is the highest form of "Objective spirit." Many of Hegel's critics point this out when they call attention to his eventual worship of the authoritarian, repressive Prussian State. Some even claim his whole system was contrived to be in the political

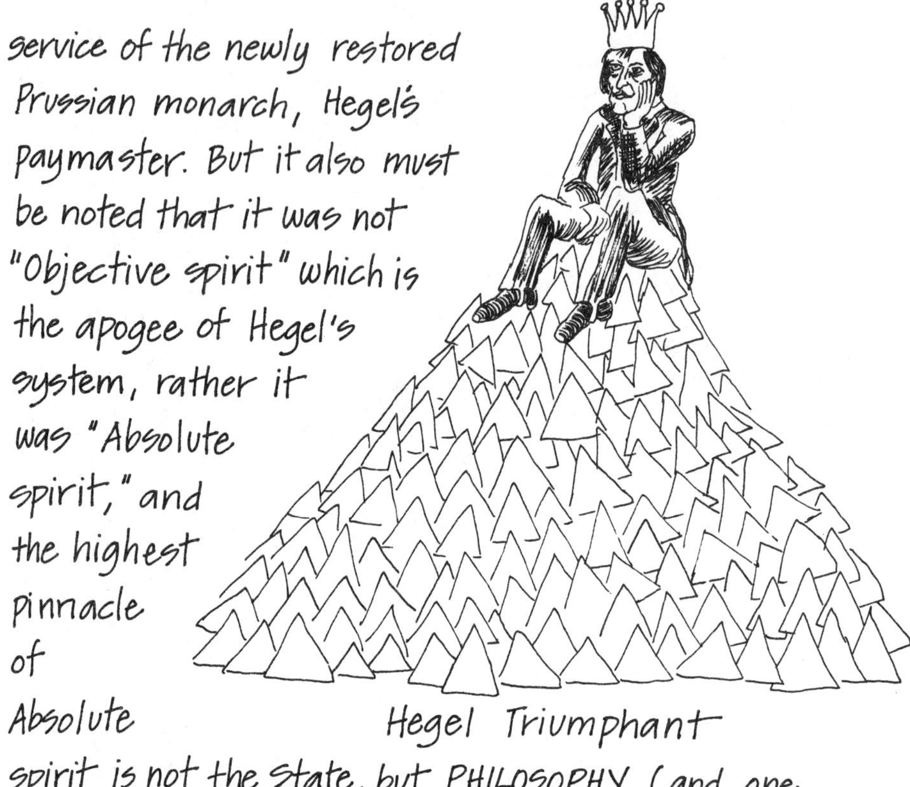

service of the newly restored Prussian monarch, Hegel's paymaster. But it also must be noted that it was not "Objective spirit" which is the apogee of Hegel's system, rather it was "Absolute spirit," and the highest pinnacle of Absolute spirit is not the State, but PHILOSOPHY (and, one assumes, particularly *Hegel's* philosophy).

Hegel Triumphant

ARTHUR SCHOPENHAUER

ARTHUR SCHOPENHAUER (1788–1860) was one of Hegel's sharpest critics. He was a younger contemporary of his who refused to be intimidated by Hegel's immense fame. As a beginning philosophy teacher at the University of Berlin, Schopenhauer had scheduled classes at the same time as Hegel's, knowing full well that thereby he was guaranteeing for himself few, if any, students. This arrogant young philosopher's opinion of Hegel was one of undisguised contempt, as can be seen in the following unflattering portrait he drew of him. "Hegel, installed from above by the powers that be as the certified Great Philosopher, was a flat-headed, insipid, nauseating, illiterate charlatan, who reached the pinnacle of audacity in scribbling together and dishing up the craziest mystifying nonsense."

Schopenhauer in fact showed deep respect for only two Western philosophers: Plato and Kant. He also admired the philosophical traditions of India. To Schopenhauer, the rest of the philosophers throughout history had been merely "windbags." Schopenhauer began his work

The History of Philosophy as the History of Windbags

demanding a return to Kant, and indeed, the first part of Schopenhauer's main work, The World as Will and Idea, was fundamentally a repetition of Kantian ideas. He agreed with Kant that the human mind is incapable of knowing ultimate reality, that the only reality we are capable of grasping intellectually is that which has passed through the gridwork of space and time, and through the categories of the understanding. Schopenhauer wrote: " 'The world is my idea:'—this is a truth which holds good for everything that lives and knows, though man alone can bring it into reflective and abstract consciousness. If he really does this, he has attained to philosophical wisdom. It then becomes clear and certain to him that what he knows is not a sun and an earth, but only an eye that sees a sun, a hand that feels an earth; that the world which surrounds him is there only as idea."

Now, when Kant turned to the noumenal world, he had claimed that we could not know it, though we had the right to hold various beliefs about it based on certain of our practical needs. It will be recalled that for Kant these beliefs were extremely optimistic ones: faith in God, freedom, immortality and eternal justice. Furthermore, Kant had pointed out certain human experiences, certain positive intuitions of ours, which he hoped might be extra-rational hints about the nature of that unknowable noumenal world. For example, there were those feelings of the sublime which we experience when we look deeply into the sky on a clear summer night, and equally inspiring to Kant were the feelings of moral duty which we experience in certain moments of crisis. As Kant put it, "two things fill the mind with ever new and increasing admiration and awe... the starry heavens above and the moral law within."

Well, Schopenhauer, too, believed that there were certain intuitive experiences which should be heeded because they might well give us an extra-rational insight into ultimate reality. But Schopenhauer's examples of such insights were very different indeed from those of Kant.

For example, Schopenhauer wondered why it is that when someone is told of the death of an acquaintance, the first impulse which that person experiences is the urge to grin — an urge which of course must be suppressed. And

It's Not Nice to Giggle at Funerals

Schopenhauer wondered why it is that a respectable businessman or government official, who may have worked tirelessly for years to achieve the success and power which he has finally obtained, is willing to risk all of it for a moment's sexual pleasure with a forbidden partner. These and similar human experiences left Schopenhauer with a much more pessimistic hunch about the nature of ultimate reality than that held by Kant. Schopenhauer's dark suspicions quickly became "truths" in his system. (The curious status of these non-epistemological truths has not escaped the eyes of Schopenhauer's critics.) Said Schopenhauer: "This truth, which must be very serious and impressive if not awful to everyone, is that a man can also say and must

SCHOPENHAUER PEERS BEYOND THE CURTAIN OF THE PHENOMENAL WORLD

say, 'The world is my will.' "

Schopenhauer's awful truth amounts to this: behind appearances, behind the phenomenal veil, there does lie a noumenal reality; but, far from being the benign sphere where Kant hoped to find God, immortality and Justice, Schopenhauer found there a wild seething, inexorable, meaningless force which he called "Will." This force

creates all and destroys all in its insatiable demand for "More!" (More of what it does not know — it only knows that it wants more.)

The best phenomenal images for understanding Schopenhauer's "Will" are images of sex and violence. Not only in nature, but even in the human sphere, every event is an act of procreation or destruction. Our actions, whether intentional or unintentional, motivated consciously or unconsciously, are in fact actions which in one way or another are in the service of procreation and destruction. (It must be obvious to you now where Freud got his idea of the "Id." Even the name "Id" [Latin for "it"] indicates the same noumenal indeterminacy as Schopenhauer's "Will." Freud himself said in 1920, "We have unwittingly steered our course into the harbour of Schopenhauer's philosophy.")

According to Schopenhauer, everything in the phenomenal

world is merely the manifestation of this perverse Will, or, as he called it, an "objectification of the Will" (that is to say, the Will passed through the Categories and the gridwork of space and time).

Even though Schopenhauer's images of the Will are ones of dumb brutality, he also conceived of it as immensely cunning. The Will is capable of disguising its heartless purposes from any of its own "experiments" which might be capable of taking offense or even taking reprisals against the Will. This means that the human mind is constructed in such a way as to be self-deceiving, even concerning its view upon the world. The Will is denatured as it passes through the gridwork and the Categories. Nevertheless, if we could strip away our natural optimism, itself a product of the "cunning of the Will," we could look into Nature and see that it cares not a whit for the happiness nor well being of any of its creatures beyond the bare needs of reproduction. Schopenhauer illustrated his point with descriptions of the giant turtles of the South Pacific which were known to have been smashed to death by the hundreds against the rocky coast in storms during mating season as they tried to get to shore to lay their eggs in the sand. Schopenhauer also called attention to that strange species of moth which emerges from its cocoon with full

Waiter, there seems to be a problem here.

reproductive and digestive systems, yet Nature forgot to give it one little detail — a mouth! So the moth reproduces, then finds food, but quickly starves to death. Yet Nature does not care; the moth has laid its little eggs. And, according to Schopenhauer, what's true of the turtle and the moth is true of the human being. If you are over eighteen years of age, your body is deteriorating. Your body, which is just the scaffolding for the reproductive system, begins to die once it has held its eggs in place and given them a chance to duplicate themselves.

This is terrible news indeed. Why do people not realize that we are all in a state of bondage to the irrational, meaningless Will? Precisely because of the cunning of the Will. Human culture itself is nothing but one more experiment of the Will, and human optimism and hope are simply the Will's gift to us to guarantee that we continue to deceive ourselves about the true state of affairs. The whole of human culture is nothing more

The Human Being in the Grip of the Will

What seems to be the case

What is the case

than a grand deception. Art, religion, law, morality, science, and even philosophy, are only sublimations of the Will, sublimations which are still acting in its service. Hegel's glorification of higher culture is simply proof of the absolute triumph of the Will.

All of our hopes and aspirations will be dashed. Happiness is an impossible dream. It is absurd that anyone could remain an optimist after even a glance at the newspaper on any given day. A mud slide swallows up whole villages. A mad assassin's bullet strikes down the hope of a people. A single parent, mother of three, is killed by a painful disease. The drums of war never cease beating, and an inglorious death awaits all. Verily, only a fool could remain optimistic in the face of the truth.

Surely philosophy was never so disheartened and disheartening as in the case of Schopenhauer. But, according to him, his pessimism was a <u>rational</u> pessimism, and he sought a rational solution to it. There had, of course, been others who understood the truth and sought rational responses to it. Both Jesus and the Buddha had been pessimists, according to Schopenhauer, but their solutions were chimerical and still in the service of the Will (besides, their doctrines were perverted by the cunning of the Will manifested in the optimism of their disciples who presented their masters' pessimistic messages as "good news"). Plato too had offered a <u>nearly</u> successful solution, but his eternal Forms were still part of the world of Idea, hence of the Will.

II might seem that suicide should be the only recommendation that Schopenhauer's philosophy could make. But, in fact, Schopenhauer recommended against suicide on the grounds that self-murder would be a last, desperate act of will, hence still a manifestation of the Will (that is to say, no act requires as much concentration of will as does suicide, hence suicide cannot possibly be the negation of the Will).

PLATO'S SOLUTION

Do not despair! There is a Schopenhauerian solution. Even though all culture is nothing but a sublimation of sex and violence, hence an experiment of the Will, there is a point at which the cultural world can achieve such a degree of subtlety that it can break off from its own unconscious origins and set up an independent sphere which is in fact counter-nature, and therefore anti-Will. This autonomy from the Will occurs in a specific corner of the art world—that of music. But not just <u>any</u> music. Certainly popular music won't do, evoking as it does the imagery and emotions of the phenomenal world. Nor will most classical music serve. For example, in Beethoven's works the imagery is still too strong, hence its link to the Will is too obvious. (When listening to the "Pastoral" we <u>see</u> the cows in the meadow, the bright green grass and the wild-flowers,

ELVIS'S SOLUTION

and the puffy little white clouds in the blue sky.) No, an escape from the Will can be achieved only in the contemplation of purely <u>formal</u> music, a music without words and without imagery. There is a kind of baroque music which fits the bill — a kind of pure mathematical formalism: point, counterpoint, point.

SCHOPENHAUER'S SOLUTION

It is possible to dedicate one's life to the disinterested contemplation of such music, and Schopenhauer recommended precisely this as his version of Nirvana — an escape from the world into Pure Form, and hence a triumph over the Will. It was this toward which Plato and the Buddha were clumsily struggling.

Schopenhauer's philosophy was deeply influential

among intellectuals in the German-speaking world. The work of Nietzsche, Freud and Thomas Mann is hardly conceivable without Schopenhauer. Yet nobody seems to have taken Schopenhauer's solution very seriously. It was perhaps too obvious, as Nietzsche was to point out, that baroque music is the most sensual of all music, and that the desire to immerse oneself in it is after all a *desire*, hence still the work of the Will.

Schopenhauer's method of dealing with Hegel was first to call him names, then to ignore him. But the generation of Continental philosophers who followed Schopenhauer had to deal more directly with Hegel, whose influence by the 1830s had become immense. One of the most curious members of this generation was the Dane, SØREN KIERKEGAARD (1813-1855). Kierkegaard, who is generally recognized today as "the father of existentialism," thought of himself primarily as a religious author and an anti-philosopher. In truth, he was not opposed to philosophy as such, but to *Hegel's* philosophy. Nevertheless, like the rest of his generation, Kierkegaard fell more under Hegel's spell than he would have liked to admit.

Kierkegaard blamed Hegel for much of what he

SØREN KIERKEGAARD

took to be the dehumanization of the intellectual life of a whole generation. This dehumanization was the result of a "correction" which Hegel made to Aristotelian logic. Aristotle had laid down the three basic principles of logic as:

(1) THE PRINCIPLE OF IDENTITY. (A = A)

(2) THE PRINCIPLE OF NON-CONTRADICTION. [not(A and not-A)]

(3) THE PRINCIPLE OF THE EXCLUDED MIDDLE [either (A) or (not-A)]

Hegel believed these principles to be erroneous. His new dialectical logic overturned them. In the Dialectic, everything is in some sense its opposite; therefore, it is not the case that "A = A", because "A = not-A." (Greek democracy was in some sense equivalent to Greek slavery, hence it was its own opposite.) If the Principle of identity falls, then the Principles of non-contradiction and of the excluded middle collapse too. Kierkegaard took offense at the pompousness of Hegel's suggestion. He mocked it with vignettes like the following:

> "If you marry, you will regret it; if you do not marry, you will also regret it; ... whether you marry or do not marry, you will regret both. Laugh at the world's follies, you will regret it; weep over them, you will regret that; laugh at the world's follies or weep over them, you will regret both, ... Believe a woman, you will regret it, believe her not, you will also regret that; believe a woman or believe her not, you will regret both.... Hang yourself, you will regret it, do not hang yourself, and you will also regret that; hang yourself or do not hang yourself, you will regret both. ... This, gentlemen, is the sum and substance of all philosophy."

I was going to hang myself, but it's just too much trouble.

This is not really the sum and substance of all philosophy. It is the sum and substance of Hegel's philosophy, a philosophy in which all oppositions are swallowed up, creating absolute apathy and demoralization, and which, by abrogating the Principle of the excluded middle, thereby annuls the "either/or" of decision making — and therewith denies freedom, which, for Kierkegaard and his existentialist followers, is the essence of human existence. Therefore Kierkegaard published the foregoing "ecstatic lecture" in a book which he called Either/Or, whose very title was an attack on Hegel.

Not only had Hegel collapsed the distinction between the "Either" and the "Or," but he had also abolished the difference between epistemology and ontology by asserting, "The Real is the Rational and the Rational is the Real," which is another way of saying that existence and thought are identical. Kierkegaard inverted Hegel's assertion, claiming that existence is the one thing which cannot be thought. This is a double-entendre meaning: (a) thought and existence are not identical, and (b) it is impossible to think "existence."

It will be recalled that Hegel's god had found himself incapable of thinking pure existence (pure Being). Kierkegaard pushed this limitation to the fore, claiming not just that pure existence was impossible to think, but that <u>any</u> existence was unthinkable. This is because, in Kierkegaard's Platonic theory of meaning, thought is always a form of abstraction. Words are signifiers which denote CONCEPTS, and concepts are general categories. Every word in the sentence, "The brown dog obeys its master," denotes for Kierkegaard an abstraction. Language abstracts from experience and suppresses differences in order to allow the possibility of thought and communication; hence, thought (which is language-bound) distances us from real existence, which is never abstract but always <u>concrete</u>.

As opposed to the abstractions of Hegelian philosophy, Kierkegaard's philosophy would return us to the concreteness of existence. But he was not so much interested in the con-

Language Alienates One from Lived Experience

creteness of existence of things in the world as he was in the concreteness of individual human existence. René Descartes had been right to begin philosophy with the self ("I think, therefore I am"), but he had been wrong, as was Hegel after him, to equate the self with thought. "To think is one thing, to exist is another," said Kierkegaard. I can think and say many things about myself — "I am a teacher, I am a man, I am an American, I am in love, I prefer chocolate to vanilla." Yet, when I am done talking and thinking about myself, there is one thing remaining which cannot be thought — MY EXISTENCE, which is a "surd" (an irrational residue). I cannot think it, rather I must live it.

My lived existence, according to Kierkegaard, is equated with passion, decision and action. None of these

When All the Roles Have Been Stripped Away, What's Left Is My Existence

categories can be exhausted by thought. But that is not to say that there is no connection between existence and thought. Kierkegaard wrote, "Existence must be interpenetrated with thought." What kind of thought? A kind of philosophical self-consciousness which he called "existential thought."

To explain this notion we must clarify a distinction which Kierkegaard drew in his Concluding Unscientific Postscript to the Philosophical Fragments between "objective thought" and "subjective thought." The first category is a kind of thinking for which there exist objective criteria of truth, such as in the case of math, science and history. If you wonder whether "3+2=5," "f=ma," or "Caesar crossed the Rubicon in 49 B.C.," there are recognized standards which can be used to determine the truth of these assertions. Objective truths exist, then, but they are "existentially indifferent." That is, they have no essential relationship to my existence. If I found out that one of them was false I might be surprised, but I would not thereby become a different person. Therefore, Kierkegaard's philosophy is uninterested in "objective truths."

Subjective thought, however, is thought for which there exist no objective criteria of truth. This is so, for example, in the case of VALUES, e.g., ethical and

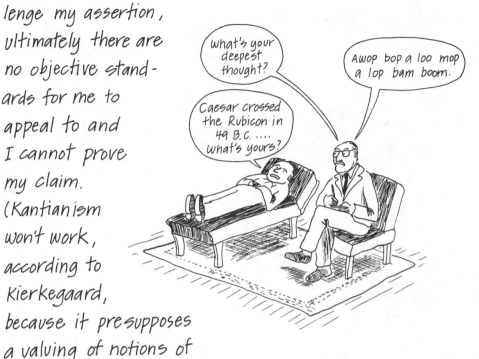

religious claims. If I tell you that it is immoral to cause unnecessary misery to others, and if you challenge my assertion, ultimately there are no objective standards for me to appeal to and I cannot prove my claim. (Kantianism won't work, according to Kierkegaard, because it presupposes a valuing of notions of consistency and non-contradictoriness. But what if you refuse to accept that value?) Similarly, if I claim that "God is love," and you challenge me, I cannot appeal to any objective criterion of truth to justify my assertion.

Nevertheless, these "subjective truths" are essential to my existence in the way that "objective truths" are indifferent. This is because we pretty much *are* what we *do*, and what we do — the actions we perform — is the result of *decisions*, which are embodiments of *values* chosen. Yet those values cannot be grounded in certainty, but are always accepted on faith — a faith in the uncertain. This need for values and decisiveness in the face of the uncertainty of all things provokes, according to Kierkegaard, a kind of dizziness and loss of footing which reveals the true human condition as one of anguish and despair. Hegel was wrong. The Real is not the Rational. Rather, the lived experience of true human reality lies underneath rationality as a kind of despairing nothingness longing to be a something. (Yet, had Hegel not said this too?)

Vertigo in the Face of the Uncertainty of Reality

There are other "subjective truths" besides those of moral and religious valuation. But these truths can only be communicated indirectly, Kierkegaard told us. They can be hinted at, alluded to, overstated, understated, misstated, joked about, poeticized or ignored. But they cannot be SAID — or at least, if they are said, they can't be directly understood. Such a truth would be the truth of "MY DEATH." Now, I know that all humans die, and that, being a human, someday I too will die. I know much about death from the studies I have made in my history and biology classes. But that does not mean that I have grasped <u>my</u> death as a subjective truth. In the <u>Postscript</u>, Kierkegaard relates the story of a man who meets a friend on a street corner of Copenhagen and is invited to dinner by him. The invitee enthusiastically promises to attend, but at that very moment the prospective guest is struck and killed by a tile which happens to fall from the roof. Kierkegaard mocks the dead man, saying that one could laugh oneself to death over this case. Here is a person who makes an absolute commitment into the future, yet whose existence is whisked away by a gust of wind. After chuckling

I'll be there. Set a place for me.

for a while over the irony of this story, Kierkegaard then asks himself if he is not being too harsh on the chap. Surely we don't expect the guest to respond to his invitation saying, "I shall attend. Set a place at the table for me, but you must make room for the contingency that a tile falls and strikes me dead, for in that case I shall not attend." Yet the reader of the Postscript comes to the realization that that is exactly what Kierkegaard wanted. When we reach the understanding that after every utterance which we make about the future, we can correctly add the rider: "However, I may be dead in the next moment, in which case I shall not attend," then we will have grasped the subjective truth of our death.

The point of Kierkegaard's story is not to provoke a sense of morbidity. According to him, the discovery of one's death as a subjective truth becomes the pre-text for another discovery — that of "one's existence" as a subjective truth. Only against a backdrop of the yawning abyss of eternity can the immediacy and fragility of existence be understood. Most people are oblivious to the proximity of nothingness, and they spend their lives engaged in petty thoughts and pointless projects. ("Do my socks have holes? What will people think of me if I wear a soiled tie?") But

The Individual Before the Yawning Abyss of Eternity

the discovery of our subjective truths concretizes and intensifies our existence. It helps us to order our priorities and clarify our values and to recover the self from its alienation into social roles, material possessions and linguistic abstractions. It reveals (and at the same time creates) the self which had been invisible to the self.

For Kierkegaard, the self is essentially subjectivity, and subjectivity is constituted by the individual's commitment to his subjective truths. The authentic self, for Kierkegaard, is one which "chooses itself" by a form of self-reflective activity which both clarifies and creates one's values while assuming total responsibility for those values. It was this which Hegel had left out of his System, according to Kierkegaard; or more correctly, it was this which <u>any</u> system would necessarily swallow up. Therefore Kierkegaard was anti-systematic, and titled one of his books <u>Philosophical Fragments</u>, yet another slap in Hegel's face.

Søren Kierkegaard saw as his task, not the development of a new epistemology, nor the creation of a new system of metaphysics, but the creation of a whole new kind of human being, one who could grasp his own freedom and create his own destiny. (In this he was joined by two other wayward nineteenth century thinkers at whom we have yet to look: Karl Marx and Friedrich Nietzsche.) Kierkegaard calls his version of the new human being "a Knight of Faith." This is a person who, for Kierkegaard, has an almost superhuman kind of strength and greatness. Kierkegaard wrote of the archetypal Knight of Faith, "Not one shall be forgotten who was great in the world. But each was great in his own way... each became great in proportion to his <u>expectation</u>. One became great by expecting the possible, another by expecting the eternal, but he who expected the impossible became greater than all. Everyone shall be remembered, but each was great in proportion to the greatness of that with which he <u>strove</u>.

That Other "Knight of Faith"

For he who strove with the world became great by overcoming the world, and he who strove with himself became great by overcoming himself, but he who strove with God became greater than all." This knight has grasped the absurdity and contingency of all existence. David Hume had meditated on the disconnectedness of all things. But Hume had <u>only</u> meditated on it while the Knight of Faith feels it in his bones. Yet he finds the strength within himself to unify his world, to hold it together with an act of will which Kierkegaard called "faith." He is an individual who has looked profoundly into the world of men and seen that at the deepest level we are alone — in "absolute isolation" — an aloneness which constitutes a kind of madness, "divine madness"; for Kierkegaard's hero is alone with his god. In fact, Kierkegaard's Knight of Faith, his "new human," is not new at all. Rather, he is based on Kierkegaard's tortured interpretation of the Biblical patriarch, Abraham, who heard a voice in the night telling him to sacrifice his son. Abraham took full responsibility for the meaning of the message — it was <u>his</u> meaning, his subjective truth — and for his actions, thereby becoming

a Kierkegaardian hero. Kierkegaard wrote of him, "Abraham was greater than all, great by reason of his power whose strength is impotence, great by reason of his wisdom whose secret is foolishness, great by reason of his hope whose form is madness." Hegel had transformed human existence into pure thought. Kierkegaard counteracted Hegel's rationalization by introducing into philosophy a new category, "the category of the absurd," and putting it in the heart of his ideal human being.

Of course, Søren Kierkegaard was not the only philosopher of his generation to be deeply influenced by Hegel. When KARL MARX (1818-1883) arrived as a young philosophy student at the University of Berlin in the mid-1830s, Hegel had been dead of cholera for five years, but his spirit still reigned supreme. To do philosophy in the Germany of the 1830s was to do Hegelian

Hegel's Spirit Reigns Supreme

philosophy. Nevertheless, the Hegelians were by no means in agreement as to what "doing philosophy" truly consisted of. In fact, they had broken into two warring camps, the "Hegelian Left" and the "Hegelian Right." The Right gave the more orthodox reading of Hegel and was composed mostly of older, more conservative members of their generation. They were primarily interested in what Hegel had to say about religion and morality. The Left was composed of younger, more radical philosophers. They sometimes called themselves "the Young Hegelians." They were mostly interested in developing what they took to be still inchoate Hegelian notions about social and political issues. They believed that Hegel's ideas as he himself understood them were false but that there was a hidden truth in them which needed revealing. Their attitude toward Hegel's writing was very much like Freud's attitude toward dreams. There is a "manifest content" [the dream images] and a "latent content" [the true meaning of the dream, which can be discovered only by interpreting the manifest content]. As with Freud, sometimes the analysis of the imagery demonstrates that its meaning is the opposite of what it appears to be.

Needless to say, Marx fell under the influence of

The Manifest Content

The Latent Content

the Hegelian Left, not the Right. The foremost practitioner of the art of Hegelian Leftism was LUDWIG FEUERBACH (1804-1872), whose *Essence of Christianity* became holy scripture to a whole generation of progressive German youth.

Feuerbach's book, which was meant to be a kind of anthropological analysis of religion, contained an inversion of a key Hegelian idea. Hegel had asserted, "Man is God self-alienated." Feuerbach reversed this proposition, saying, "God is man self-alienated." That is, the idea of God is the perversion of the idea of

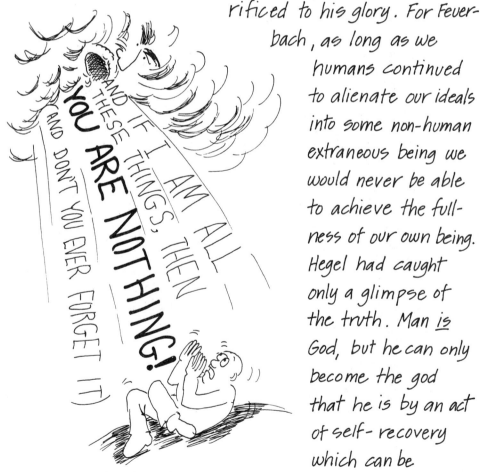

man. Feuerbach believed that there were certain (Platonic) universal values to which all humans aspired. Every culture throughout history has longed for truth, beauty, justice, strength and purity. It is part of the human essence to have these longings. But as historical peoples were frustrated in their attempts to achieve these ideals, the ideals themselves became alienated from the human and were projected onto an ideal being, a God who demanded that all be sacrificed to his glory. For Feuerbach, as long as we humans continued to alienate our ideals into some non-human extraneous being we would never be able to achieve the fullness of our own being. Hegel had caught only a glimpse of the truth. Man *is* God, but he can only become the god that he is by an act of self-recovery which can be

AND IF I AM ALL
THESE THINGS, THEN
YOU ARE NOTHING!
(AND DON'T YOU EVER FORGET IT)

brought about exclusively by annulling our traditional concept of religion. For example, consider the Feuerbachian concept of "the Holy Family":

This is the HEAVENLY FAMILY. It is the idealization of the earthly family. Here peace, happiness and love reign.

This is the EARTHLY FAMILY. The frustrated father comes home drunk from the tavern where he has spent much of the pittance that is his weekly wage. He expends his rage terrorizing his wife and children.

According to Feuerbach, only by abolishing the image of the Heavenly Family can we bring peace, happiness and love into the Earthly Family, because as long as we hold the image of the former before us, we will consider the Earth merely a place of trial and punishment. The worker will attend church on Sunday, confess his sins, become resigned to misery as the human lot, and on the next payday return to the tavern to drink away his meager salary.

Marx fell directly under Feuerbach's influence. As a young philosophy student Marx wrote, "One cannot do philosophy without passing through the fiery brook." (In German, "Feuerbach" means "fiery brook.") But Marx soon became disenchanted with Feuerbach, and his own philosophy began with a critique of his old mentor. Feuerbach had prided himself on having escaped from Hegel's idealism, proclaiming himself a materialist. But Marx criticized Feuerbach as a crypto-idealist, that is, an idealist who believes himself to be a materialist. Marx pointed out the idealistic implications of Feuerbach's account of the Heavenly Family. According to it, we could bring about changes in the MATERIAL configurations of the earthly family by changing the IDEA of the heavenly family. Marx, to the contrary, argued that all change must begin at the level of material configurations. In his _Theses Against Feuerbach_, he wrote, "Once the earthly family is discovered to be the secret of the holy family, the former must then itself be theoretically criticized and radically changed in practice." Consistent with this attitude, Marx ended his tract against Feuerbach with the following famous line: "The philosophers have only interpreted the world in various ways: the point however is to change it." Marx believed that once the family was revolutionized (i.e., once its hierarchy of power was restructured, along with the hierarchy of power in the society of which the family was the mirror image), then the idea of the holy family would simply disappear.

The Disappearance of the Heavenly Family

Religion would not need to be abolished; it would simply dissolve. This is because, contrary to Feuerbach, religion is not the cause of alienation; it is, rather, a symptom of alienation, and sometimes even a remonstration against it. Marx's statement that religion is the opiate of the masses is often taken out of context and misunderstood. What he actually said in The German Ideology is this: "Religious distress is at the same time the expression of real distress and the protest against real distress. Religion is the sigh of the oppressed creature, the heart of a heartless world, just as it is the spirit of an unspiritual situation. It is the opium of the people." Here the word "opium" refers to the drug's medicinal powers.

Like Feuerbach, and Hegel before him, Marx was interested in analyzing ALIENATION (the process of the subject being split from its natural object). Although Marx discussed alienation in a number of its manifestations (alienation from nature, social alienation and self-alienation), he was most philosophically original perhaps in his account of "the alienation of labor." Marx believed that it was of the nature of human beings to be producers. We create of necessity, Marx thought. He preferred the designation homo faber (man the maker) to homo sapiens (man the knower) because our knowing is dependent on our doing. According to Marx, to a great extent we are what we make. We create our products and our products re-create us. Our minds begin to take on the features of

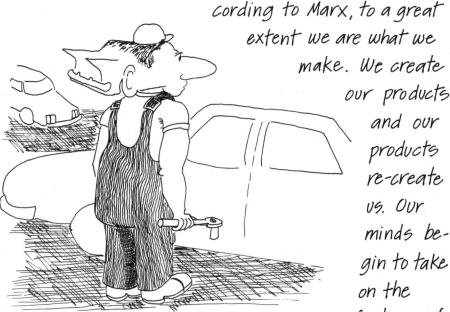

You Are What You Make

the objects which we create. If we create in piecemeal, fragmented ways, we become piecemeal and fragmented ourselves. If we create useless objects, we ourselves become useless human beings. Unfortunately, the processes of production are influenced by historical forces which are not always in our control. When these forces, usually socio-politico-economic ones, drive a wedge between individual humans and their products, the result is "alienated labor." This happens if the work which one performs is not the expression of a natural creative need, but is motivated by the necessity of fulfilling other needs, such as economic or avaricious ones. Further alienation occurs if the product one creates is for the profit of another, and if the product enters into an economic system meant to fulfill desires of greed rather than true human needs. And above all, alienated labor comes about if the worker's product returns to the worker as a disabling alien force. (Extreme case: the worker produces cigarettes, which give him lung cancer.) It will come as no surprise to you to hear that, according to Marx, of all the historical socio-economic systems, with the exception of slavery, capitalism is the one which promotes the most intense forms of alienated labor. Alienated labor in turn produces self-alienation—the worker confronts himself as a stranger, and as a stranger

The Worker Confronts Himself As an Alien

to the human race. (This is Marx's version of Hegel's divine identity crisis.) The goal of the young Karl Marx's communism was to create a society in which all alienation would be overcome and where humans would recover their lost essence as homo faber.

In converting Hegel's idealism into a form of materialism (thereby "standing Hegel on his head") Marx created a philosophy unique in history. We have run across materialists before, of course; Democritus and Hobbes were such. But each of them, in claiming that ultimately everything resolves into matter, chose to define his key category in terms of physics. Their "material reality" was simply mass in motion. But Marx chose

Marx Stands Hegel on His Head

his key category not from physics but from economics. He did not try to explain the whole of reality, but only human reality. Marx used an analytic model involving a foundation and a superstructure. According to him, the foundations of the social world are material ones: natural resources, means of production and means of distribution, as well as the human work relations involved at this

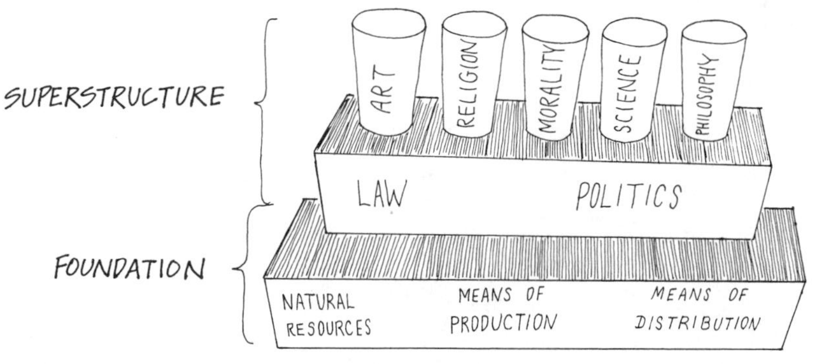

level. Built upon this foundation there is a level composed of certain other social relations, such as legal and political arrangements, and above this there is yet another level comprising "higher culture": such social features as art, religion, morality, science and philosophy. In *A Contribution to the Critique of Political Economy*, Marx wrote:

> "In the social production of their life, men enter into definite relations that are indispensable and independent of their will, relations of production which correspond to a definite stage of development of their material productive forces. The sum total of these relations of production constitutes the economic structure of society, the real foundation, on which

rises a legal and political superstructure and to which correspond definite forms of social consciousness. The mode of production of material life conditions the social, political, and intellectual life process in general. It is not the consciousness of men that determines their social being, but, on the contrary, their social being that determines their consciousness."

In this and similar passages, Marx made the relationship between the foundation and the superstructure seem simple. Higher culture, or what he called the "ideological" sphere, was merely a "reflex" or a "sublimate" of the socio-economic foundation. Later he modified this,

ART AS IDEOLOGY

admitting that the ideational superstructure and the material foundation mutually influenced each other, though ultimately it was the foundation which dominated. The ideational features of society never ceased to be IDEOLOGY, that is, a system of unconscious propaganda for the foundational economic structure. Therefore, to find out the true status of the symbols in a society, one simply asks, "Who owns the foundation?" Find out who controls the natural resources, the means of production and the means of distribution (the raw materials, the factories, the trucking lines and distribution outlets) and you will discover the secret behind the laws, the politics, the science, the art, the morality, and the religion of any society. As the old saw has it, "He who pays the piper calls the tune." Marx's version is, "The ruling ideas of each age have ever been the ideas of its ruling class."

Add to Marx's materialistic model of "foundation and superstructure" his dialectical interpretation of the foundation. The possession of a society's material wealth by a specific group of people automatically creates a class system — basically, the owning class (the "haves") and the class controlled by the owning class (the "have nots"). Since the interests of these two classes are always in opposition, these classes must be in perpetual conflict. In

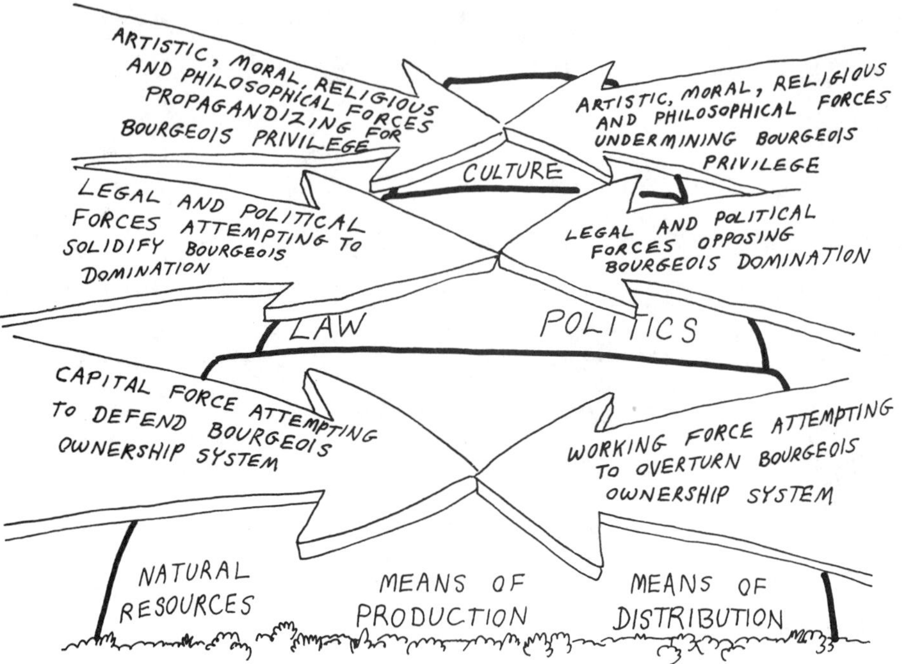

the first line of The Communist Manifesto Marx announced, "The history of all hitherto existing society is the history of class struggle." This conflict, which began in prehistoric times with the creation of tools, had, in Marx's time, reached what he took to be its most clearly-delineated stage, and indeed, according to him, it had reached its final stage, a struggle between the owning class of capitalism – the bourgeoisie — and the working class which capitalism exploited – the proletariat. Marx spent the bulk of his mature years describing the structure of capitalism in all of its internal contradictions (memories of the Hegelian dialectic!), e.g., capitalism's emphasis on competition leading to its own opposite, monopoly — and the consequent expulsion of some former members of the economic elite into the ranks of the paupers; capitalism's constant need for new sources of raw materials, cheap labor, and dumping grounds for its products — leading to imperialistic wars among capitalist states; capitalism's need to solve the problem of unemployment, achieved by pumping more money into the system, thereby creating inflation, and its need to solve the problem of inflation, achieved by increasing unemployment. Marx thought that these internal contradictions of capitalism, along with the massive unrest which would be caused by the ever-growing misery of its dispossessed, would necessarily bring on a simultaneous internal collapse of capitalism and a revolt of the working class which would produce Marx's notorious "dictatorship of the proletariat," whose function it would be to ensure that the victorious proletariat did not reconstitute the institutions of classism. (After all, these

As Per Karl Marx's Prediction, Capitalism Collapses in the Middle Due to Its Own Excesses conquering street fighters themselves grew up in conditions of alienation, and hence in "false consciousness.") According to Marx, once this dictatorship has performed its essential service, it will simply step down from power — "wither," as Marx had it. Marx's critics are quick to point out that he does not deal with the question of the abuse of power in his socialistic utopia. Perhaps this is due to the philosophical optimism he inherited from Hegel. Unfortunately, as the Stalinist period in the Soviet Union proved, Lord Acton's pessimism was more realistic than Marx's optimism. (It was Acton who said, "Power corrupts, and absolute power corrupts absolutely.") This relinquishing of control by the dictatorship will usher in a classless society, which will end the dialectic of conflict, and therefore end history as we know it. (History was defined, after all, as "the history of class conflict.") Humans will live under optimum conditions for the first time since aboriginal times. Private ownership will be abolished, as well as "the division of labor" (i.e., the type of specialization where one is defined throughout life by the practice of <u>one</u> special-

ity). We will all be artists and philosophers, and we shall "hunt in the morning, fish in the afternoon, rear cattle in the evening, criticize [poetry] after dinner, just as [we] have in mind, without ever becoming hunter, fisherman, shepherd or critic." Elsewhere Marx includes in his picture of the ideal world: socializing in the pub, going to dances, going to the theater, buying books, loving, theorizing painting, singing, and even fencing. (Fencing?) Sometimes Marx's "true communist society" seems more like a bourgeois pastoral than a working-class paradise; and sometimes, as in the case of Kierkegaard, his "new human being" seems to be a very "old human being," though not one from the historical past, but from the mythical Golden Age.

The New Golden Age?

FRIEDRICH NIETZSCHE

FRIEDRICH NIETZSCHE (1844-1900) was the third post-Kantian who responded to the crisis of his time not by demanding a new "critique of reason," but by calling for a new kind of human existence. (The other two, as we have seen, were Kierkegaard and Marx.) Nietzsche was a solitary thinker who liked Alpine trails more than the halls of academia (which he abandoned in his mid thirties). He spent most of his life using his authorship in an attempt to triumph over the powerful influences on his childhood: Lutheranism, German nationalism, and the domination of his forceful mother, granny, aunts and sister. (His attempts were more successful in some of these endeavors than in others.) The material result of his efforts was an unprecedented stream of the most eccentric books ever to have been introduced into the history of philosophy, including such titles as: _The Birth of Tragedy_, _Beyond Good and Evil_, _The Genealogy of Morals_, _Thus Spoke Zarathustra_, and his outrageous intellectual autobiography, pretentiously titled _Ecce Homo_ ("behold the man"— the phrase with which Pilate introduced Jesus to the masses), with such chapter headings as "Why I Am So Wise," "Why I Am So Clever," and "Why I Write Such Good Books." Nietzsche's short, prolific authorship ended in 1888 with the onset of syphilis-induced insanity.

Nietzsche's epistemological theory constituted a radical return to the Sophistic period. It is usually called "perspectivism." It derived from Nietzsche's early training as a philologist. Philologists, those students of ancient languages, knew that what was called _The Bible_, _The Vedas_, _The Upanishads_ or _The Iliad_ were not direct translations of single existing documents; rather, they were compilations of fragments of conflicting evidence derived from a dizzying number of sources. The dream of the philologists was to find _the_ original texts of each of the great scriptures in history. Nietzsche's conclusion as a philologist was that *there is no original text*. Each of these books is simply the result of a *decision* to let a particular interpretation represent an end product, even though in fact that "end product" is merely an emblem of a relationship which exists among a number of fragmentary documents, reports, historical studies, and items of gossip.

There is no original text.

Nietzsche translated his philological insight into an ontological and epistemological doctrine. Just as in philology there is no original text, so in reality and knowledge there is no "pure being" nor "original datum." There are no gods, no Platonic Forms, no substances, no "Things-in-themselves," nor even any "things." There exist only flux and chaos upon which we must impose our will. Therefore, said Nietzsche, there can be no such thing as *knowing* in the Platonic sense. All "knowing" is inventing, and all inventing is lying. But then, there are lies, and there are *lies*. Inauthentic lying is self-deception. According to Nietzsche, self-deceivers are those who "lie traditionally," that is, who lie in terms of established traditions.

Nietzsche's recommendation in the face of what appears to be a condemnation to a life of lying is to "lie creatively," which is to say to invent, or "know" creatively. To do this is to express what Nietzsche, borrowing and subverting a Schopenhauerian idea, calls "Will to Power." To express Will to Power is to force "reality" to submit to one's own creative might. Nietzsche also calls Will to Power "the urge to freedom." All of our biological instincts expend themselves as manifestations of this desire for freedom, even though in most cases these instincts have been constrained by the forces of normalization (themselves other manifestations of Will to Power, or, manifestations of the Will

Forcing Reality to Bend to One's Will

to Power of <u>others</u>).

Not only our biology, but our thought and language are manifestations of Will to Power. But at the same time, language and thought are the main vehicles of self-deception. According to Nietzsche's radical account of language (reminiscent of Kierkegaard's), language functions precisely by lying, that is, by denying real dissimilarities and inventing fictitious similarities. For example, the only way we can classify as "leaves" all the forms of foliage which sprout from trees and shrubs is by ignoring, and indeed <u>suppressing</u>, the fact that no two of these entities are alike, and by asserting an identity among them which does not in fact

The Tyranny of Language

exist. So language can be, and usually is, a medium of reification and petrification of being. It produces errors which "tyrannize over us as a condition of life." But the fact that language _must_ lie is also the source of the creative possibilities inherent in language. Nietzsche rejected the traditional view of language, viz., that its poetic function is peripheral to its literal function. He felt that the so-called literal function was merely a sub-class of its poetic nature. Language, according to Nietzsche, is "a mobile army of metaphors, metonyms and anthropomorphisms." [Reminder: A metaphor is a form of speech in which one image replaces another, importing the new meaning into the old context. ("Achilles is a lion in battle.") A metonym is a form of speech in which meaning is displaced from one image onto an adjacent image which now bears the weight of both images. ("He likes the bottle too much.") Anthropomorphisms — the projection of human traits onto the non-human world ("The rose is striving to reach the light") — are themselves usually unconscious metaphors or metonyms.] There can be whole chains of metaphors and metonyms which create a poetic rendition of reality. Nietzsche recognized these as felicitous expressions of Will to Power.

LANGUAGE: A Mobile Army of Metaphors, Metonyms and Anthropomorphisms

In fact, as Nietzsche understood full well, his own term "Will to Power" was the product of such a metaphorical/metonymical chain of reasoning, as were his other key terms, such as "the Overman," "Eternal Recurrence," and "the Death of God." It follows, then, that a claim of Nietzsche's such as this: "All being is Will to Power," constitutes not a philosophical insight into the ultimate nature of being, but simply another poetic interpretation of being. (When confronted with this charge, Nietzsche responded, "Well, all the better!")

If it is true that there are only interpretations, are all interpretations equally valid? It is clear that, in spite of his relativism, Nietzsche did not think so. Only those "lies" which affirm life are truly noble lies for him. All other lies are nihilistic and on the side of death. This is why Will to Power must be full of laughter, dancing, and affirmation, and why we must condemn Platonism ("that fear of time") and Christianity ("Platonism for the masses"), which in longing for another world, deny reality as it is (i.e., they refuse to recognize reality as chaos and flux which must be molded in the image of each Will), and thereby long not for being but for nothingness and death. (One smells Hegel in all this, somehow.)

Nietzsche embodied his doctrine in a goal which he

DER ÜBERMENSCH?

called "the Overman" (<u>der Übermensch</u>). The Overman represents the triumph of the Will to Power. Besides teaching laughter and dance, the Overman teaches "the Death of God" and "Eternal Recurrence." Of course, there can be no single correct answer to the question, "What did Nietzsche mean by 'the Death of God'?" (anymore than there can be to the question concerning what Prufrock meant when he said, "I should have been a pair of ragged claws scuttling across the floors of silent seas"), but surely Nietzsche at least meant to announce the end of traditional forms of authority: historical, political, religious, moral and textual. (For an interesting reading of Nietzsche's phrase, "God is dead," try replacing the term "God" with the term "Santa Claus." Why is the claim, "Santa Claus does not exist," less tragic than the claim, "Santa Claus is dead"?)

The Death of Santa Claus

What is true of "the Death of God" is true of "Eternal Recurrence." There has been a great river of literature trying to interpret this enigmatic doctrine. But whatever else it means, it was certainly meant to assert Nietzsche's allegiance to reality as it is. Nietzsche advocated what he took to be the opposite of the Schopenhauerian ideal of pessimism, namely, "the ideal of the most high-spirited, alive and world-affirming human being who has not only come to terms and learned to get along with whatever was and is, but who wants to have what was and is repeated into all eternity.... Let us think this thought in its most terrible form: existence as it is, without meaning or aim, yet recurring inevitably without any finale of nothingness: the eternal recurrence."

It is easy enough to criticize Nietzsche for his inconsis-

The Thought in Its Most Terrible Form: The Eternal Recurrence tency and faulty logic. (How can we will life as it really is if there is no such thing as life nor will — only interpretations of interpretations? If everything is a lie, then isn't the claim that everything is a lie also a lie?) But this misses Nietzsche's point. He meant to teach neither consistency nor logic, but a radically new kind of subversive subjectivity which would undermine all previous forms of thought and being. However, there is a price to pay for such subversiveness. One will have disciples which one might not have hoped for. And indeed, many diverse groups have claimed the Nietzschean heritage, including Nazis, psychoanalysts, existentialists, and currently, a group called "deconstructionists," whom some see as the new liberators, and others as the new nihilists.

Let us leave the extravagant frenzy of Nietzsche's (ultimately) deranged mind and turn to the orderly and complacent minds of his contemporaries in the British Isles (whom Nietzsche dismissed as "blockheads"). In spite of Hume's facetious suggestion that philosophy

Nietzsche's View of a Meeting of the Utilitarian Society

be abandoned altogether, a philosophical empiricism was alive and thriving in mid-19th century Britain. It derived from a side of Hume's thought which was not explored in this book, and which is difficult to square with his radical skepticism. Despite his denial of the possibility of true knowledge concerning causality, self and the external world, Hume held that what is commonly taken as "Knowledge" in these areas is really a set of reasonable beliefs which are well-founded because they are based on experience. The tradition deriving from this more practical side of Hume was inherited by a group of philosophers known as THE UTILITARIANS, headed by JEREMY BENTHAM (1748-1832) and his wayward follower, JOHN STUART MILL (1808-1873), who were interested

John Stuart Mill with the Mummified Head of Jeremy Bentham

in applying the principles of empiricism to moral and social issues. The eccentric Bentham (whose fully dressed, mummified body still presides over the trustees' meetings at University College in London because his fortune was left to them with the provision that he be able to attend all of their meetings) concluded that all theory, including moral and political theory, must be grounded in empirical fact. He claimed that in the case of the human sciences this fact would have to be the primacy of the pleasure principle. That is to say, all analyses of human behavior and all recommendations for change in behavior would have to begin with the fact that humans are motivated by the desire for pleasure and by the aversion to pain. In this, of course, he was not unlike Hobbes, though Bentham's conclusions were much more liberal.

The doctrine that only pleasure can (or should) have value is known as HEDONISM, and we have seen this philosophy before, not just with Hobbes, but also with Epicurus and Callicles. Bentham's innovation was the claim that hedonism doesn't have to be egoistic; it can be social. That is, one can (and should) be motivated to act in the name of the pleasure of others as well as for one's own pleasure. His SOCIAL HEDONISM is reflected in his most famous maxim, "The greatest amount of happiness for the greatest number" (where "happiness" is defined in terms of pleasure). This principle, in association with the "one person, one vote" principle (i.e., each person gets to define his or her version of happiness), gave Bentham's utilitarianism a distinctly democratic cast. Furthermore, it meant that the moral worth of an act depended exclusively on the amount of happiness or unhappiness which that act promoted. This view is sometimes called "consequentialism" (because it is the consequence of the act which determines the act's value), and it is the opposite extreme from Kant's moral perspective, according to which the moral worth of an action depended on the <u>intention</u> of the agent, on whether or not the act was motivated by a desire to do one's duty, and on whether the act was consistent with the laws of rationality.

Kant and Bentham between them have provided us with the two key moral models used in Western ethics. Unfortunately the conclusions drawn from these two models sometimes contradict each other, and, when applied to specific cases, sometimes the utilitarian view seems much more reasonable than the Kantian one; yet in other cases, the Kantian view seems better than the utilitarian one. For instance, the Kantian ethic tells us we are duty-bound never to lie. But what if an armed man, frothing at the mouth, asks us where Bill Jones is? Do we have a duty to tell the truth, knowing full well that doing so may lead to Jones' death? Here Bentham's principle seems better: the act of lying is not immoral if by lying we can prevent grievous harm. But consider another famous example: what if you pay a visit to a friend in the hospital, and a utilitarian physician decides to sacrifice you, and distribute your vital organs to five patients who will die if they do not receive immediate organ implants? The doctor is acting on the "greatest amount of happiness for the greatest number of people" principle, and maybe even on the "one person, one vote" principle. But in this case, most of us probably feel that Kant would be right to call this sacrifice immoral.

As we saw, Bentham believed that happiness could be defined in terms of pleasure, and he held that the study of pleasure could be refined to a science. Pleasures could be experienced in terms of seven categories. These categories could be articulated in terms of a set of seven questions:

1) INTENSITY (How intense is the pleasure?)
2) DURATION (How long does the pleasure last?)
3) CERTAINTY (How sure is the pleasure?)
4) PROXIMITY (How soon will the pleasure be experienced?)
5) FECUNDITY (How many more pleasures will follow

in the train of this pleasure?)

6) PURITY (How free from pain is the pleasure?)

7) EXTENT (How many people will experience the pleasure? [It is this category which makes Bentham's hedonism a social one.])

When considering any act whatsoever, one should analyze it in terms of the pleasure it will produce in these seven categories which Bentham called "The Calculus of Felicity."

On a scale of one to ten, this is about a "ten" in all categories.

He thought that after some practice one could learn to apply this calculus rather intuitively, but until that point, one should actually work out the figures as often as possible. (Indeed, the story goes that he himself did this in choosing between remaining a bachelor or marrying. [He married!]) Try out the Calculus on a decision such as that between studying for a chemistry mid-term and going to the beach with some friends. Obviously the beach party will be strong in some categories (#1, #3, #4, #6), and weaker in others (#2, #5). Studying will be weak in most categories, but strong in a few (#2 and #5, and #7 also, if other persons have an interest in your succeeding in college). Are the assets of studying strong enough to overcome its deficits, in the face of the fun enticing you to the beach? (Of course, the guilt you would experience at the beach has to be taken into consideration too.) According to the "one person, one vote" principle, each person must decide for him or herself.

BEACH GUILT

JOHN STUART MILL, who was raised in strict adherence to Benthamite tenets, developed certain qualms about those views after suffering a nervous breakdown at 21 years of age. Among other concerns, he was worried about the beach/chemistry-type decision, or perhaps more about the six-pack of beer/Shakespearean sonnet-type decision. If the average person were given the choice between reading a Renaissance poem or guzzling beer while watching the Forty-niners on the tube... Well, you can't force people to read poetry or watch football if they don't think it's fun. But in a democracy, under the "one person, one vote" principle, what if you gave people a choice of making public expenditures for the teaching of Shakespeare in universities, or receiving a tax rebate? Mill feared the worst, and thought it bode ill for the advancement of civilization. If we let ourselves be guided by the Calculus of Felicity, perhaps the pig would prove to be right; wallowing in the mud might

rank higher than studying philosophy.

Mill solved the problem by saying that only those who were competent judges of both of two competing experiences could "vote" for one or the other of them. (You get a vote only if you know beer and Shakespeare, or have wallowed and read Plato.) Mill's conclusion was that "some kinds of pleasure are more desirable and more valuable than others." One assumes that he had in mind the reading of Shakespeare and Plato.

Mill claimed that in abandoning the Calculus of Felicity, he was simply defining pleasure in qualitative and not merely quantitative terms, but his critics charge that in asserting that some pleasures are better than others, Mill had abandoned the "Principle of Utility" (i.e., the pleasure principle) altogether. They have also charged him with elitism and with undermining the democratic foundation which Bentham had given utilitarianism. For what it's worth, Mill's doctrine did leave us some questions to ponder: In a democracy, must the "one person, one vote" principle apply at all levels of decision making? And if so, are democracy and higher culture compatible?

In his most famous book, On Liberty, Mill outlined his doctrine of laisser-faire (hands off!). There were certain spheres where the government had no business interfering in the lives of its citizens. Mill's "Principle of Liberty" states, "... the only purpose for which power can be rightfully exercised over any member of a civilized community, against his will, is to prevent harm to others." In other words, Mill was against "state paternalism," the condition in which the state orders a citizen what to do for his or her own good. For Mill, there could be no such thing as a "victimless crime." If a man decides to ride his Harley without a helmet, get bombed on "Ripple" or drugs in the privacy of his own house, visit a prostitute, or even <u>become</u> a prostitute, that's his own business and not the state's.

A Drunken Male Prostitute Without a Helmet Riding His Motorcycle in the Privacy of His Own Home.

For moral reasons we should perhaps try to persuade him of the error of his ways, but we have no business passing laws to protect him from himself as long as he is doing no harm to others. (Contemporary commentators point out that it was probably easier to draw this distinction in Mill's day than in our own. In today's world there are very few acts which are purely private. If you go to a hospital because of a motorcycle injury, my tax dollars may well have to nurse you back to health.)

Mill also believed in the "hands-off" doctrine in the marketplace. He said, "Laisser-faire ... should be the general practice: every departure from it, unless required by some great good, is a certain evil." He thought that under most conditions, the government should not interfere in the exchange of commodities, that the law of supply and demand should determine the nature and quality of production.

Even though Mill was considered a liberal in his own day, in many ways his views sound to us more like those which today we associate with political conservatism. But the proof that he was not a pure "supply side" theorist can be seen in the restrictions he placed on the laisser-faire doctrine. He excluded from the application of his "hands off" policy any products which the buyer is not competent to judge, or any product "in the quality of

"The Uncultivated Cannot Be Competent Judges of Cultivation"

which society has muchat stake." Mill said, "There are ... things of the worth of which the demand of the market is no test, things ... the want of which is least felt where the need is greatest. This is peculiarly true of those things which are chiefly useful as tending to raise the character of human beings. The uncultivated cannot be competent judges of cultivation."

VII. THE 20th CENTURY

Let us cross at last from Old Europe to the New World and visit the PRAGMATISTS — a school which makes the first truly American contribution to the history of philosophy, and one which also provides a bridge between the 19th and the 20th centuries. The logician and semiologist CHARLES PEIRCE (1839-1914) invented the term "pragmatism," and meant it to be the name of a method whose primary goal was the clarification of thought. Perhaps pragmatism was conceived in Peirce's mind when he read the definition of "BELIEF" offered by the psychologist Alexander Bain. Belief is "that upon which a man is prepared to act," said Bain. Peirce agreed, and decided that it followed from this definition that beliefs produced habits, and that the way to distinguish between beliefs was to compare the habits they produced. *Beliefs*, then, were *rules for action*, and they got their meaning from the action for which they were rules. With this definition, Peirce had bypassed the privacy and secrecy of the Cartesian mind, and had provided a direct access to mental processes (because a person's belief could be established by observing that person's actions).

Providing Direct Access to the Cartesian Mind

In its inventor's hands, pragmatism was a form of radical empiricism, and some of Peirce's claims are reminiscent of Berkeley's. For example, what Berkeley said about ideas ("... our idea of anything is our idea of its sensible effects") is not unlike what Peirce said about belief.

Peirce's essay, "How to Make our Ideas Clear," published in 1878, was generally ignored until interpreted by WILLIAM JAMES (1842-1910) some twenty-five years later. James swore allegiance to what he took to be Peircean principles, and set about to promote the doctrine of pragmatism. But Peirce was so chagrined at what James was doing to pragmatism that he changed its name to "pragmaticism," which he said was "ugly enough to be safe enough from kidnappers."

Where Peirce had meant for pragmatism merely to provide a formula for making ordinary thought more scientific, James saw it as a philosophy capable of resolving metaphysical and religious dilemmas. Furthermore, he saw it as both a theory of meaning and a theory of truth. Let us first look at James' pragmatic theory of meaning. In _Pragmatism_, he wrote:

Ugly Enough to be Safe From Kidnappers

> "Is the world one or many? —fated or free? —material or spiritual? —here are notions either of which may or may not hold good of the world; and disputes over such notions are unending. The pragmatic method in such cases is to try to interpret each notion by tracing its respective practical consequences. What difference would it practically make to anyone if this notion rather than that notion were true? If no practical difference whatever can be traced, then the alternatives mean practically the same thing, and all dispute is idle."

James concluded from this the following principle: "There can _be_ no difference anywhere that doesn't _make_ a difference elsewhere."

To clarify James' point, we will take three sentences, each quite different from the others, and test them for pragmatic meaning:

(A) "Steel is harder than flesh."

(B) "There is a Bengal tiger loose outside."

(C) "God exists."

From a pragmatic point of view, the meanings of (A) and (B) are unproblematical. We know exactly what it would be like to believe them, as opposed to believing their opposites. If we believed an alternative to (A), it is clear that in many cases we would behave very differently from the way we do behave

I now believe that steel is harder than flesh.

now. And what we believe about (B) will also have an immediate impact on our behavior. What about (C)? Here we see what James himself would admit to be the subjective feature of his theory of meaning. If certain people believed that God existed, they would conceive of the world very differently from the way they would conceive of it if they believed God did not exist. However, there are other people whose conceptions of the world would be <u>practically</u> identical (i.e., identical in practice) whether they believed that God did or did not exist. For these people, the propositions "God exists," and "God does not exist," would <u>mean</u> (practically) the same thing. For certain other people who find themselves somewhere between these two extremes, the proposition "God exists" <u>means</u> something like this: "On Sunday, I put on nice clothes and go to church." That is because, for them, engaging in this activity is the only practical outcome of their belief (and a belief just is a rule for action, as Peirce had said).

I am dressed up, therefore God exists.
A Pragmatic Proof of God's Existence

So much for the pragmatic theory of meaning. Now for the pragmatic theory of truth. James had this to say about truth: "... ideas (which themselves are but parts of our experience) become true just insofar as they help us to get into satisfactory relation with other parts of our experience, ... Truth in our ideas means their power to 'work'." James also said (perhaps less felicitously) that the issue was that of the "cash value" of ideas.

If we return to our three model sentences, we will see that (A) certainly <u>works</u>. Believing that steel is harder than flesh definitely puts us in a much more satisfactory relation to the rest of our experience than does believing the opposite. For most of us, (B) usually does <u>not</u> work. Under typical conditions, believing that there is a Bengal tiger loose outside the room we now occupy would put us in a paranoid relation with the rest of our experience. Of course, <u>some</u>times believing it to be true <u>would</u> work. (Namely, we are tempted to say, when there really is a tiger outside.)

What about the third example? Obviously the truth or falsity of the claim that God exists cannot even come up for those people for whom there is no practical difference whether they believe it or not. But for those people for whom the distinction

is meaningful, the pragmatic test of truth is available. Unlike the cases of (A) and (B), there is no direct pragmatic test of the proposition, "God exists." In fact, the empirical evidence, according to James, is equally indecisive for or against God's existence. About this and similar cases, James said: "Our passional nature not only lawfully may, but must, decide an option between propositions, whenever it is a genuine option that cannot by its nature be decided on intellectual grounds." (In saying this, James sounded very much like Kant.) James went on to say that for many, the belief in God does work, though he was prepared to admit that for a few it did not work. Rather, it put them in a state of paranoic fear vis-à-vis the rest of their experiences. So, for the first group, the proposition, "God exists," is true, and for the second group, it is false.

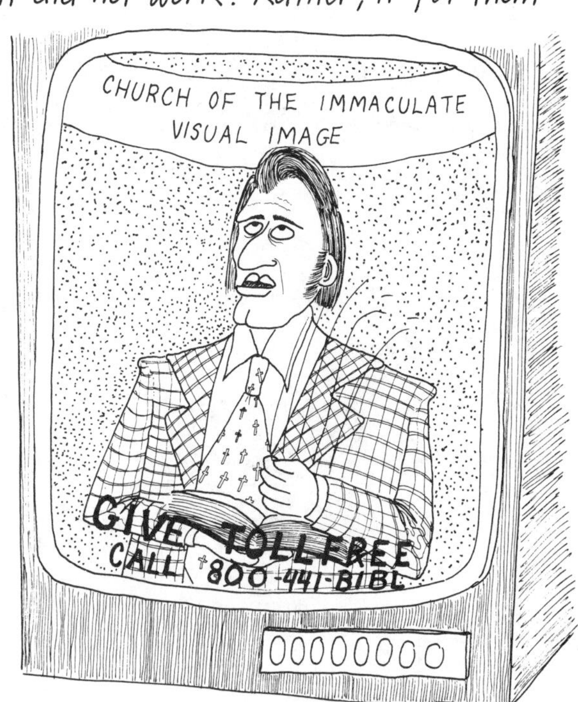

For Some, a Belief in God Definitely Has Cash Value

It was this subjective side of James' theory of truth which displeased many, including Peirce. This feature of pragmatism was somewhat ameliorated by the work of JOHN DEWEY (1859-1952), who backed off from what he took to be James' metaphysical excesses. But Dewey did not address exactly the same issues as James. His concerns were not religious in nature. He was interested in the application of pragmatic principles to moral, social, educational and aesthetic problems. Even though all three of the pragmatist leaders wrote on a great number of issues, it would be fair to say that Peirce was a philosopher of science, James was a philosopher of religion, and Dewey was a social philosopher.

One last point about James: the allusion earlier to the similarity between him and Kant is not gratuitous. Both Kant and James tried to justify on practical grounds our right to hold certain moral and religious values which could not be justified on purely intellectual grounds. Furthermore, just as Kant had seen himself as trying to mediate between the rationalists and the empiricists, so did James see himself as mediating between what he called the "tender-minded" and the "tough-minded" philosophers:

THE TENDER-MINDED	THE TOUGH-MINDED
Rationalistic (going by "principles")	Empiricist (going by "facts")
Intellectualistic	Sensationalistic
Idealistic	Materialistic
Optimistic	Pessimistic
Religious	Irreligious
Free-willist	Fatalistic
Monistic	Pluralistic
Dogmatical	Skeptical

The trouble with these alternatives, said James, was that "you find an empirical philosophy that is not religious enough, and a religious philosophy that is not empirical enough...." Obviously, James thought that his pragmatism offered a third, more satisfying, alternative.

Shortly before the turn of the century, an amazing phenomenon occurred in Britain, and the ripple effect brought it to America. The British discovered Hegel! This was long after Hegelianism had been declared dead on the Continent. Neo-Hegelianism found some able defenders in men like F.H. Bradley at Oxford, J.E. McTaggart at Cambridge, and Josiah Royce at the University of California. But the Anglo-American national characters (if there are such things) could not have been very comfortable with Hegelian idealism, and it is not surprising that a "realist"

The British Discover Hegel

reaction was soon provoked. (Notice that "realism" is used here in the Lockean sense of naming a <u>real</u> external world and not in the Medieval sense of naming the reality of Platonic Forms.) This revolt was led by GEORGE EDWARD MOORE (1873-1958) and BERTRAND RUSSELL.

Moore had come to Cambridge to study classical literature ("the Greats," as it is known there), and part of his program involved taking philosophy classes, where, according to him, he heard the most astonishing things asserted — things to which he could attach no precise meaning. It seemed to him that the lectures were full of denials of things that every sane human knew to be true. Moore must have been an annoying undergraduate. If McTaggart asserted that space was unreal, Moore would ask if that meant that the wall next to him was not nearer than the library building, and if McTaggart asserted that time was unreal, Moore wanted to know if that meant that the class would not end at noon. Russell found Moore's "naive" questions to be very exciting. In his autobiography, Russell wrote: "Moore took the lead in rebellion, and I followed, with a sense of emancipation. Bradley argued that everything common sense believes in is mere appearance; we reverted to the opposite extreme, and thought that everything is real that common sense, uninfluenced by philosophy or theology, supposes real. With a sense of escaping from prison we allowed ourselves to think that grass is green, that the sun and stars would exist if no one was aware of them...."

Young George Moore and Bertie Russell Discover That the Grass Is Green

Moore continued to defend

common sense throughout his life, even though Russell would go on later to find his own reasons for doubting it. (Russell: "Science ... has shown that none of these common-sense notions will quite serve for the explanation of the world.") Indeed, Moore came to be known as the "philosopher of common sense." Common sense became for him what sense-data had been for the empiricists and reason had been for the rationalists — namely, the foundation of certainty. In one of his most famous essays, "A Defense of Common Sense," Moore listed a series of propositions which he claimed <u>to know with certainty to be true</u>, including these:

A) There exists at present a living human body, which is <u>my</u> body.

B) This body was much smaller when it was born than it is now.

C) Ever since it was born it has been in contact with, or not far from, the surface of the earth.

D) Ever since it was born it has been at various distances from a great number of physical objects.

E) The earth had existed many years before my body was born.

F) Many other human bodies had existed before my body was born, and many of them had already died before my birth.

This list goes on and on. It is a rather boring list, but Moore knew full well that his list was tedious. The point is that, according to him, every one of these propositions

G.E. Moore Reads to His Students the List of Things He Knows for Certain

has been denied by some philosopher, somewhere, sometime. The truth usually _is_ boring, and we should get suspicious when we hear dramatic metaphysical theses which deny commonplace beliefs, such as the Hegelian claims: Time and space have no objective reality; the individual is an abstraction; mathematics is only a stage in the dialectic; the Absolute is expressed, but not revealed, in the world. Moore did not necessarily want to claim that these assertions were untrue, rather that they were _strange_, and that no obvious meaning could be attached to them. As Moore's student and friend, John Maynard Keynes, said, the question most frequently on Moore's lips was, "What _exactly_ do you mean?" And, said Keynes, "If it appeared under cross-

What **EXACTLY** do you mean?

examination that you did not mean <u>exactly</u> anything, you lay under a strong suspicion of meaning nothing whatever."

The Hegelian philosophers at Cambridge and Oxford in the 1880s and 90s had spent a lot of time inventing new philosophical terminology in order to devise novel ways of talking, because they all seemed to agree that there was something defective about our ordinary discourse concerning the world. Moore was not a bit convinced that these new ways of speaking were really necessary. He wanted to know <u>exactly</u> what was wrong with ordinary language. Moore's commitment to our normal way of thinking and talking about the world is seen very clearly in this passage from "A Defense of Common Sense:"

> "I [assume] that there is some meaning which is <u>the</u> ordinary ... meaning of such expressions as 'The earth has existed for many years past.' And this, I am afraid is an assumption which some philosophers are capable of disputing. They seem to think that the question 'Do you believe that the earth has existed for many years past?' is not a plain question, such as should be met either by a plain 'Yes' or 'No,' or by a plain 'I can't make up my mind,' but is the sort of

question which can be properly met by: 'It all depends on what you mean by 'the earth' and 'exists' and 'years': If you mean so and so, and so and so, and so and so, then I do; but if you mean so and so, and so and so, and so and so, or so and so, and so and so, and so and so, or so and so, and so and so, and so and so, then I don't, or at least I think it is extremely doubtful.' It seems to me that such a view is as profoundly mistaken as any view can be."

It is very clear that with Moore, the aim of philosophy was not that of generating grandiose metaphysical schemes, nor was it even that of arriving at the truth (much less, the Truth), rather its goal was the clarification of meaning. Moore is not the first philosopher we've seen with that conception of philosophy. Much of Peirce's work had the same thrust, and some of British empiricism did as well. (Locke had said, "It is ambition enough to be employed as an under-laborer in clearing the ground a little, and removing some of the rubbish that lies in the way of knowledge.") Even though this view was not original to Moore, in adopting it he became the forerunner of a method of philosophizing which, for better or for worse, was to dominate a great part of the 20th century. He was the initiator of what might almost be called a movement: one which was anti-metaphysical, purely analytical, obsessed with the problem of meaning, and one which was far removed from the social, political, and personal problems which afflicted people of his day. Furthermore, with his concern with precise language, Moore took the first step in the direction which has since been called "the linguistic turn." We will see all these features again in Russell, the logical positivists, and in Wittgenstein.

For all his virtues, Moore seems a bit too complacent to many today His perhaps overly satisfied attitude toward the world can be easily detected in the following passage:

> "I do not think that the world or the sciences would ever have suggested to me any philosophical prob-

I do not think that the world would have suggested to me any philosophical problems.

lems. what has suggested philosophical problems to me is things which other philosophers have said about the world and the sciences."

Moore's friend at Cambridge, BERTRAND RUSSELL (1872-1969), was born into a prominent noble family. His grandfather, Lord John Russell, was a British prime minister. Bertrand himself inherited an earldom. He was privately educated, and early demonstrated unusual mathematical skills. His temporary flirtation with Hegelianism must have gone against all his native instincts and abilities. The philosophy of McTaggart and Bradley had no use for the mathematical and scientific precision for which Russell had a natural affinity. As we saw,

Hegelianism's Fatal Attraction

Moore helped Russell break away from Hegelianism's fatal attraction, and for a brief period, Moore and Russell thought alike. But Moore did not know mathematics and was uninterested in science, so even though Moore and Russell always agreed that the main job of the philosopher was that of analysis, they soon went their separate philosophical ways.

In 1900 Russell went to the International Congress of Philosophy in Paris and met the great mathematician and logician Giuseppe Peano. Conversations with him and other mathematical luminaries set Russell on a path which led to one of his major works, Principia Mathematica, written in collaboration with Alfred North Whitehead in 1910-1913, in which they tried to prove that all of arithmetic is an extension of the basic principles of logic. Probably Russell's major contribution to the history of philosophy was his demonstration of the power of symbolic logic as a tool of philosophical analysis.

Reading PRINCIPIA MATHEMATICA

A Key feature of Russell's overall view was his belief in

philosophy's subordination to science. Russell wrote, "... we shall be wise to build our philosophy upon science, because the risk of error in philosophy is pretty sure to be greater than in science." The fact that Russell saw philosophy as ancillary to science, along with the fact that science was changing so rapidly during the period in which Russell wrote, partially explains why Russell's philosophy evolved so much over the many years that he developed it. His most uncharitable critics claimed that Russell made a philosophical career for himself by writing a book every year in which he refuted his book of the previous year. And indeed, it is difficult to state exactly what Russell's philosophy _is_, precisely because of its many transformations over the years. But there were certain common denominators which survived and unified his views in spite of all the changes. One constant in his thought was his view of philosophy as essentially analytical. In 1924 he wrote:

> "Although ... comprehensive construction is part of the business of philosophy, I do not believe it is the most important part. The most important part, to my mind, consists in criticizing and clarifying notions which are apt to be regarded as fundamental and accepted uncritically. As instances I might mention: mind, matter, consciousness, knowledge, experience, causality, will, time. I believe all these notions to be inexact and approximate, essentially infected with vagueness, incapable of forming part of any exact science."

Another constant in Russell's philosophy was his commitment to Occam's Razor, which, as we have seen, is a plea for theoretical simplicity, an injunction not to "multiply entities beyond necessity." Russell formulated it thus: "Wherever possible, substitute constructions out of known entities for inferences to unknown entities." He thought we should try to account for the world in terms of those features of it with which we have direct acquaintance, and we should avoid the temptation of positing the existence of anything with which we cannot be acquainted, unless we are forced to do so by undeniable facts or by a compelling logical argument.

Lord Russell With Razor

We will let Russell's "Theory of Descriptions," which he took to be one of his major contributions to philosophy, represent his views for us: From Plato forward, philosophers had struggled with the logic of the concept of existence, and many of them, including Plato, were driven to create grandiose metaphysical schemes to accommodate the problems caused by that concept. Russell found most of these schemes to be too metaphysical (i.e., too much in violation of the strictures of Occam's Razor), or to be simply too paradoxical. Let us look at three such problems dealing with the question of existence:

(1) I say, "The golden mountain does not exist." You ask, "What is it that does not exist?"

The Golden Mountain — Which (Unfortunately) Does Not Exist

I answer, "The golden mountain." By doing so, I seem to be attributing a kind of existence to the very thing whose existence I just denied. (And what thing is that?) Furthermore, if I say, "Unicorns do not exist," and "Round squares do not exist," I seem to be saying that golden mountains, unicorns, and round squares are three different things, and none of them exists! — The Platonists' solution to this problem was to say that terms like "the golden mountain" designate ideals which exist in a realm of pure being, but not in the physical world. Clearly, such a view would be too metaphysical for Russell, and would cry out for the application of Occam's Razor.

(2) Take the sentence, "Scott is the author of Waverly." Logicians have held that if two terms denote the same object, these terms could be interchanged without changing the meaning or truth of the proposition being expressed by the sentence. (If A=B, then [A=B]=[B=A]=[A=A]=[B=B].) Now, the novel, Waverly, was published anonymously, and many people wanted to know who wrote it. (King George IV was particularly interested to know, because he wanted to find out who was maligning his ancestors.) The King did not want to know whether the sentence, "The author of Waverly is the author of Waverly," was true, nor if the

sentence, "Sir Walter Scott is Sir Walter Scott," was true. (Though a Platonic/Leibnizian solution to the problem would be that, indeed, <u>all</u> sentences are versions of the proposition, "Everything is everything" — "A = A". But such a metaphysical "solution" could never satisfy a Bertrand Russell.)

(3) Consider this sentence: "The present King of France is bald." This assertion seems false (since there is no such person); but, according to the Law of the Excluded Middle, the negation of any false proposition must be true, so it follows that there must be truth to the claim, "The present King of France is not bald." Yet surely that sentence is false too. Must we once again accept some kind of metaphysical solution to the dilemma by consigning to an ideal realm of being the object designated by the term, "the present King of France," along with the ideal characteristics, "bald" and "hairy"? The Platonic logicians thought so. Russell thought not. (Russell said that the Hegelians would find the solution in a synthesis: "The present King of France wears a toupee.")

The Hegelian Solution

so here we have three different logical problems concerning the concept of "being" or "existence." The goal of Russell's "Theory of Descriptions" was to unveil the true logical structure of propositions about existence in order to eliminate paradoxes and metaphysical obfuscations. Russell discovered a formula which he thought could perform this job:

There is an entity C, such that the sentence 'X is Y' is true if and only if X=C.

In this formula, C is an entity, and Y is a characteristic, and X is the subject of the prediction of the characteristic Y. For example, the sentence, "The golden mountain does not exist," is rendered by Russell as: "There is no entity C, such that the sentence, 'X is golden and mountainous,' is true if and only if X=C." In other words, the offending term, "the golden mountain" (offending because it seems to <u>denote</u> an entity — name a thing —, has been transformed into a DESCRIPTION [golden and mountainous], and the real assertion of the proposition is that the description is not a description <u>of</u> anything. Notice that the notion of "existence" has been analyzed out of the term, "the golden mountain.")

Concerning the second problem, the sentence, "Scott is the author of <u>Waverly</u>," becomes: "There is an entity C, such that 'X wrote <u>Waverly</u>' is true if and only if X is C; moreover, C is Scott." So the characteristic "authorly" properly describes an existing entity (Scott), and does so in a way which is not merely tautological. Notice once again that the notion of existence has been analyzed out of the description, "the author of Waverly."

Finally, the sentence, "The present King of France is bald," means "There is an entity C, such that 'X is Kingly, French, and bald' is true if and only if X=C." But there is no entity to which such a description correctly applies, so the sentence is false; and so is its negation, because there is also no entity which is correctly described as being "Kingly, French and hairy." So we can assert that both sentences are false without violating the Law of the Excluded Middle.

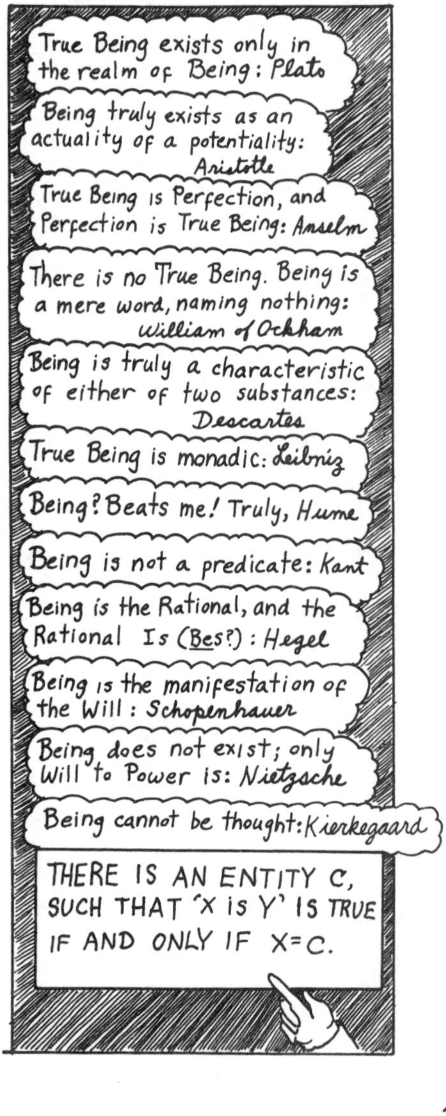

True Being exists only in the realm of Being: Plato

Being truly exists as an actuality of a potentiality: Aristotle

True Being is Perfection, and Perfection is True Being: Anselm

There is no True Being. Being is a mere word, naming nothing: William of Ockham

Being is truly a characteristic of either of two substances: Descartes

True Being is monadic: Leibniz

Being? Beats me! Truly, Hume

Being is not a predicate: Kant

Being is the Rational, and the Rational Is (Bes?): Hegel

Being is the manifestation of the Will: Schopenhauer

Being does not exist; only Will to Power is: Nietzsche

Being cannot be thought: Kierkegaard

THERE IS AN ENTITY C, SUCH THAT 'X IS Y' IS TRUE IF AND ONLY IF X=C.

In each of these three cases, Russell applied Occam's Razor and excised the concept of existence. Russell rather immodestly said of his solution,

"This clears up two millennia of muddle-headedness about 'existence,' beginning with Plato's Theaetetus."

The exposition of the Theory of Descriptions has probably been the most technical presentation in this book, and even then, it has been greatly simplified. Much of Russell's philosophy was highly specialized, but Russell the technical philosopher contrasted greatly with Russell the social critic and activist. He spent part of World War I in jail as a pacifist. (He was disappointed that Moore joined the war effort as a British officer; and he was even more disappointed that his student, Wittgenstein, returned to the Continent to join the Austrian army as a private.) He was a harsh critic of the social policies of both the United States and the Soviet Union, and, after World War II, he became an active protester against nuclear weapons. (He was jailed when he was 89 years old for inciting the public to civil disobedience after an illegal rally in Hyde Park to protest the presence of American atomic weapons in Britain, and in his nineties he was actively engaged in preaching against the American involvement in Vietnam.) In this respect, Russell was the very opposite of G.E. Moore, who, as we've seen, never found anything to engage his intellect and passions except things said by other philosophers. In 1960, when the journalist Ved Mehta went to Russell's home to interview him about his philosophy, Mehta was met by Russell at the door and was asked by Russell if he had not heard about The Bomb. Russell told Mehta that in the face of the implications of the nuclear crisis, there was no time to discuss philosophy.

The paradigmatic case of the view that philosophy's job is that of logical analysis came from a group of European philosophers who are known as the LOGICAL POSITIVISTS. Their movement grew out of some seminars in the philosophy of science offered at the University of Vienna in the early 1920's by Professor MORITZ SCHLICK. The original group, which called itself "the Vienna Circle," was composed mostly of scientists with a flair for philosophy and a desire to render philosophy respectable by making it scientific. Their technical inspiration came primarily from the work of Ernst Mach, Jules Poincaré, and Albert Einstein. The models for their idea of logical analysis came from _Principia Mathematica_, by Russell and Whitehead, and from _Tractatus Logico-philosophicus_, recently published by Ludwig Wittgenstein. (Much to the great annoyance of its members, Wittgenstein stayed aloof from the Vienna Circle — we will hear a lot more about Wittgenstein shortly.) The Vienna Circle was positively antagonistic toward most of the history of philosophy, finding only Hume's empiricism and Kant's anti-metaphysical stance worthy of respect.

Wittgenstein Aloof from the Vienna Circle

Besides Schlick (who was murdered in 1936 by an insane student on the steps of the University of Vienna), other names associated with the movement were OTTO NEURATH, HANS REICHENBACH, A.J. AYER, and RUDOLF CARNAP. By the early 1930s their passion for scientific truth was well known, so they were not much liked by the Nazis (whose views did not fare well in the light of scientific scrutiny), nor did the members of the "Circle" like the Nazis much, and the advent of Hitler's regime scattered the group throughout British and American universities, where they exerted even more influence than perhaps they might have done had they remained in Austria.

At the risk of oversimplifying the platform of logical positivism (but only slightly), we can say that the main project of the Vienna Circle was the resurrection and up-dating of "Hume's Fork." All putative propositions would be shown to be either _analytic_ (tautologies whose negation leads to self-contradiction), _synthetic_ (propositions whose confirmation depends on observation and experimentation), or _nonsense_. The positivists' conclusions were therefore like Hume's in many respects. For example, Carnap wrote: "In the domain of _metaphysics_, including all philosophy of value and normative theory, logical analysis yields the negative result _that the alleged statements in this domain are entirely meaningless_." Take a look at Carnap's analysis of the function of language:

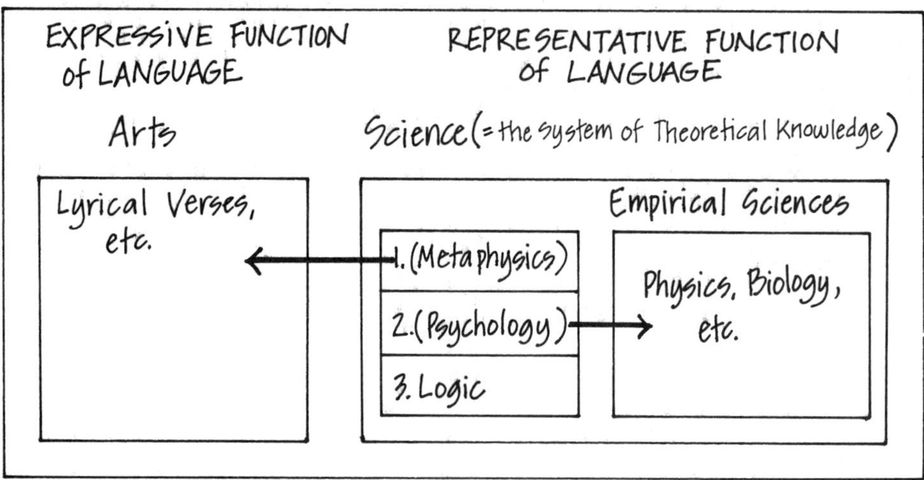

We see that language has only two duties: expression and representation. Once psychology has been correctly established as an empirical science, and metaphysics correctly recognized as an art form, philosophy is seen to be nothing but logic. According to Carnap, there is nothing wrong with the poetic function of metaphysics as long as it is identified and treated as such. Carnap wrote: "The non-theoretical character of metaphysics would not be in itself a defect; all arts have this non-theoretical character without thereby losing their high value for personal as well as social life. The danger lies in the deceptive character of metaphysics; it gives the illusion of knowledge without actually giving any knowledge."

Even some of Hume's skeptical musings were too metaphysical for the positivists Hume had claimed that there was no good reason to believe that any event ever caused another event, because there was no sense-datum representing any cause, only sense-data representing series of events. But for Schlick, Hume's search for an entity to correspond to the name, "cause," was itself suspect. Schlick said: "The word cause, as used in everyday life, implies nothing but regularity of sequence because nothing else is used to verify the propositions in which it occurs..... The criterion of causality is successful prediction. That is all we can say."

Schlick's comments about causality reveal another feature of the positivistic view, namely, that (in the case of synthetic claims) the meaning of a proposition is its method of verification. Furthermore, the language of verification would have to be reduced to what were called "protocol sentences." Protocol sentences were to be assertions which expressed the raw verifiable facts with complete simplicity. These sentences would be "the absolutely indubitable starting points of all knowledge," according to Schlick. An example

would be: "Moritz Schlick perceived red on the 6th of May, 1934, at 3:03 pm in the room numbered 301 in the Philosophy Hall at the University of Vienna." The logical positivists, looking for incorrigibility as the foundation of science, decided that even protocol sentences were not certain enough because they did not designate the simplest facts, so they tried to reduce protocol sentences yet further to what they called "confirmation sentences," an example of which would be: "Red here now." These were more certain because they were less complex than protocol sentences; but the trouble with them turned out to be that the act of writing down the phrase, "here now," produced a meaning not identical to the actual pointing which took place when the confirmation sentence was uttered. Not only that, but to name the experience as "red" seemed to transcend the perceptual event by categorizing it as a member of the class of red experiences, thereby referring to more than what was actually present in the experience. Ultimately, it was suggested that certainty could only be found in an act of <u>pointing</u> and <u>grunting</u>.

Logical Positivists Arguing

By now it was beginning to become obvious that something had gone very wrong, and that this part of the positivist program was hopeless. The logical positivists had tried to find the foundations of science, and instead they had reverted to the cave man mentality. They fell to squabbling over this problem, and it was never resolved to anyone's satisfaction, including their own.

We have seen Carnap's demonstration that metaphysics is only an "expressive," not representative, form of language. The positivists performed a similar outrage on moral language, claiming that it was simply a disguised display of emotion, often coupled with "commands in a misleading grammatical form," according to A.J. Ayer. So the sentence, "stealing is immoral," really means something like this:

STEALING!
DON'T DO IT!
I DON'T LIKE IT!!

Only the third part of this division could have truth value, therefore the whole sentence, "stealing is immoral," can be neither true nor false. It expresses what Ayer called a "pseudo-concept." — Such were the moral consequences of the positivists' radical application of "Hume's Fork."

Needless to say, most philosophers were not very satisfied with this account of ethics. Furthermore, as has been indicated, logical positivism began to come undone over its failure to find the much-heralded incorrigibility in protocol sentences and confirmation sentences. (As one commentator put it, the positivists set out to sea unfurling the sails of what they took to be a water-tight man o'war, only to find that it leaked badly. They began patching the leaks, and discovered that the patches leaked. By the time the ship sank, they were patching patches on patches.) Logical positivism came to its final grief over another internal question: if all propositions are either analytic, synthetic, or nonsense, what is the status of the proposition, "All propositions are either analytic, synthetic, or nonsense"? It too must be either analytic, synthetic, or nonsense. If it is analytic (Ayer's view), it is a mere tautology, and tells us nothing about the world. Furthermore, in this case, we should be able to look up the word "proposition" in the dictionary and discover it to be defined in terms of analyticity and syntheticity. But this is not the case. If it is synthetic (Carnap's view), then we should be able to verify the proposition empirically. But this isn't possible either. So it looks as though the key principle of positivism is neither analytic nor synthetic. Ludwig Wittgenstein, whose <u>Tractatus Logico-philosophicus</u>, had been the main

inspiration of positivism, took the heroic step of claiming that it was nonsense (though, as we shall see, he thought some nonsense was better than other nonsense). This pretty much spelled the end of logical positivism. Perhaps Professor Jon Wheatley was writing its obituary when he said, "Logical positivism is one of the very few philosophical positions which can be easily shown to be dead wrong, and that is its principal claim to fame."

Some Nonsense Is Better Than Other Nonsense

(after Sir John Tenniel)

There were a number of European thinkers who had continued to work well within the Continental philosophical tradition in spite of the unrelenting attack upon that tradition by the logical positivists. Primary among them was EDMUND HUSSERL (1859-1938), the founder of a philosophy which he called "phenomenology" (from the Greek *phainómenon* — appearance — hence, the study of appearances). He traced the roots of his view to the work of Descartes. Like Descartes, Husserl placed consciousness at the center of all philosophizing, but Husserl had learned from Kant that a theory of consciousness must be as concerned with the FORM of consciousness as with its CONTENT (Descartes had failed to realize this), so he developed a method which would demonstrate both the structure and the content of the mind. This method would be purely descriptive and not theoretical. That is, it would describe the way the world actually reveals itself to consciousness without the aid of any theoretical constructs from either philosophy or science. This method laid bare the world of what Husserl called, "the natural standpoint," which is pretty much the everyday world as experienced unencumbered by the claims of philosophy and science. Writing about "the natural standpoint" in Ideas: General Introduction to Pure Phenomenology, Husserl said:

> "I am aware of a world, spread out in space endlessly, and in time becoming and become, without end. I am aware of it, that means, first of all, I discover it immediately, intuitively, I experience it. Through sight, touch, hearing, etc., ... corporeal things ... are for me simply there, ... 'present,' whether or not I pay them special attention...."

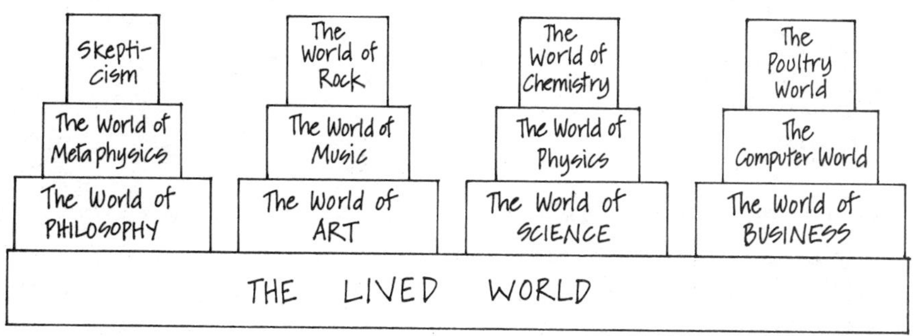

Worlds Upon Worlds

This "world of the natural standpoint" is the absolute beginning of all philosophy and science. It is the world as actually LIVED. Other worlds can be built up upon the "LIVED WORLD," but can never replace it, nor undermine it. For human beings, ultimately there is only the lived world of the natural standpoint. But Husserl wanted to "get behind" the content of the natural standpoint to reveal its structure. To do so, he employed a method like Descartes' "radical doubt," a method which Husserl called "phenomenological reduction" (or <u>epochê</u>: a Greek word meaning "suspension of belief").

This method "brackets" any experience whatsoever, and describes it while suspending all presuppositions and assumptions normally made about that experience. "Bracketing" the experience of looking at a coffee cup, for instance, requires suspending the belief that the cup is <u>for</u> holding coffee, and that its handle is <u>for</u> grasping. Bracketing reveals

Prof. Edmund Husserl Performs An Epochê On a Coffee Cup

the way the cup presents itself to consciousness as a number of possible <u>structures</u>. (I can't see the front and the back at the same time, nor the top and the bottom, nor see more than one of its possible presentations at any given moment.)

If we apply the "epochê" to the more philosophically significant example of the experience of <u>time</u>, we must suspend all belief in clocks, train schedules and calendars. Then we will discover that LIVED TIME is always experienced as an eternal NOW, which is tempered by a memory of earlier "nows" (the "then-ness" of the past) and is always rushing into the semi-experienceable, but ultimately non-experienceable then-ness of the future. Phenomenologically speaking, the time is always "Now." To do anything is to do something <u>now</u>. You can never act <u>then</u>.

Similarly, a phenomenological reduction of the experience of <u>space</u> reveals the difference between LIVED SPACE and MAPPED SPACE. Lived space is always experienced in terms of a "HERE/THERE" dichotomy, in which I am always "here," and everything

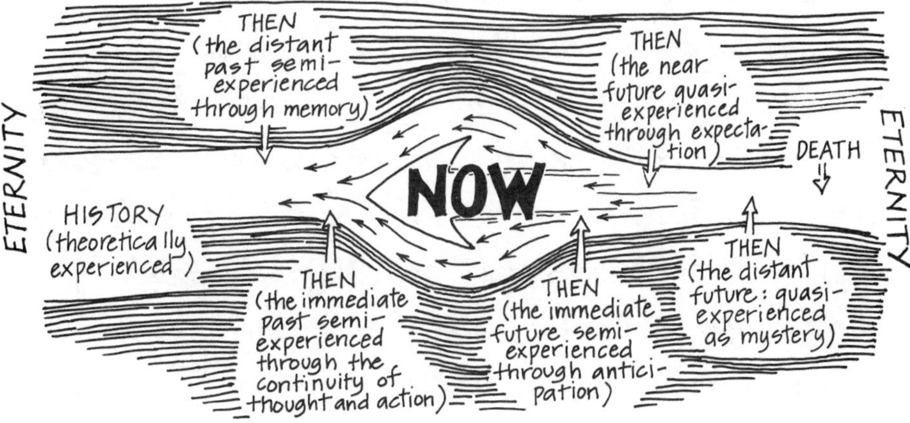

From the Natural Standpoint

From the Standpoint of the Epochê

else is always at different intensities of "there-ness." (Jean-Paul Sartre, Husserl's errant disciple, would later draw very pessimistic conclusions from this discovery.) So the "HERE/NOW" experience is the "ground zero" of the experience of space and time. It is somehow the locus of the self.

One of Husserl's main insights (actually derived from the work of his teacher, Franz von Brentano), and one which was to be incorporated into both the later phenomenological tradition and the analytic tradition, was his treatment of the INTENTIONALITY of all consciousness (i.e., its referentiality). The Husserlian motto here is, "All consciousness is consciousness of ..." (That means there is no such thing as self-enclosed thought; one thinks about something: You can't be just aware — you have to be aware of something, and afraid of something, and concerned about something. There are no intransitive mental states, not even Kierkegaard's "dread" — the fear of absolutely nothing. It is still the fear *of* nothing.) It is this "intentionality" (or referentiality) which distinguishes consciousness from everything else in the universe.

Husserl claimed that the phenomenological suspension could be performed on the *object* of intentionality (e.g., the coffee cup), or on the act of consciousness itself. Therefore, he believed it was possible to step back from normal consciousness into a kind of pure consciousness, a transcendental ego, a self-behind-the-self, which, like Descartes' "I AM" (but more deeply real), would be the starting point of all knowledge. Husserl's ideas get very complex here, and few of his disciples have chosen to follow him into these ethereal regions.

Today, Husserl is most admired for his METHOD. This method has had a number of outstanding adherents, including Martin Heidegger, Maurice Merleau-Ponty, and

The Self Behind the Self (But Is There a Self Behind the Self Behind the Self?)

Jean-Paul Sartre. Shortly, we will review the philosophy of Sartre, Husserl's best known, if most wayward, disciple, and we will let him represent the outcome of the evolution of phenomenology into existentialism. First, however, one last look at the analytic tradition.

Was sich überhaupt sagen lässt, lässt sich klar sagen; und wovon man nicht reden kann, darüber muss man schweigen.

The author of the Tractatus Logico-philosophicus, the book that so inspired the logical positivists, was LUDWIG WITTGENSTEIN (1889–1951). He has earned himself a longer chapter in this overview than have most philosophers because he has the unusual distinction of having inspired two philosophical movements: logical positivism and what came to be known as "ordinary language philosophy." Each of these movements dominated a large portion of the analytic tradition in this century, and, ironically, in many respects the later movement refutes the earlier movement.

Wittgenstein was born into a wealthy, refined, Viennese family. Uninterested in material riches, he gave away his entire inheritance. In 1911 he went to Manchester, England, to study aeronautical engineering. His genius for mathematical thinking was soon recognized, and he was directed to Cambridge to study with Bertrand Russell. When Wittgenstein returned to Austria to enlist in the army during the First World War, the story has it that he put a ream of paper in his backpack and went into the trenches with it. He was soon taken captive by the Italians, and as a prisoner of war, set about writing the Tractatus (which puts that work in the category of "great books written in jail," along with Boethius' The Consolations of Philosophy, and part of Cervantes' Don Quixote).

Prop. 1 : The World Is All That Is the Case

The Tractatus, which is barely 100 pages long, is set up as a series of seven propositions. Each proposition is followed by a sequence of numbered observations about each proposition, or observations about the observations, or observations about the observations about the observations. For instance, the first page begins thus:

1. The world is all that is the case.

1.1 The world is the totality of facts, not of things.

1.11 The world is determined by the facts, and by their being <u>all</u> the facts.

1.12 For the totality of facts determines what is the case, and also whatever is not the case.

1.13 The facts in logical space are the world.

1.2 The world divides into facts.

1.21 Each item can be the case or not the case while everything else remains the same.

2. What is the case — a fact — is the existence of states of affairs.

Wittgenstein held the view that, because we can say true things about the world, the structure of language must somehow reflect the structure of the world. That is part of what it means to say in #1.1, "The world is the totality of facts, not of things." Now, what are the facts of which the world consists? They are, to use Russell's term, "atomic facts." They are the simplest facts which can be asserted, and are the simple truths into which all other more complex truths can be analyzed. In the *Tractatus*, Wittgenstein did not say exactly what these facts were, and it was these which the positivists were seeking with their attempts to construct "protocol sentences" and "confirmation sentences."

The positivists liked other features of the *Tractatus* as well. They particularly approved of the conception of philosophy which Wittgenstein put forth:

"Most of the propositions and questions to be found in philosophical works are not false but nonsensical. Consequently we cannot give any answer to questions of this kind, but can only establish that they are nonsensical" (4.003).

"The correct method in philosophy would really be the following: to say nothing except what can be said, i.e., the propositions of natural science — i.e., something that has nothing to do with philosophy —and then, whenever someone else wanted to say something metaphysical, to demonstrate to him that he had failed to give a meaning to certain signs in his propositions .... this method would be the only strictly correct one" (6.53).

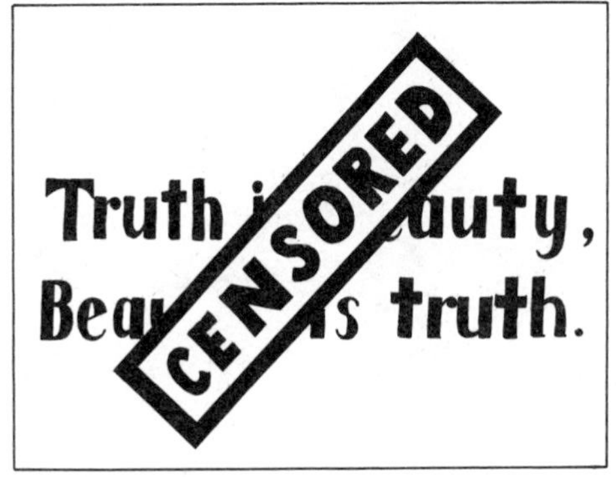

It Cannot Be Said

These paragraphs seem to express perfectly the "hard liner" position of the logical positivists. No surprise that the latter thought of Wittgenstein as one of their own. However, there were certain puzzling statements in the Tractatus which created quite a bit of discomfort for the members of the Vienna Circle. For example, Wittgenstein wrote: "The whole sense of this book might be summed up in the following words: what can be said at all can be said clearly and what we cannot talk about we must consign to silence." Now, the positivists wanted to interpret Wittgenstein as saying here,

"Metaphysicians, shut up!" But Wittgenstein himself seemed curiously attracted to what he called "the silence", and made further enigmatic allusions to it. In proposition 6.54 he wrote:

> "My propositions serve as elucidations in the following way: anyone who understands me eventually recognizes them as nonsensical, when he has used them — as steps — to climb up beyond them. (He must, so to speak, throw away the ladder after he has climbed up it.)
> He must transcend these propositions and then he will see the world aright."

It was here that Wittgenstein was admitting that his own propositions were nonsense, but apparently a special kind of higher nonsense. What would higher nonsense be like? Wittgenstein continued:

"*How* things are in the world is a matter of complete indifference for what is higher. God does not reveal himself *in* the world" (6.432). "It is not *how* things are in the world that is mystical, but *that* it exists" (6.44). "... The solution to the enigma of life in space and time lies *outside* space and time" (6.4312).

Slowly and in horror the truth dawned on the Vienna Circle. Wittgenstein was a mystic! He was *worse* than the metaphysicians.

For a while, Wittgenstein seemed satisfied with the *Tractatus*. It had answered all the philosophy questions which could be sensibly asked.

As he had written: "When the answer cannot be put into words, neither can the question be put into words. The *riddle* does not exist. If a question can be framed at all, it is possible to answer it" (6.5).

Wittgenstein dropped out of philosophy. He went off into the villages of the Austrian Alps as a primary school teacher. But he was not completely happy in his new work, and his mind was not at rest. Russell spearheaded a move to get Wittgenstein to return to Cambridge and to have the *Tractatus* accepted as Wittgenstein's doctoral dissertation.

Wittgenstein was given the professorial chair of the retiring G. E. Moore, and much excitement was generated over the fact that Wittgenstein had returned to philosophy.

However, word soon got around that what Wittgenstein was now saying about philosophy was not what had been expected of him. It was not easy to know exactly what *was* going on, however, because the eccentric Wittgenstein was very secretive about his new views, and he insisted that his students be so too. Nevertheless, some mimeographed copies of notes from his lectures began to circulate. It was not until after his death that his work from this period was published as *Philosophical Investigations*. But long before the appearance of that book, it had become clear that a major shift had taken place in Wittgenstein's thinking. Both the positivism and the mysticism of the *Tractatus* were gone, for better or for worse. Yet there continued to be some common denominators between the two works. Philosophy was still seen as essentially the concern with meaning, and it was still very much language oriented. In the *Tractatus*, Wittgenstein had written: "*The limits of my language* are the limits of my

Psst! Ya wanna buy some Wittgenstein notes?

world." That view continued to hold in the Investigations, but language itself now seemed much less limited than it had been in the earlier book.

Let us start our discussion of the Investigations with a look at the problem of meaning. Throughout the history of philosophy, from Plato to the Tractatus, the key model of meaning was that of denotation, that is, of naming. Even where philosophers like Russell and the author of the Tractatus had distinguished between denotation and connotation (that which is implied about the thing named), the former was given priority. According to Wittgenstein, the historical prioritizing of naming as the key feature of meaning had generated a certain kind of metaphysical picture which was pervasive in Western thought, and which was in error. Plato thought that words had to be names of things which existed unchanging and eternally, and because there was no such thing in the observable world,

he developed his theory of the otherworldly Forms. Aristotle thought words named something unchanging *in* the world, namely, substances. In the Medieval period, the nominalists also thought of words as names, but thought that they named *nothing*. Their conclusion, therefore, was like that of the last sentence of Eco's novel, *The Name of the Rose*, viz., "we have only names." The empiricists held that words named sense-data, and that any word which did not do so was suspect. The pragmatists thought that words named actions, and the positivists, Russell, and the early Wittgenstein thought they named atomic facts.

The later Wittgenstein broke completely with this tradition, claiming that THE MEANING OF A WORD IS ITS USE. He wrote:

Wittgensteinians Arguing

"Think of the tools in a tool box: there is a hammer, pliers, a saw, a screwdriver, a rule, a glue pot, glue, nails and screws.—The functions of words are as diverse as the functions of these objects. (And in both cases there are similarities.) .... It is like looking into the cabin of a locomotive. We see handles all looking more or less alike. (Naturally, since they are all supposed to be handled.) But one is the handle of a crank which can be moved continuously (it regulates the opening of a valve); another is the handle of a switch, which has only two effective positions, it is either off or on; a third is the handle of a brake-lever, the harder one pulls on it, the harder it brakes; a fourth, the handle of a pump: it has an effect only so long as it is moved to and fro."

So language, like tools or like the gadgets in the cabin of a locomotive, can get jobs done, and its meaning is found in the work it accomplishes. — Suppose two people are driving rapidly toward a certain destination, trying to arrive before sunset because the headlights are broken, and suppose the driver says, "Well, bad luck! The sun just went down." Now, what if the passenger says, with a look of superiority, "We now know that the sun does not

Well, the sun's going down. Or the Earth's coming up, as the fashionable theory has it.

from "ROSENCRANTZ and GUILDENSTERN ARE DEAD," a play by Tom Stoppard 'go down,' and that the illusion that it does is the result of the earth turning on its axis." Does what he said mean anything? No, because in that context, it gets no job done (even though in another context that same sentence would get a job done). In fact, there is something mad about inserting this scientific fact into the context described. There would also be something mad if the passenger, having found a hammer in the glove compartment, began hitting the driver with it, and explained the action by saying, "Hammers are for hitting." Yes, but not for hitting just anything, any time, any place. And the same is the case with language.

Still, a tool can serve a number of functions. In some contexts, a hammer can serve as a weapon, or as a paper weight. How about language? Does it have only two uses, as the logical positivists suggested (an expressive function and a representative function)? Wittgenstein asked:

> "But how many kinds of sentence are there? Say assertion, question, and command? — There are countless kinds: countless different kinds of use of what we call 'symbols,' 'words,' 'sentences.' And this multiplicity is not something fixed, given once for all; but new types of language, new language-games, as we may say, come into existence, and others become obsolete and get forgotten."

This brings up another feature of Wittgenstein's theory

of meaning related to his claim that "the meaning is the use." He wrote: "The question 'What is a word really?' is analogous to 'what is a piece in chess?'... Let us say that the meaning of a piece is its rôle in the game." Wittgenstein generalized his claim when he called any language "a language-game." Let's consider this point. All games are rule-governed. The "meaning" of a piece (or a chip, or card, or mitt) in the game is derived from its use according to the rules. What is a pawn? A pawn is a piece which moves one square forward, except on its first move, when it may move two squares. It may take the opponent's piece laterally, and is converted to a queen if it reaches the opposite side of the board, etc. Similarly with words, phrases and expressions — they are rule-governed and their meaning is derived from the use to which they may be put according to the rules of the language-game. There are lots of kinds of rules determining language use: grammatical rules, semantical rules, syntactical rules, and what could generally be called rules of context. Some of these are very rigid, some very flexible, and some are negotiable. This is true in comparing various games (the rules of chess are more rigid than those of ring-around-the-rosy), or even <u>within</u> games (rules governing the pawn's moves are rigid, but those governing the pawn's size are flexible). But even flexible rules are rules, and they can't be broken without certain conse-

quences. When some of the rules of a given "language-game" are broken in subtle ways, "language goes on holiday," as Wittgenstein said, and one result is a certain kind of _philosophy_ (as in the case of metaphysicians), and another result is a certain kind of _madness_ (as in the case of _Alice in Wonderland_). The allusion to _Alice_ is not gratuitous. The "Alice" books were among Wittgenstein's favorites, no doubt because they are compendiums of linguistic jokes showing the lunacy which results when the function of certain features of language are misunderstood. Think of the episode when the White King tells Alice to look down the road, and asks her if she sees anyone there. "I see nobody on the road," said Alice. "I only wish _I_ had such eyes," responded the King. "To be able to see Nobody! And at that distance too!" What has gone wrong here? The joke is based on what some of Wittgenstein's followers called a "category mistake"— the miscategorization of certain linguistic facts, and the drawing of absurd conclusions from the miscategorization. (According to the "ordinary language philosopher," GILBERT RYLE, this was the error made by Descartes which resulted in the mind/body problem. He had placed "minds" in a similar category with bodies, making them "thinking <u>things</u>"— ghostly, spiritual <u>beings</u> which somehow cohabitated with physical beings, but no one could figure out how.)

Or consider the case of the White Queen, who promises to pay her lady's maid "Twopence a week, and jam every other day," but then refuses to provide the jam on the grounds that it never <u>is</u> any other day. Surely this is language gone on holiday.

The Elusiveness of Jam

What about the positivists' search for the most simple constituents of reality on which to base the scientific edifice? Wittgenstein asked:

"But what are the simple constituent parts of which

reality is composed? — What are the simple constituent parts of a chair? — The bits of wood of which it is made? or the molecules, or the atoms? — 'Simple' means: not composite. And here the point is: in what sense 'composite'? It makes no sense at all to speak absolutely of the 'simple parts of a chair.'"

So much for the search for "atomic facts."

In the _Tractatus_, Wittgenstein had written, "Most of the propositions and questions of philosophy arise from our failure to understand the logic of our language." He still held more or less the same view in the _Investigations_, but by then his conception of "the logic of our language" had changed radically. It was no longer the philosopher's job to reveal the hidden logic _behind_ language, rather to reveal the implicit logic of ordinary language (hence the term, "ordinary language philosophy"), showing how a failure to grasp that logic could result in "a bewitchment of our intelligence by means of language," and to show that unwarranted tampering with our ordinary way of thinking and talking about the world produces a "linguistic holiday" which generates the jokes which comprise much of the history of philosophy. Wittgenstein said: "[My aim in philosophy:] To show the fly the way out of the fly bottle." Apparently in Wittgenstein's native Vienna, a common flytrap was made by putting some honey in a vinegar bottle.

The fly, travelling on its merry way, would smell the honey, deviate from its path into the bottle, and either drown in the sticky, sweet stuff, or buzz to death. For Wittgenstein, much of philosophy was like that buzzing. To "show the fly the way out of the fly bottle"

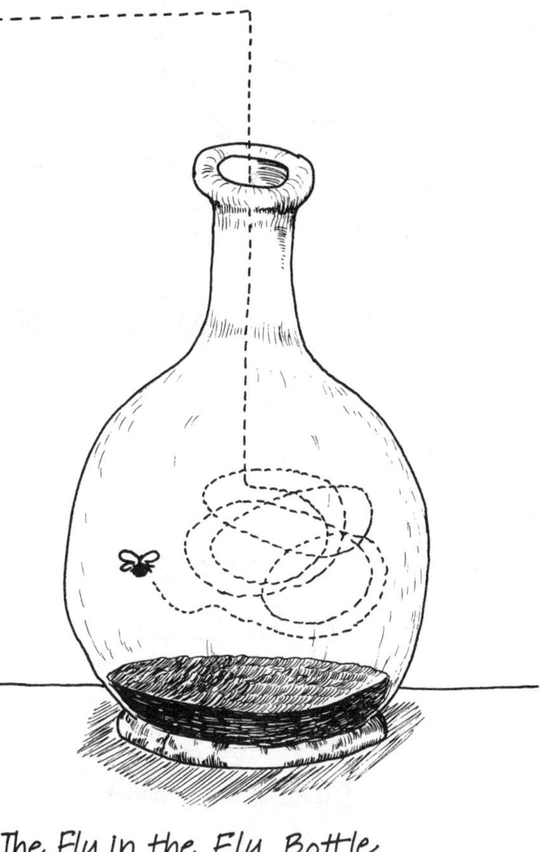

The Fly in the Fly Bottle

was not to solve philosophical problems, but to dissolve them, by showing that they were the result of deviating from the path of everyday language. This is the conservative side of Wittgenstein's thought. According to him, "Philosophy can in no way interfere with the actual use of language; it can in the end only describe it. For it cannot give it any foundation either. It leaves everything just as it is."

The apparent complacency here is reminiscent of G.E. Moore, but the analogy, though good in some respects, is bad in others. Wittgenstein's mind was in constant turmoil and perplexity. There was a brooding disquietude about the man and his thought which belied the Vermeer-like bourgeois self-satisfaction of passages like the one above.

JOHN-PAUL SARTRE (1905-1980), besides being one of the most important philosophers of the 20th century, was also an essayist, novelist, and playwright. His early philosophical ideas are developed in his novel, Nausea (1938), in his treatises, Transcendence of the Ego (1936), Being and Nothingness (1943), and in his essay "Existentialism is a Humanism" (1946). In these works we see the influence not only of Husserl, but of Heidegger and Kierkegaard.

First, let us look at Sartre's theory of consciousness. From Husserl, Sartre had learned that consciousness is always referential, in that it always refers beyond itself to an <u>object</u>. "Unreflected consciousness" is consciousness before it is reflected upon or philosophized about. When I read a novel, the object of unreflected consciousness is the hero of the novel. When I run to catch a trolley, the object of unreflected consciousness is "streetcar-to-be-caught." In unreflected consciousness, there is no self, no "I" to be found—only its objects exist, Don Quixote, or the streetcar. "Reflective consciousness" is consciousness which reflects on itself. According to Sartre (and contrary to Descartes), the "ego," or the "I," is to be discovered only in reflected consciousness. It is not only <u>discovered</u> there, it is actually created there.

consciousness always refers

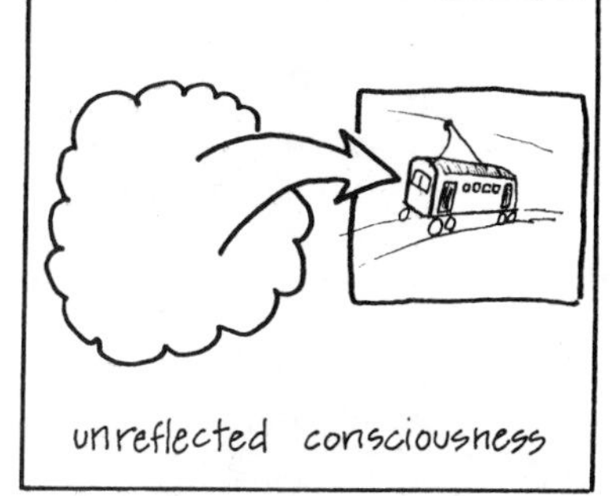
unreflected consciousness

reflective consciousness—
consciousness reflecting on consciousness

Once we study consciousness phenomenologically ("bracket" it, make it the object of reflective consciousness), we discover that it is "a monstrous, impersonal spontaneity," in which thoughts come and go at <u>their</u> will, not ours. This spontaneity is a form of

dizzying freedom, according to Sartre, and contemplation of it leads to anguish. We actively struggle to impose order on this free spontaneity, and when we fail, neurosis and psychosis ensue.

Sartre mentions the case of a woman who dreaded her husband's leaving for work because she feared that upon his departure she would sit nude in the window like a prostitute. Because she knew she was *free* to do so, she feared she *would* do so. (This theme was inspired by Kierkegaard's account of DREAD. When God told Adam not to eat the apple, Adam then knew that he *could* eat it — that he was *free* to do so — and he knew that if he could, he *might*. That is, he experienced his freedom as dread.)

In our own case, as in the case of that woman, sometimes the order we impose upon consciousness breaks down and consciousness is revealed to us as the monstrous spontaneity that it is. As a philosophical exercise, Husserl had suspended all beliefs and all "normality" in the epochê, but Sartre discovers that an epochê can break in upon us when we least expect it, not as a philosophical exercise, but as a crisis of consciousness, as when we look into a chasm, and suddenly feel the urge to throw ourselves in.

This is what happens to Roquentin, the "hero" of Sartre's novel, *Nausea*, as he sits on a park bench looking at the knotted roots of a chestnut tree.

Suddenly, all the old assumptions break down, and he sees the tree not as a *tree*, but as a "black, knotty, raw, doughy, melted, soft, monstrous, naked, obscene, frightening lump of existence." Suddenly, the tree's BEING has presented itself to him. Roquentin discovers that Being, as it reveals itself in the crisis of consciousness, is pure superfluity, pure excess.

The Rationalists, Spinoza and Leibniz, were badly mistaken. Not only is Being not necessary, it is ABSURD. Far from there existing a "sufficient reason" for the being of Being, there is no reason for it to exist at all. So the Sartrean existentialist finds his own existence as a superfluity in an absurd world. Yet the human being <u>does</u> exist. He has been thrown into a meaningless world without his permission. What is the relation between the human being and the world?

The most significant form of this relationship is that of "the question." By questioning the world, I reveal a <u>Nothingness</u> in Being. When I seek Pierre in a café and discover that Pierre is NOT there, I reveal a nothingness in reality. (Pierre's absence is REAL.)

In the same way, I discover that a nothingness separates me from myself. There is a nothingness between me and my past (I am NOT who I was), and between me and my future (the person I will be is NOT who I am).

This realization again makes me aware that "I await myself in the future. Anguish is the fear of not finding myself there, of no longer even wishing to be there." This anguish stems from my discovery that my "self" is not a stable, solid entity which lasts through time; rather, it is a <u>creation</u> which I must make and re-make from moment to moment.

I Await Myself
in the Future

Not only must I create myself, I must create my world. I do so by bestowing values on the world. According to the pre-Sartrean view of freedom, values pre-exist my freedom. I am placed between these values, and my freedom consists in my ability to choose between these pre-existing values. According to the Sartrean view, through freedom, I bestow value on the world by choosing aspects of it. Freedom pre-exists values. Life has no meaning or value except that which I give to it. Ultimately, my choice of values cannot be justified, since there are no eternal (Platonic) values, no stone tablets, no scriptures, to which I can appeal to justify my choices. In the final analysis, no set of values is objectively any more valuable than any other set. This discovery leads to more anguish (of course!).

The Old View of Freedom

The Sartrean View of Freedom

"My freedom is anguished at being the foundation of values while being itself without foundation."

Certainly my freedom is not absolute. Consciousness runs up against "facticity" in existence (i.e., that which cannot be changed). If a boulder falls in my path, I cannot change the fact that it is there, nor that it is impenetrable. But I am free to interpret the meaning of its "there-ness" for me. It may mean an obstacle to be conquered, or it may mean that

my goal of reaching the mountain top is defeated, or I may interpret it as an object of aesthetic contemplation, or as a scientific specimen. The interpretation of facticity Sartre calls "situation." To interpret facticity is to create a world for me to inhabit. I am always "in situation," and am always freely creating worlds. In fact, in this respect ...

" . . . I AM CONDEMNED TO BE FREE."

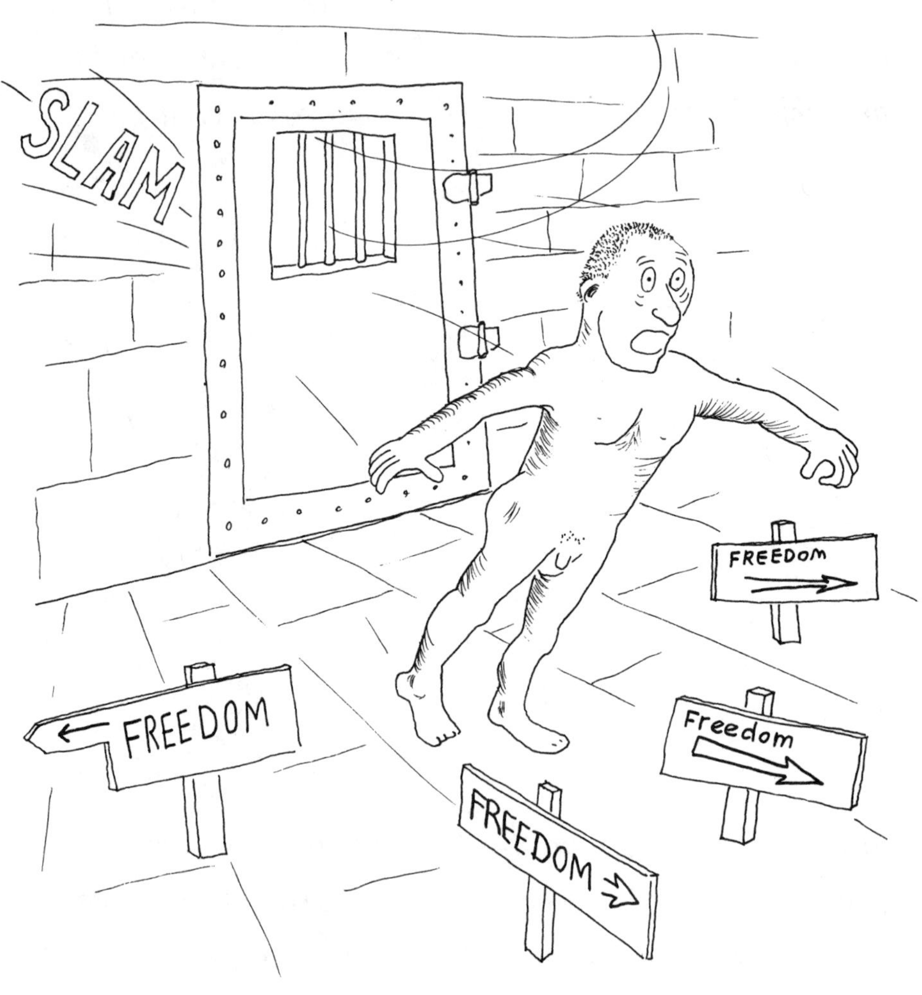

Most people create worlds in "bad faith." That is, rather than facing up to their responsibility and freedom, they flee from them by denying them, by blaming them on others, on fate, or on "the Establishment."

But there can be no blaming in good faith. We cannot blame our upbringing, our parents, our poverty (or our wealth), nor the "hard times," because we alone determine the meaning that these things have for us.

We are always free because there are always alternative choices — the ultimate alternative is death. If I do not shoot myself, then I have chosen whatever is the alternative to death.

A major complication in the experience of our freedom is that we must encounter other free beings. The unity which I have imposed upon my consciousness is momentarily shattered when the Other <u>LOOKS</u> at me and

transforms me into the <u>object</u> of his gaze. I can recover my own selfhood only by looking at him and transforming him into my object. (This is like Hegel's Master / Slave relation, except that no synthesis is possible.) "Hell," says Sartre, "is other people."

Sartre's philosophy ends with what many take to be a pessimism which reflects the plight of the human in the modern world. Sartre denies that he is a pessimist. He makes heroes of us all. The authentic human being knows that all her acts are ultimately futile in the face of death and the absurdity of existence, yet she chooses to persevere. In God-like fashion she creates worlds upon worlds. Like Sisyphus, she pushes her boulder daily up the steep incline of existence, without excuse and without complaint. It is, after all, her boulder. She created it.

Afterword

The most recent treatise referred to in this book was Wittgenstein's Philosophical Investigations, which was published in 1953. What has happened to philosophy in the thirty-five years since that date? First, the Anglo-American tradition: by the mid 1950s, the British and American thinkers in the "philosophical mainstream" were pretty much in agreement that their job was that of the analysis of meaning and clarification of concepts (hence the "Anglo-American tradition" and the "Analytic tradition" were more or less synonymous), but there were basically two different notions about what philosophical analysis should look like. One, in the tradition of Russell and Carnap, considered symbolic logic to be the key tool of analysis. Philosophers in this tradition refused to be governed by the strictures of ordinary language and deviated from it whenever they found it expedient to do so. The other, following the lead of the later Wittgenstein, saw ordinary language as the best hope for correct thinking, and they rejected as false pretensions the claims of the formal logicians. Oxford became the spiritual center of this "linguistic philosophy," and it produced a number of remarkable thinkers, including J.L. Austin, Gilbert Ryle, and Paul Grice. The writings of the philosophers in both analytic camps were usually highly technical and were addressed only to fellow initiates. There were very few large books published, and relatively few articles, and then only in a handful of professional journals.

By 1965 there was a noticeable tendency for much of the work in logic which previously had been done by philosophers to be taken over by mathematicians, and by that date, the Oxford variety of ordinary language philosophy was losing its grip on the hearts and minds of Anglo-American philosophers. There was still a great deal of interest about language among the analytic philosophers (as among all students of human affairs in the twentieth century), but now there was a distinction between LINGUISTIC PHILOSOPHY (the view that all philosophy problems could be shown to be based on confusions about language), and PHILOSOPHY OF LANGUAGE (the analysis of those features of language which are philosophically significant). Key names associated with the philosophy of language in the 1970s were John Searle, Donald Davidson, Michael Dummett and Gilbert Harman. Many of these philosophers were influenced by the writings of the linguist, Noam Chomsky.

Meanwhile, on the Continent, existentialism and phenomenology had passed their heyday by 1960. They were sur planted by a view called STRUCTURALISM, which w consciously anti-phenomenological, and in some ways even anti-philosophical. Its main promoter was not a philosopher at all, but an anthropologist: Claude Lévi-Strauss. To the extent that he thought of himself as a philosopher, Lévi-Strauss associated himself with Kant (who had claimed that behind all the apparent differences in the minds of humans in different places at different times, there were certain universal structures which were geographically and historically constant), and with Marx (who denied the validity of phenomena as experienced, arguing that a special kind of theory was required to get at the truth behind the appearances). Like the Anglo-American analytic philosophers, Lévi-Strauss prioritized language, basing his structuralism on the work of the Swiss linguist, Ferdinand de Saussure.

But by 1970, structuralism was declared dead by the Parisian pundits (about the same time that it was beginning to be taken seriously by many in American and British universities), and was displaced by various forms of "post-structuralism," such as that of Michel Foucault in history, Jacques Lacan in psychoanalysis, and Jacques Derrida in philosophical and literary criticism. All of these theorists were influenced by Marx, Freud, de Saussure, Lévi-Strauss, and, in the case of Foucault and Derrida, by Nietzsche and Hegel. Together, they disagreed with the "totalizing" tendency of structuralism and Marxism, claiming that it is impossible to give a theoretically complete, consistent account of the totality of human life and language. (Indeed, Derrida's philosophy—called "deconstruction"— seems to claim that, due to the paradoxical nature of human thought and language themselves, it is impossible to give a complete, consistent account of <u>anything</u>, while Foucault's work stresses the discontinuities rather than the continuities in history.)

By 1980, the main claim of the analytic tradition (viz., that the job of the philosopher was exclusively that of analyzing and clarifying concepts) began to buckle, somewhat belatedly, under the pressure of the socially and politically turbulent sixties and seventies. Philosophers in America and Britain had begun to write shamelessly about concerns like nuclear warfare, the environmental crisis, abortion, feminism, and social justice. Furthermore, the distinction between Anglo-American and Continental traditions had begun to blur. This healthy sign is due not only to the fact that the British and American philosophers were now ready to speak out on social issues (as the Continental philosophers had been doing since World War II), but to a number of other factors as well: the splintering within the two traditions, which broke down the forbidding monolithic front that each presented to the other, the discovery that both traditions were interested in the same problems, in spite of major differences in styles and vocabularies, the centrality of the concern for language, which had developed independently in each tradition, and the evolution of a general cultural pluralism which is anti-ethnocentric and hence conducive to the cross-fertilization of ideas. It is to be hoped that this rapprochement (championed in the U.S. by philosophers such as Richard Rorty, Hilary Putnam, and Hubert Dreyfus) proves to be a momentous, and not merely momentary, event.

Glossary of Philosophical Terms

employed but not defined in the text.

(An asterisk * indicates the possibility of cross-referencing within the Glossary.)

AESTHETICS. The philosophy of art. The branch of philosophy which investigates questions such as; what makes something a work of art? Are there absolute values in art, or are aesthetic values always relative? Can there be aesthetic arguments, or are aesthetic judgments based only on preference? What is the status of art among other human intellectual and creative endeavors?

ALIENATION. A term usually associated with Hegelian or Marxian philosophy, designating the estrangement of a subject from its own essence, or the rupture between a subject and its natural object.

A POSTERIORI. A belief, proposition,* or argument is said to be _a posteriori_ if its truth can be established only through observation. Classical empiricism* was an attempt to show that all significant Knowledge about the world is based on _a posteriori_ truths.

A PRIORI. A belief, proposition,* or argument is said to be _a priori_ if its truth can be known independently of observation. Definitions, arithmetic, and the principles of logic are usually held to be _a priori_. Classical rationalism* was an attempt to show that all significant Knowledge of the world is based on _a priori_ truths, which most of the rationalists associated with innate ideas.

ARIANISM. A fourth century heresy named after its leader, Arius, who denied the doctrine of the Trinity, holding that Christ had his own essence, which was divine, but which was independent of God's essence.

DECONSTRUCTION. The creation of the contemporary French philosopher Jacques Derrida, based on his eccentric but provocative reading of the linguistic theory of Ferdinand de Saussure, deconstruction is a theory of TEXTS (philosophical, fictional, legal, scientific), according to which, due to the very nature of thought and language, almost all traditional texts can be shown to "deconstruct" themselves, i.e., to undermine and refute their own theses.

DEDUCTION. A form of argument in which the conclusion follows necessarily from the premises.

DETERMINISM. The view that every event which occurs, occurs necessarily. Every event follows inevitably from the events which preceded it. There is no randomness* in reality; rather, all is law-governed. Freedom* either does not exist (hard determinism), or exists in such a way as to be compatible with necessity* (soft determinism).

DIALECTIC. In the philosophies of Hegel and Marx, the Dialectic is a mechanism of change and progress, in which every possible situation exists only in relation to its own opposite. This relationship is one both of antagonism and mutual dependency, but the antagonism (a form of violence) eventually undermines the relationship and overthrows it. (However, sometimes the term "dialectical" is used only to emphasize a relationship of reciprocity between two entities or processes.)

DONATISM. A fourth century heresy named after its founder, Donatus, who claimed that he had the right to reject the authority of prelates which he took to be unworthy.

DUALISM. The ontological view that reality is composed of two kinds of beings, usually (as in Descartes) minds and bodies.

EMPIRICISM. The epistemological view that true knowledge is derived primarily from sense experience (or, in "purer" strains of empiricism, _exclusively_ from sense experience). For these philosophers, all significant knowledge is _a posteriori_,* and _a priori_* knowledge is either non-existent, or tautological. The "classical" empiricists were the 17th and 18th century Britons, Locke, Berkeley and Hume, all of whom denied the existence of innate ideas, and conceived of the human mind as a "blank slate" at birth.

EPISTEMOLOGY. Theory of knowledge: answering questions such as: What is knowledge? What, if anything, can we know? and What is the difference between opinion and knowledge?

ETHICS. Moral philosophy: the branch of philosophy which answers questions such as: Is there such a thing as the Good? What is "the good life"? Is there such a thing as absolute duty?

Are valid moral arguments possible? Are moral judgements based only on preference?

EXISTENTIALISM. A twentieth century philosophy associated principally with Jean-Paul Sartre, but also thought to encompass the work of Karl Jaspers, Martin Heidegger, Gabriel Marcel, Albert Camus, and Miguel de Unamuno, among others. More of a shared attitude than a school of thought, it can nevertheless be roughly defined by saying with Sartre that existentialists are those who believe that, in the case of humans, "existence precedes essence." This is the thesis that there is no human nature which precedes our presence in the world. All humans individually create humanity at every moment through their free acts.

FALSE CONSCIOUSNESS. A term in Marxian philosophy, originating with Friedrich Engels, designating the psychological state of mind of members of a society dominated by ideology.*

FORMS. Usually associated with the philosophies of Plato or Aristotle. For Plato (in whose philosophy the word "Form" is capitalized), everything which exists in the physical or conceptual world is in some way dependent upon Forms, which exist independently of the world, but are the models (essences, universals, archetypes) of all reality. Forms are eternal and unchangeable, and the ultimate object of all true philosophizing. — For Aristotle, forms are also the essences of things, but they exist _in_ things, and are not independent of them. The form of an object and its function are ultimately related.

FREEDOM. Freedom exists if there are such things as free acts and free agents, that is, if some acts are performed in such a way that the authors of those acts could be held responsible for them. Some philosophers (called "libertarians") say that these acts _do_ exist, that some acts are freely chosen from among genuine alternatives, and that therefore determinism* is false. ("I did X, but under exactly the same circumstances, I could have done Y instead. Therefore, X was a free act.") Other philosophers (called soft determinists) also say that free acts exist, but define "free acts" not in terms of genuine alternative choices, but in terms of voluntary acts. ("I wanted to do X, and I did do X, therefore X was a free act.") Still other philosophers (called hard determinists), while agreeing with the definition of "free act" given by libertarians, deny that any such free acts or agents exist.

HEDONISM. Either the view that pleasure and pain <u>should</u> be the only motives for correct action (called "moral hedonism," defended by Epicurus and Bentham), or the view that pleasure and pain <u>are</u> the only motives for voluntary action (called "psychological hedonism," defended by Hobbes).

IDEALISM. The ontological view that, ultimately, every existing thing can be shown to be spiritual or mental (hence, a version of monism*), usually associated in Western philosophy with Berkeley and Hegel.

IDEOLOGY. A term in Marxian philosophy designating the status of cultural phenomena (such as art, religion, morality and philosophy) as systems of propoganda supporting a specific socio-economic system and its beneficiaries.

INCORRIGIBILITY. An empirical statement has incorrigibility if a person who believed it could not be wrong. An example might be, "I feel pain now," uttered in a case where one in fact does feel intense pain. Whether such statements actually exist is controversial, but empiricism* in its classical form (Locke) and modern form (logical positivism) put great stock in them.

INDUCTION. A form of argument in which the "premises" are empirical observations; generalizations are made from these observations. In induction, the conclusion stands in only a probabilistic relation to the observations on which it is based.

LAW OF IDENTITY. See "Principle of identity."

LAW OF NON-CONTRADICTION. See "Principle of non-contradiction."

LAW OF THE EXCLUDED MIDDLE. See "Principle of the excluded middle."

LOGIC. The branch of philosophy which studies the structure of valid inference. A purely <u>formal</u> discipline, interested in the structure of argumentation rather than in its content.

MATERIALISM. The ontological view that, in the final analysis, all phenomena can be demonstrated to be material in nature, and that mental and spiritual phenomena are either non-existent, or have no existence independent of matter (e.g., as in

Democritus, Hobbes and Marx).

METAPHYSICS. The branch of philosophy which attempts to construct a general, speculative world view: a complete, systematic account of all reality and experience, usually involving an epistemology,* an ontology,* an ethics,* and an aesthetics.* (The adjective "metaphysical" is often employed to stress the speculative, as opposed to the scientific, or common-sensical, features of the theory or proposition it describes.)

MONISM. The ontological view that only one entity exists (e.g., as in Spinoza), or that only one kind of entity exists (e.g., as in Hobbes and Berkeley).

MORAL PHILOSOPHY. See "Ethics."

MYSTICISM. The view that reality reveals its true nature only in a super-rational ecstatic vision.

NATURALISM. As employed in this text, naturalism is the ontological view that all is nature, that there are no supernatural or unnatural phenomena, and that there is no natural hierarchy of value. E.g., humans are no more valuable per se than coyotes.

NECESSITY. (A) LOGICAL necessity: There is a relation of logical necessity (or "logical entailment") between two propositions if the assertion of one of them, together with the denial of the other, results in a contradiction. E.g., there is a relation of logical necessity between the sentences, "Linda is my sister," and "Linda has at least one brother," because the assertion of the one and the denial of the other would result in a contradiction. (B) ONTOLOGICAL necessity: There is a relation of ontological necessity between two events X and Y if the occurrence of the first event X must be followed by the second event Y. (Determinists* claim that every event is necessary, i.e., every event follows necessarily from the events preceding it; and indeterminists claim that no events are necessary.)

NIHILISM. Either the view that nothing exists, or the view that nothing deserves to exist.

ONTOLOGICAL ARGUMENT. An _a priori_* attempt to prove God's existence by showing that, from the very concept of God, his existence can be deduced. This argument has been defended by a number of religious philosophers in the Platonic tradition. It was first formulated by St. Anselm, and appears in one form or another in the work of Descartes, Spinoza, Leibniz, and Hegel. It has some able contemporary defenders, e.g., Charles Hartshorne and Norman Malcolm. But it has been rejected by some notables, too, including St. Thomas, Hume, Kant and Kierkegaard.

ONTOLOGY. Theory of being. The branch of philosophy pursuing such questions as What is real? What is the difference between appearance and reality? What is the relation between minds and bodies? Are numbers and concepts real, or are only physical objects real?

PANTHEISM. The view that everything is divine. God's "creation" is in fact identical with God: from the Greek _pan_ (all) and _theos_ (god).

PHILOLOGY. The study of ancient written records, usually of "dead" languages.

PLURALISM. The ontological view that reality is composed of a plurality of beings, rather than just of one kind of being (monism*), or of two kinds of beings (dualism*).

PRINCIPLE OF IDENTITY. Claimed to be one of the three basic laws of thought, this principle states that everything is identical to itself: Fido is Fido; A=A.

PRINCIPLE OF NON-CONTRADICTION. Claimed to be one of the three basic laws of thought, this principle states that it is not the case that something both is and is not A at the same time (where A is any identity or characteristic): it is not the case that Fido is brown all over and not brown all over; ~(A.~A).

PRINCIPLE OF THE EXCLUDED MIDDLE. Claimed to be one of the three basic laws of thought, this principle states that, given anything in the world, it is either A, or not-A (where A is any identity or characteristic): Either Fido is brown all over, or Fido is not brown all over; A v ~A.

PRISCILLIANISM. A fifth century heresy originated by a Spanish bishop, Priscillian, attacked by St. Augustine in his book, Ad Orosium, contra Priscillianistas et Origenistas.

PROPOSITION. As employed in this text, a proposition is whatever is asserted by a sentence. The sentences, "It's raining," "Es regnet," and "Llueve," all assert the same proposition.

PSYCHOLOGICAL ATOMISM. The view held by Locke, Berkeley and Hume (though not named as such by them) that all knowledge is built up from simple, discrete psychological data, such as the primitive sensorial experiences of colors, sounds and tastes. (See also: "sense-data."*)

RANDOMNESS. If there are events which are totally uncaused and in principle unpredictable, then those events are random events. If there is randomness (that is, if random events exist), then determinism* is false.

RATIONALISM. The epistemological view that true knowledge is derived primarily from "reason" (or exclusively from "reason," in the purer strains of rationalism). Reason is conceived as the working of the mind on material provided by the mind itself. In most versions, this material takes the form of innate ideas. Therefore, for the rationalists, a priori* knowledge is the most important kind of knowledge. In rationalistic ontologies,* the mind and the world are seen to be in conformity — the real is the rational. The classical rationalists were the 17th and 18th century Continental philosophers, Descartes, Spinoza and Leibniz, but the concept is broad enough to include such philosophers as Parmenides, Plato and Hegel.

REIFICATION. The result of illegitimately concretizing that which is abstract or that which is general, or that which defies concretization. From the Latin, res (thing), hence, to "thingify."

RELATIVISM. In ethics* and aesthetics,* relativism is the view that there are no absolute values; all values are relative to time, place and culture. In epistemology,* relativism is the view that there are no absolute truths; all truths are relative to time, place and culture.

SCHOLASTICISM. The name given to the philosophy practiced in the "schools" of the Medieval universities, where all branches of philosophy, logic, and linguistics were developed and systematized according to theological schemata.

SEMIOLOGY (sometimes called SEMIOTICS). The study of the system of signs. A "sign" is an arbitrary mark or sound which has become imbued with meaning by virtue of its membership in a system of conventionality. Language is the most obvious case of such a system of signs, but behaviors and rituals can also be studied semiologically.

SENSE-DATA. A sense-datum is that which is perceived immediately by any one of the senses, prior to interpretation by the mind. Sense-data include the perceptions of colors, sounds, tastes, odors, tactile sensations, pleasures and pains. Classical empiricism* based itself on the supposedly epistemologically foundational nature of sense-data.

SKEPTICISM (or SCEPTICISM). A denial of the possibility of knowledge. General skepticism denies the possibility of <u>any</u> knowledge; however, one can be skeptical about specific fields of inquiry (e.g., metaphysics*), or specific faculties (e.g., sense perception), without denying the possibility of knowledge in general.

SOLIPSISM. The view that the only true knowledge one can possess is knowledge of one's own consciousness. According to solipsism, there is no good reason to believe that anything exists other than oneself.

STRUCTURALISM. Based on the philosophical anthropology of the contemporary French theorist Claude Lévi-Strauss (but also finding followers in all the human sciences), structuralism is the view that the human mind is universal in that, everywhere and in every historical epoch, the mind is structured in such a way as to process its data in terms of certain general formulae which give meaning to those mental data.

SUBJECTIVISM. The view that there are no objective truths or values; all truths and values are relative to the subjectivity of the individual. (Subjectivism is a version of relativism.*)

SUBLIMATION. A term usually associated with Freud, but employed earlier by Schopenhauer, Marx, and Nietzsche, naming the process of refinement or of spiritualization whereby the more base and crass elements are transformed into more subtle or sublime elements, e.g., the sexual or aggressive drives are transformed into art.

SUBSTANCE. In philosophy, "substance" has traditionally been the term naming whatever is thought to be the most basic, independent reality. Aristotle defined a substance as whatever can exist independently of other things, so that a horse or a man (Aristotle's examples) can exist independently, but the <u>color</u> of the horse, or the <u>size</u> of the man cannot. The 17th and 18th century rationalists took the idea of substance as <u>independent being</u> so seriously that one of their members, Spinoza, claimed there could be only one substance in the world (i.e., only one <u>thing</u>), namely, God, because only God could exist independently. Under Berkeley's criticism of material substance, and Hume's criticism of spiritual substance, the concept of substance was very much eroded away. It turned up again in Kant, but only as a "category" of knowledge, not as a basic reality itself.

TELEOLOGY. A teleological explanation is an explanation in terms of goals, purposes or intentions (from the Greek <u>telos</u> = goal). E.g., "John closed the window because he didn't want his budgie to escape" is a teleological explanation because it explains John's behavior in terms of his intentions.

THEOLOGY. The systematic study of God and his properties, from the Greek <u>theos</u> (God) and <u>logos</u> (theory, or study of).

Index

Abelard, Peter, 128
Abraham, 262-63
Absolute, The, 101, 102, 315
Absurd, The, 120, 261, 263, 365, 375
Achilles, 3, 30, 286
Acton, Lord, 278
Actuality, 78-79, 80
Adam, 363
Aesthetics, 64, 73, 87, 88, 310, 371, 381, 385, 387
Alexander the Great, 89
Alienation, 164, 225, 252, 259, 265, 266, 269, 270, 271, 272, 278, 381
Alpha and Omega, 115
Altruism, 160
Analytic propositions (or analytic sentences), 170, 171, 174, 196-97, 198, 199, 200, 201, 202, 204, 208, 332, 337
Anarchy, 163
Anaxagoras, 35
Anaximander, 11-12, 15
Anaximenes, 13-15
Anguish, 256, 362, 368, 369, 370
Anscombe, G.E.M., xi
Anselm of Canterbury, 116-19, 123, 131, 153, 200, 328, 386
Antipodes, 111
A posteriori, 131, 170, 196, 198, 208, 210, 381, 382
A priori, 119, 132, 153, 164, 170, 196, 197, 208, 209, 210, 211, 212, 214, 217, 225, 381, 382, 386, 387. *See also* Synthetic *a priori*
Arete, x
Arianism, 105, 381
Aristophanes, 40
Aristotle, 34, 74-88, 90, 96, 100, 121, 122, 125, 126, 128, 131, 132, 249, 328, 352, 383, 389
Arius, 381
Art, 68, 73, 233, 243, 246, 273, 274, 275, 276, 279, 332, 333, 339, 381, 384, 389
Asceticism, 96, 101
Aspasia, x
Atheism, 159
Atomic facts, 346, 352, 358
Atomism, 36-37, 39, 90, 94, 111, 158. *See also* Psychological atomism
Augustine of Hippo, 103-09, 116, 176, 387
Austin, John Langshaw, 376
Averröes, 121, 125
Ayer, Sir Alfred Jules, 331, 336, 337

Bacon, Roger, 134
Bad faith, 373
Bain, Alexander, 303
Beatific vision, 133
Beauty, 54, 68, 73, 132, 266, 347
Beauvoir, Simone de, xi
Becoming, 227, 229, 232
Beethoven, Ludwig van, 246
Being, 26, 27, 65, 69, 113, 118, 225, 227, 228, 229, 232, 251, 266, 287, 291, 325, 326, 327, 328, 357, 360, 364, 365, 366, 382, 386
Belief, 64, 66, 217, 221, 236, 292, 303, 304, 307, 340

Bentham, Jeremy, 292-97, 298, 299, 384
Berkeley, George, 188-95, 201, 223, 304, 382, 384, 385, 387, 389
Boethius, 110, 121, 345
Bourgeoisie, The, 276, 279, 360
Bracketing, 340, 362
Bradley, Francis Herbert, 311, 313, 320
Brahe, Tycho, 134
Brentano, Franz von, 342
Brutus, 174
Buddha, 244, 247
Buridan, John, 134

Caesar, Julius, 171, 174, 254, 255
Calculus of Felicity, The, 295-97, 298, 299
Callicles, 47, 293
Camus, Albert, 383
Capitalism, 271, 276, 277
Carnap, Rudolf, 331, 332, 335, 337, 376
Categorical imperative, 218, 220
Categories of the understanding, 211, 212, 213, 236, 241
Category mistake, 356
Catholicism, 142, 149
Causality, 75, 79, 80, 108, 129, 130, 131, 132, 180, 202, 203, 206, 211, 212, 213, 215, 216, 292, 322, 333
Certainty, 100, 145, 148, 149, 150, 151, 152, 204, 295, 314, 315, 335
Cervantes Saavedra, Miguel de, 345
Chancellor, John, 65
Charles the Bald, 111
Chomsky, Noam, 377
Christianity, 80, 98, 99, 100, 103, 104, 105, 112, 113, 117, 126, 128, 164, 167, 217, 287
Christina of Sweden, 157
Common sense, 14, 177, 202, 209, 211, 214, 216, 313, 314, 316, 385
Communism, 72, 272, 279
Complex ideas, 179, 180
Concepts, 64, 66, 68, 101, 128, 213, 214, 215, 252, 336, 376, 379, 383, 386
Conceptualism, 129
Confirmation sentences, 334, 336, 346
Conjecture, 64, 65, 66, 73
Connotation, 351
Consciousness, 152, 176, 274, 278, 322, 339, 341, 342, 343, 361, 362, 363, 364, 371, 388
Consequentialism, 294
Constantine, 103
Constitution, the American, 188
Copernicus, Nikolaus, 134
Courage, 86
Critias, 47-48
Cunning of Reason, The, 229
Cunning of the Will, The, 241, 242, 244

Dark Ages, The, 108, 111, 126
Darwin, Charles, 38, 141
David, Jacques-Louis, 56
Davidson, Donald, 377
Death, 98, 101, 238, 257, 258, 287, 288, 289, 341, 373, 375
Death of God, The, 287, 288, 289
Declaration of Independence, The, 188

Deconstruction, 291, 379, 381
Deduction, 210, 382
Democracy, 48, 49, 229, 230, 231, 249, 294, 298, 299
Democritus, 36–37, 90, 94, 158, 180, 272, 385
Denotation, 327, 351
Derrida, Jacques, 378, 379, 381
Descartes, René, 135–57, 158, 159, 163, 164, 165, 167, 170, 175, 177, 178, 181, 182, 200, 205, 212, 253, 303, 304, 328, 338, 339, 340, 343, 357, 361, 382, 386, 387
Desire, 90, 91, 92, 93, 97, 248, 293
Determinism, 37, 159, 382, 383, 385, 387
Dewey, John, 310
Dialectic, The, 114, 227–31, 249, 275, 315, 382
Dictatorship of the proletariat, 277, 278
Dignity, 220, 229
Dionysius the Areopagite, 112
Diotima, x
Doctrine of the Double Truth, The, 121
Dominican order, The, 125
Donatism, 105, 382
Donatus, 382
Don Quixote, 345, 361
Dread, 343, 362, 363
Dreyfus, Hubert, 380
Dualism, 78, 156, 157, 158, 165, 167, 177, 382, 386
Dummett, Michael, 377
Duns Scotus, John, 134
Duty, 132, 160, 217, 219, 220, 221, 237, 294, 382
Economics, 273
Eco, Umberto, 352
Efficient cause, 79, 129, 130
Egoism, 160, 163, 293
Einstein, Albert, 38, 330
Elitism, 84, 299
Emanations, 101–102, 115
Empedocles, 32–34, 35, 36
Empiricism, 31, 177, 180, 183, 188, 189, 195, 196, 197, 198, 201, 204, 205, 213, 292, 293, 304, 309, 310, 311, 314, 318, 331, 352, 381, 382, 384, 388
Engels, Friedrich, 383
Enlightenment, The, 96, 98, 217, 221
Epictetus, 95, 98, 99
Epicureanism, 89–94, 95
Epicurus, 89–94, 293, 384
Epi-phenomena, 159
Epistemology, 64, 71, 73, 177, 179, 183, 251, 260, 281, 282, 382, 385, 387, 388
Epochê, The, 340, 341, 342, 363
Erigena, John Scotus, 111–15, 116, 120
Eros, 33
Essence, 75, 77, 80, 166, 225, 251, 265, 266, 272, 381, 383
Eternal recurrence, 287, 288, 289, 290
Ethics, 81, 87, 88, 132, 217, 218, 220, 221, 222, 233, 254, 294, 336, 382, 385, 387
Euclid, 17
Evil, 104, 149, 150, 151, 153, 154, 187, 281
Evil genius, The, 149, 150, 151, 153, 154
Evolution, 34, 38, 225

Excellence, 96
Existentialism, 248, 251, 254, 291, 344, 360, 365, 377, 383
Ex nihilo nihil, 12
Expediency, 43, 49

Facticity, 371
Faculty of intuition, The (or The faculty of perception), 209, 210, 211
Faculty of reason, The, 209, 214
Faculty of understanding, The, 209, 211
Faith, 120, 121, 128, 129, 236, 256, 260, 261, 262
False consciousness, 278, 383
Fatalism, 305, 311
Feudalism, 230, 231
Feuerbach, Ludwig, 265–68, 269
Fichte, Johann Gottlieb, 223
Final cause, 80
Five ways, The, 129, 132
Foot, Philippa, xi
Formal cause, 79
Forms, Platonic, 64, 67, 68, 69, 70, 72, 75, 76, 77–79, 113, 115, 122, 128, 244, 247, 282, 312, 352, 383
Foucault, Michel, 378, 379
Four causes, The, 79
Four roots, The, 32, 35, 39
Freedom, 37, 95, 97, 107, 108, 159, 160, 168, 176, 215, 217, 229, 230, 231, 232, 236, 251, 260, 283, 305, 362, 363, 369, 370, 371, 372, 373, 374, 382, 383
Freud, Sigmund, x, 33, 70, 73, 93–94, 141, 240, 248, 264, 378, 389

Galilei, Galileo, 134, 137, 138, 141, 142, 154, 180
Garden of Eden, The, 139
Gaunilon, 118
Geist, 224
Genus, 122
George IV, 325
God, 80, 101, 102, 107, 108, 113, 114, 115, 116, 117, 119, 120, 121, 126, 129, 130, 132, 139, 149, 152, 153, 154, 156, 160, 164, 166, 167, 168, 170, 171, 173, 174, 176, 184, 185, 193, 194, 195, 200, 201, 203, 206, 214, 215, 216, 217, 221, 224, 225, 226, 229, 236, 239, 251, 255, 261, 262, 266, 282, 285, 287, 288, 289, 306, 307, 308, 349, 363, 375, 381, 386, 389
Golden mean, The, 85
Good, The, 64, 69, 70, 74, 80, 82, 83, 96, 281, 382
Good life, The, 87, 90, 382
Grice, Paul, 376

Hades, 53
Happiness, 83, 85, 87, 90, 97, 126, 132, 267, 294, 295
Harman, Gilbert, 377
Hartshorne, Charles, 386
Harvey, William, 134
Hedonism, 94, 293, 296, 384
Hegel, G.W.F., 114, 223–34, 235, 243, 248, 249, 250, 251, 252, 253, 256, 260, 263, 264, 265, 266, 268, 272, 276, 278, 287, 311, 312, 315, 316, 320, 326, 328, 374, 378, 381, 382, 384, 386, 387
Heidegger, Martin, 343, 360, 383
Heraclitus, 19–24, 25, 76
Heresy, 105, 115, 381, 382, 387
Hitler, Adolf, 331

Hobbes, Thomas, 158–63, 183, 184, 185, 187, 272, 293, 384, 385
Homer, 3, 73
Homo faber, 270, 272
Homo mensura, 43
Homo sapiens, 270
Honorius III, 115
Hume, David, 130, 195–206, 207, 208, 209, 210, 212, 214, 216, 261, 291, 292, 328, 330, 332, 333, 382, 386, 387, 389
Hume's fork, 204, 331, 336
Husserl, Edmund, 338–44, 360, 361, 363
Hypatia, x

Id, The, 240
Idealism, 78, 167, 189, 192, 222, 223, 224, 268, 272, 311, 384
Ideology, 269, 274, 275, 383, 384
Images, 64, 65, 66, 67, 73, 101, 246, 247, 269, 286
Immortality, 215, 216, 217, 236, 239
Incorrigibility, 334, 336, 384
Induction, 204, 384
Infinite regress, 130, 131, 132
Infinite seeds, 35, 39
Innate ideas, 70, 152, 154, 178, 182, 381, 382, 387
Inquisition, The, 137, 138, 141
Intention, 217, 294, 389
Intentionality (or Referentiality), 342, 343, 361
Irigaray, Luce, xi
Irony, 53, 258
Isidore of Seville, 110, 111

James, William, 304–11
Jaspers, Karl, 383
Jesus, 107, 244, 281, 381
Jewish, 163, 164, 167
John of Salisbury, 123
Judas, 107
Justice, 46, 54, 66, 68, 183, 215, 216, 217, 236, 239, 266

Kant, Immanuel, 38, 119, 206–22, 223, 235, 236, 237, 238, 239, 255, 280, 294, 295, 309, 310, 328, 331, 338, 378, 386, 389
Kepler, Johannes, 134
Keynes, John Maynard, 315
Kierkegaard, Søren, 248–63, 279, 280, 284, 328, 343, 360, 363, 386
Knowledge, 64, 66, 67, 69, 70, 81, 96, 108, 132, 144, 145, 148, 163, 168, 178, 179, 182, 198, 211, 216, 217, 221, 270, 282, 292, 318, 322, 332, 333, 343, 381, 382, 387, 388, 389
Kristeva, Julia, xi

Lacan, Jacques, 378
Laisser-faire (or *Laissez-faire*), 299, 301
Langer, Susanne, xi
Language, 101, 192, 193, 228, 252, 284, 285, 316, 318, 332, 336, 346, 350, 351, 353, 354, 355, 356, 357, 358, 359, 376, 377, 378, 379, 380, 386, 388
Language-game, 354, 355, 356
Latin Averröism, 121
Law of identity, The. *See* Principle of identity, The
Law of non-contradiction, The. *See* Principle of non-contradiction, The
Law of the excluded middle, The. *See* Principle of the excluded

middle, The
Leibniz, Gottfried, 167-77, 196, 207, 214, 326, 328, 365, 386, 387
Leucippus, 36
Lévi-Strauss, Claude, 378, 388
Libertarianism, 383
Lived world, The, 339, 340
Locke, John, 177-88, 189, 190, 195, 312, 318, 382, 384, 387
Logic, 87, 88, 116, 169, 171, 232, 249, 291, 303, 321, 323, 325, 326, 327, 332, 346, 358, 376, 377, 381, 384, 385, 388
Logical positivism, 318, 330-38, 344, 346, 347, 350, 352, 354, 357, 384
Logos, 24
Louis XIV, 274
Love, 33-34, 36, 267
Lucretius, 94
Lutheranism, 221, 280
Lyceum, The, 74

Mach, Ernst, 330
McTaggart, John Ellis, 311, 313, 320
Maimonides, 125
Malcolm, Norman, 386
Mani, 104
Manicheanism, 104, 105, 106
Mann, Thomas, 248
Marcel, Gabriel, 383
Marcus Aurelius, 95, 99
Marx, Karl, 260, 263-79, 280, 378, 379, 381, 382, 383, 385, 389
Material cause, 79
Materialism, 37, 95, 158, 167, 268,
Materialism cont., 272, 275, 305, 311, 384
Mathematics, 16, 17, 70, 137, 149, 154, 155, 158, 247, 254, 315, 320, 340, 345, 377
Meaning, 305, 306, 307, 309, 315, 316, 318, 325, 332, 334, 347, 350, 351, 352, 353, 354, 355, 369, 373, 376, 388
Mechanism, 158
Mehta, Ved, 329, 330
Meno, 70
Merleau-Ponty, Maurice, 343
Metaphysics, 57, 78, 80, 81, 83, 87, 88, 102, 111, 125, 134, 164, 170, 173, 177, 181, 183, 198, 207, 214, 215, 216, 217, 221, 222, 260, 304-05, 315, 317, 318, 324, 325, 326, 327, 331, 333, 335, 339, 347, 348, 351, 356, 385, 388
Miletus (the Milesians), 6, 15, 16
Mill, John Stuart, 292, 298-302
Mind/Body problem, The, 165, 357, 386
Moderation, 47, 85, 93
Modes, 156, 166
Monads, 175-76
Monism, 15, 31, 170, 311, 384, 385, 386
Moore, George Edward, 312-19, 320, 329, 350, 359
Morality, 46, 47, 81, 84, 161, 217, 218, 221, 233, 237, 243, 256, 264, 273, 275, 276, 281, 289, 293, 301, 310, 336, 382, 383, 384, 385
Moses, 226
Motion, 29, 30, 39, 75, 76, 78, 80
Murdoch, Iris, xi
Music of the spheres, The, 17

Mysticism, 100, 101, 105, 168, 349, 350, 385
Myth of the cave, The, 58-64, 65, 67, 69

Napoleon, 169
Narcissism, 81
Naturalism, 15, 170, 385
Natural law, 24, 204
Natural right, 161, 184, 185, 186, 187
Natural standpoint, The, 339, 340, 342
Nature, 80, 96, 112, 122, 134, 160, 161, 163, 167, 168, 170, 183, 184, 185, 186, 187, 204, 232, 240, 241, 242, 270, 385
Nazism, 291, 331
Necessity, 37, 108, 168, 170, 171, 173, 196, 197, 200, 201, 202, 203, 204, 216, 217, 270, 323, 365, 382, 385
Neo-Platonism, 100-02, 103, 104, 112, 113, 115, 121
Nero, 98
Neurath, Otto, 331
Newton, Isaac, 170
Nietzsche, Friedrich, ix, x, 248, 260, 280-91, 328, 378, 389
Nihilism, 49, 287, 291, 385
Nominalism, 123-24, 180, 189, 352
Nothingness, 225, 227, 228, 229, 232, 256, 258, 287, 290, 360, 366, 367
Noumenal world, The, 213, 215, 222, 223, 236, 239. See also, Thing-in-itself, The
Nous, 36

Occam's razor, 178, 189, 195, 201, 323, 324, 325, 328
Ockham, William of. See William of Ockham; see also Occam's razor
Ontological proof, The (or ontological argument), 116-19, 131, 153, 200, 386
Ontology, 64, 73, 251, 282, 382, 384, 385, 386, 387
Optimism, 229, 236, 241, 242, 243, 244, 278, 311
Ordinary language philosophy, 344, 350-57, 358, 376, 377
Oresme, Nicholas of, 134
Other-worldliness, 75, 100, 125, 287
Overman, The, 287, 288. See also Übermensch, der

Pantheism, 102, 112, 115, 167, 170, 224, 386
Parmenides, 25-27, 28, 31, 37, 76, 387
Paul of Tarsus, 112
Peano, Giuseppe, 321
Peirce, Charles, 303-04, 307, 310, 318
Pelagianism, 105, 106
Pelagius, 105
Peloponnesian War, The, 88
Perfection, 80, 81, 97, 101, 119
Pericles, 229
Perspectivism, 281
Pessimism, 5, 23, 160, 238, 244, 278, 290, 311, 342, 375
Phenomenal world, The, 213, 214, 239, 240-41, 246
Phenomenological reduction, 340
Phenomenology, 338-44, 362, 377,

Phenomenology cont., 378
Philology, 281, 282, 386
Philosopher King, The, 74
Physics, 137, 143, 154, 272, 273, 332, 339
Pilate, Pontius, 280
Plato (and Platonism), 17, 24, 49, 54-74, 75, 76, 77, 78, 100, 101, 103, 112, 113, 115, 119, 122, 123, 125, 131, 132, 152, 168, 180, 212, 214, 235, 244, 245, 247, 252, 262, 282, 287, 299, 312, 323, 325, 326, 328, 329, 351, 369, 383, 386, 387
Pleasure, 47, 90, 91, 92, 93, 94, 96, 293, 294, 295, 296, 299, 384
Plotinus, 100-02, 115
Pluralism, 31, 78, 311, 380, 386
Poincaré, Jules, 330
Political science, 71, 72, 87, 160-63, 183-88
Porphyry, 121
Potentiality, 78-79, 80
Power, 46, 47, 160, 163, 269, 278, 283, 284, 286, 287, 288, 300
Pragmaticism, 304
Pragmatism, 303-11, 352
Presley, Elvis, 246
Primary qualities, 179, 180, 181, 189, 190
Prime mover, The, 80, 81
Principle of identity, The, 170, 171, 249, 386
Principle of individuation, The, 78
Principle of internal harmony, The, 170, 173-74
Principle of liberty, The, 300
Principle of non-contradiction, The, 171, 249, 386
Principle of sufficient reason, The, 170, 172, 365
Principle of the excluded middle, The, 249, 251, 326, 328, 386
Principle of utility, The, 299
Priscillian, 387
Priscillianism, 105, 387
Problem of induction, The, 204,
Proletariat, The, 276, 277
Protagoras, 43-44, 49, 50
Protocol sentences, 333, 334, 336, 346
Pseudo-Dionysius, The, 111, 112, 114
Psychological atomism, 179, 189, 387
Psychology, 71, 160, 232, 332, 383, 384, 387
Pure reason, 31, 64, 67, 87, 119
Purpose, 81, 82
Putnam, Hilary, 380
Pythagoras, 16-18, 136

Quietism, 99

Radical doubt, 145, 146, 147, 148, 149, 340
Randomness, 168, 382, 387
Rarefaction, 14
Rationalism, 31, 163, 168, 177, 197, 207, 208, 213, 310, 314, 365, 381, 387, 389
Realism, 123, 128, 155, 180, 181, 194, 311, 312
Recollection, The doctrine of, 70
Reductio ad absurdum, 28
Referentiality. *See* Intentionality.
Reichenbach, Hans, 331
Relativism, 43, 287, 387, 388
Religion, 2, 18, 40, 44, 48, 98, 100, 103, 120, 142, 143, 209, 233, 243, 248, 255, 256, 264, 265, 267,

Religion cont., 269, 273, 275, 276, 289, 305, 310, 311, 384
Renaissance, The, 134, 135, 139, 298
Resignation, 99
Responsibility, 373, 383
Rhetoric, 41, 45
Rigaud, Hyacinthe, 274
Rorty, Richard, 380
Roscelin, 123
Royce, Josiah, 311
Russell, Bertrand, 164, 169, 312, 313, 314, 318, 319-30, 331, 345, 346, 349, 351, 352, 376
Ryle, Gilbert, 357, 376

Sartre, Jean-Paul, 342, 344, 360-75, 383
Satan, 225, 226
Saussure, Ferdinand de, 378, 381
Schelling, Friedrich Wilhelm Joseph Von, 223
Schlick, Moritz, 330, 331, 333, 334
Scholasticism, 133, 134, 388
Schopenhauer, Arthur, x, 234-48, 283, 289, 328, 389
Science, 121, 134, 140, 142, 202, 209, 214, 216, 243, 254, 273, 275, 293, 295, 304, 310, 314, 318, 319, 320, 322, 330, 331, 332, 334, 335, 339, 340, 347, 354, 357, 371, 381, 385, 388
Scott, Sir Walter, 325, 326, 327, 328
Scotus, John Duns, *See* Duns Scotus, John
Searle, John, 377
Secondary qualities, 179, 180, 189, 190
Second way, The, 131
Self-actualization, 80
Selfhood, 152, 155, 200, 204, 205, 206, 231, 253, 259, 292, 342, 343, 361, 368, 374
Semiology, 303, 388
Seneca, 95, 98
Sense-data, 190, 191, 192, 193, 194, 199, 201, 202, 204, 205, 209, 210, 213, 314, 333, 352, 387, 388
Shadows, 58, 59, 60, 62, 65, 67, 68
Shakespeare, William, 298, 299
Simile of the Line, The, 64-69, 73, 101, 102, 105, 119
Simonides, 5
Simple ideas, 179, 180, 190
Sisyphus, 375
Skepticism, 42, 49, 207, 292, 311, 339, 388
Slavery, 95, 98, 229, 230, 231, 249, 271
Social contract, 163, 187
Socialism, 278
Socrates, 49, 50-56 57, 58, 60, 63, 70, 96
Solipsism, 152, 193, 388
Sophism, 42-50, 281
Soul, The, 51, 70, 71, 73, 83, 85, 87, 96, 102, 104, 126, 204, 216, 217
Space, 26, 27, 29, 37, 156, 157, 158, 215, 216, 236, 241, 313, 315, 339, 341, 342, 346, 349
Species, 122
Spinoza, Baruch (or Spinoza, Benedictus), 163-69, 170, 200, 224, 365, 385, 386, 387, 389
Spivak, Gayatari Chakravorty, xi

Stalinism, 278
State of nature, The, 160-61, 163, 183, 184, 185, 187
State paternalism, 300
Stebbing, L. Susan, xi
Stoicism, 89, 95-99, 108, 168
Stoppard, Tom, 353
Strife, 33, 36
Structuralism, 377, 378, 379, 388
Subjectivism, 49, 388
Subjectivity, 43, 152, 192, 254, 255, 256, 258, 259, 260, 262, 291
Sublimation, x, 243, 245, 274, 389
Substance, 78, 79, 80, 152, 154, 156, 159, 164, 165, 166, 167, 174, 181, 182, 183, 189, 190, 192, 194, 195, 201, 203, 211, 212, 213, 215, 282, 352, 389
Suicide, 96, 98, 99, 244
Sun, The, 61, 62, 63, 64, 66, 69, 140, 236, 313, 353
Synthetic _a priori_, 208, 209, 210, 211, 212, 214, 217
Synthetic propositions (or synthetic sentences), 170, 171, 196, 197, 198, 199, 201, 202, 204, 208, 209, 210, 211, 212, 214, 217, 332, 333, 337

Tabula rasa, 178
Tautology, 197, 200, 208, 328, 332, 337, 382
Teleology, 79, 80, 81, 132, 389
Tenniel, Sir John, 338
Tertullian, 120
Thales of Miletus, x, 6-11, 15, 38
Thanatos, 33, 94
Theology, 121, 128, 129, 134, 143, 167, 215, 216, 217, 232, 313, 388, 389
Theory of Descriptions, The, 323-29
Thesis/antithesis/synthesis, 114, 374
Thing-in-itself, The, 213, 222, 282. _See also_ Noumenal world, The
Thirty Tyrants, The, 48
Thomas Aquinas, 116, 120, 124-34, 173, 386
Thompson, Judith Jarvis, xi
Thrasymachus, 46
Time, 30, 107, 108, 215, 216, 236, 241, 287, 313, 315, 322, 339, 341, 342, 349, 368
Transcendental deduction (or Transcendental analysis), 209, 210, 214
Truth, 51, 54, 56, 64, 68, 70, 97, 100, 225, 226, 238, 239, 255, 256, 257, 258, 259, 260, 262, 264, 266, 305, 307, 308, 309, 317, 325, 326, 346, 347, 381, 387, 388

Übermensch, Der, 288. _See also_ Overman, The
Unamuno, Miguel de, 383
Unconscious, The, 70, 80, 246
Understanding, 64, 67, 86-87, 209, 211
Universals, 120, 121, 124, 128, 383
Utilitarianism, 291, 292-302

Values, 254, 255, 256, 259, 260, 332, 333, 369, 370, 385, 387, 388

Vandals, The, 108
Venerable Bede, The, 110
Vermeer, Jan, 360
Via affirmativa / via negativa, 113-14
Victimless crime, 300
Vienna Circle, The, 330, 331, 347, 349
Virtue, 54, 83, 84, 85, 86, 87, 96, 126
Voltaire, 175

Wheatley, Jon, 338
Whitehead, Alfred North, 74, 321, 330
Will, 97, 168, 239, 240, 241, 242, 243, 244, 245, 246, 247, 248, 273, 282, 283, 284, 286, 287, 288, 291, 300, 322
William of Ockham (also William of Occam), 123, 134, 178, 328. See also Occam's razor
Will to Power, 283, 284, 286, 287, 288
Wisdom, 85, 86, 87, 96, 97, 114, 236
Wittgenstein, Ludwig, vii, 318, 329, 330, 331, 337, 344-60, 376
Wittig, Monique, xi
Wolff, Christian von, 207

Zarathustra, 281
Zeno of Cyprus, 95
Zeno of Elea, 28-31, 33
Zeus, 40